The Reception of Derrida

The Reception of Derrida

Derrida

Translation and Transformation

Michael Thomas

First published in 2006 by
PALGRAVE MACMILLAN
Houndmills, Basingstoke, Hampshire RG21 6XS and
175 Fifth Avenue, New York, N.Y. 10010
Companies and representatives throughout the world

PALGRAVE MACMILLAN is the global academic imprint of the Palgrave
Macmillan division of St. Martin's Press, LLC and of Palgrave Macmillan Ltd.
Macmillan® is a registered trademark in the United States, United Kingdom
and other countries. Palgrave is a registered trademark in the European
Union and other countries.

ISBN-13: 978–1–4039–8992–5 hardback
ISBN-10: 1–4039–8992–3 hardback

This book is printed on paper suitable for recycling and made from fully
managed and sustained forest sources.

A catalogue record for this book is available from the British Library.

Library of Congress Cataloging-in-Publication Data

Thomas, Michael, 1969–
       The reception of Derrida : translation and transformation / Michael
    Thomas.
           p. cm.
       Includes bibliographical references and indexes.
       ISBN 1–4039–8992–3
           1. Derrida, Jacques. 2. Translating and interpreting. I. Title.
    B2430.D484T47 2006
    194—dc22   2005056413

10 9 8 7 6 5 4 3 2 1
15 14 13 12 11 10 09 08 07 06

Printed and bound in Great Britain by
Antony Rowe Ltd, Chippenham and Eastbourne

for
Madoka
and
William

Contents

vii

Acknowledgements

The author and publisher wish to thank the following for permission to reproduce copyright material from:

Apostolides, J.-M., 'On Paul de Man's War', *Critical Inquiry* 15:4, pp. 765–6. Copyright © 1989 The University of Chicago Press. Used by permission of The University of Chicago Press. Copyright © 1996 from *Derrida and the Political*, by R. Beardsworth. Reproduced by permission of Routledge/Thomson Publishing. *Blindness and Insight*, by Paul de Man, copyright © 1988 Paul de Man. Used by permission of Oxford University Press, Inc. Brenkman, John, Brenkman, Jules, and Law, David., 'Resetting the Agenda', *Critical Inquiry* 15:4, pp. 804–11. Copyright © 1989 The University of Chicago Press. Used by permission of The University of Chicago Press. Callinicos, A. 'Reactionary Postmodernism?', reprinted from *Postmodernism and Society*, edited by R. Boyne and A. Rattansi. Copyright © 1990 Macmillan. Used by permission of the publisher, Palgrave Macmillan. Copyright © 1988 from *Paul de Man: Deconstruction and the Critique of Aesthetic Ideology*, by C. Norris. Reproduced by permission of Routledge/Taylor Francis Group LLC. Copyright © 1994 from *Specters of Marx: the State of the Debt, the Work of Mourning, and the New International*, by J. Derrida. Reproduced by permission of Routledge/Taylor & Francis Group, LLC. Critchley, S., *The Ethics of Deconstruction*. Copyright © 1992 Blackwell Publishing. Used with permission of the publisher, Blackwell Publishing. Culler, J., 'Paul de Man's War and the Aesthetic Ideology', *Critical Inquiry* 15:4, pp. 777–83. Copyright © 1989 The University of Chicago Press. Used by permission of The University of Chicago Press. Derrida, J., 'Languages and Institutions of Philosophy', *Semiotic Inquiry*, 4:2, 91–154. Copyright © 1984 *Semiotic Inquiry*. Reprinted with the permission of *Semiotic Inquiry*. Derrida, J. 'The Principle of Reason', *Diacritics* 13:3. Copyright © 1983 The Johns Hopkins University Press. Reprinted with permission of The Johns Hopkins University Press. Derrida, J., *Writing and Difference*. Copyright © 1978 The University of Chicago Press. Used by permission of the publisher, The University of Chicago Press. Derrida, J., 'Biodegradables: Seven Diary Fragments', *Critical Inquiry* 15:4, 812–73. Copyright © 1989 The University of Chicago Press. Used by permission of The University of Chicago Press. Derrida, J., 'Before the Law', trans. A. Ronell and C. Roulston, in *Acts of Literature: Jacques*

The Johns Hopkins University Press. Reprinted with permission of The Johns Hopkins University Press. Judt, T., *Past Imperfect: French Intellectuals, 1944–56*. Copyright © 1992 The Regents of the University of California. Used by permission of the publisher, the University of California Press. Man, P. de, *Allegories of Reading*. Copyright © 1979 by Yale University Press. Used by permission of the publisher, Yale University Press. *Memoires for Paul de Man*, by J. Derrida. Copyright © 1986 Columbia University Press. Reprinted with permission of the publisher. Michaels, W. B., *Glyph* 8, Textual Studies. pp. 233. © 1980 The Johns Hopkins University Press. Reprinted with permission of The Johns Hopkins University Press. Nietzsche, Friedrich, *On the Future of Our Educational Institutions*, translated by Michael W. Grenke (South Bend, Ind.: St. Augustine's Press, 2004). Norris, C., *Derrida*. Reprinted by permission of HarperCollins Publishers Ltd. © Christopher Norris 1987. Proust, M., *Swann's Way*, translated by C. K. Scott Moncrieff and Terence Kimartin, published by Chatto & Windus. © 2004 The Random House Group Ltd. Reprinted by permission of The Random House Group Ltd. Readings, B., 'The Deconstruction of Politics', from *Reading de Man Reading*, edited by L. Waters and W. Godzich. © 1989 The University of Minnesota Press. Reprinted by permission of The University of Minnesota Press. Reprinted J. Derrida: 'Des Tours de Babel' from *Difference in Translation*, edited and translated by Joseph F. Graham. Copyright © 1985 by Cornell University. Used by permission of the publisher, Cornell University Press. Soper, K., 'The Limits of Hauntology'. Copyright © 1995 *Radical Philosophy*. Reprinted with permission of *Radical Philosophy*.

The Ear of the Other, by Jacques Derrida, copyright © 1985 by Schocken Books, a division of Random House, Inc. Used by permission of Schocken Books, a division of Random House, Inc. *The Prelude*, by William Wordsworth, copyright © 1960. William Wordsworth. Used by permission of Oxford University Press, Inc. *The Rhetoric of Romanticism*, by Paul de Man. Copyright © 1984 Columbia University Press. Reprinted with permission of the publisher. Weber, S., and Sussman, H., *Glyph* I. pp. 207–8. © 1977 The Johns Hopkins University Press. Reprinted with permission of The Johns Hopkins University Press. Weber, S., and Sussman, H., *Glyph* I. pp. 172–1970. © 1977 The Johns Hopkins University Press. Reprinted with permission of The Johns Hopkins University Press. Weber, S., and Sussman, H., *Glyph* II. pp. 162–254. © 1977 The Johns Hopkins University Press. Reprinted with permission of The Johns Hopkins University Press. Wiener, J., 'The Responsibilities of Friendship: Jacques Derrida on Paul de Man's Collaboration', *Critical Inquiry* 15:4, 797–803. Copyright © 1989 The University of Chicago

Abbreviations

I have referred throughout to the English translations of Derrida's works. They are ordered alphabetically below and referenced in the text using the mnemonic as shown below.

AL   *Acts of Literature: Jacques Derrida*, ed. Derek Attridge (London and New York: Routledge, 1992).

B   'Biodegradables: Seven Diary Fragments', trans. Peggy Kamuf, *Critical Inquiry* 15:4 (1989), 812–73.

BB   'But, Beyond ... (Open Letter to Anne McClintock and Rob Nixon)', trans. Peggy Kamuf, *Critical Inquiry* 13 (1986), 155–70.

BL   'Before the Law', trans. Avital Ronell and Christine Roulston, in *Acts of Literature: Jacques Derrida*, ed. Derek Attridge (London and New York: Routledge, 1992), 181–220.

CH   'Choreographies', trans. Christie V. McDonald, in *Points: Interviews, 1974–1994*, ed. Elisabeth Weber (Stanford: Stanford University Press, 1995), 89–108.

DIA   'Deconstruction in America: an Interview with Jacques Derrida', trans. James Creech, *Critical Exchange* 17 (1985), 1–33.

DIS   *Dissemination*, trans. Barbara Johnson (Chicago: University of Chicago Press, 1981).

DO   'Deconstruction and the Other', Interview with Richard Kearney, in Richard Kearney, *Dialogues with Contemporary Continental Thinkers* (Manchester: Manchester University Press, 1984), 105–26.

DOA   'The Deconstruction of Actuality: an Interview with Jacques Derrida', trans. Jonathan Rée, *Radical Philosophy* 68 (1994), 28–41.

DOI   'Declarations of Independence', trans. Tom Keenan and Tom Pepper, *New Political Science* 15 (1986), 7–15.

DTB   'Des Tours de Babel', *Semeia: an Experimental Journal of Biblical Criticism* 54 (1991), 3–54.

EO   *The Ear of the Other: Otobiography, Transference, Translation: Texts and Discussions with Jacques Derrida*, trans. Peggy Kamuf, ed. Christie V. McDonald (New York: Schocken Books, 1985).

FL   'Force of Law: the "Mystical Foundation of Authority" ', trans. Avital Ronell, in *Deconstruction and the Possibility of Justice*,

OH   *The Other Heading: Reflections on Today's Europe*, trans. Pascale-Anne Brault and Michael B. Naas (Bloomington: Indiana University Press, 1992).

OS   *Of Spirit: Heidegger and the Question*, trans. Geoffrey Bennington and Rachel Bowlby (Chicago: University of Chicago Press, 1989).

PA   'Passions: an Oblique Offering', trans. David Wood, in *Derrida: a Critical Reader*, ed. David Wood (Oxford: Oxford University Press, 1992).

PAF   'Politics and Friendship: an Interview with Jacques Derrida', in *The Althusserian Legacy*, eds Anne E. Kaplan and Michael Sprinker (London: Verso, 1993), 183–231.

PF   'The Politics of Friendship', *Journal of Philosophy* 75:11 (1988), 632–45.

PFSF   *The Postcard: From Socrates to Freud and Beyond*, trans. Alan Bass (Chicago: University of Chicago Press, 1987).

POF   *Politics of Friendship*, trans. George Collins (London: Verso, 1997).

POI   *Points: Interviews*, 1974–94, ed. Elisabeth Weber, trans. Peggy Kamuf (Stanford: Stanford University Press, 1995).

POR   'The Principle of Reason: the University in the Eyes of Its Pupils', trans. Catherine Porter and Edward P. Morris, *Diacritics* 13:3 (1983), 3–20.

POS   *Positions*, trans. Alan Bass (London: Athlone, 1981).

RLW   'Racism's Last Word', trans. Peggy Kamuf, *Critical Inquiry* 12:1 (1985), 290–9.

SM   *Specters of Marx: the State of the Debt, the Work of Mourning, and the New International*, trans. Peggy Kamuf (London and New York: Routledge, 1994).

SN   *Spurs: Nietzsche's Styles/Eperons: les Styles de Nietzsche*, trans. Barbara Harlow (Chicago: University of Chicago Press, 1979).

SO   'Sendoffs', *Yale French Studies* 77 (1990), 7–43.

SP   *Speech and Phenomena: And Other Essays on Husserl's Theory of Signs*, trans. David B. Allison (Evanston, Ill.: Northwestern University Press, 1983).

TOJ   'The Time Is Out of Joint', trans. Peggy Kamuf, in *Deconstruction is/in America: a New Sense of the Political*, ed. Anselm Haverkamp (New York: New York University Press, 1995), 14–38.

WD   *Writing and Difference*, trans. Alan Bass (London: Routledge and Kegan & Paul, 1978).

Introduction

The death of Jacques Derrida in October 2004 leaves behind an immense corpus of work, interviews, essays, films, TV documentaries, almost eighty books, as well as literally thousands of critical studies spanning many disciplines, languages and intellectual contexts. What is the legacy of Jacques Derrida? What will 'live on' and 'survive'? 'Live on' and 'survive' are of course two of Derrida's own phrases, and it is remarkable how Derrida's thoughts on the theme of translation, interpretation, the proper name, biodegradability and the signature, to name but a few of his concerns, illuminate the reception history and intellectual legacy of his own work. In an essay on *Hamlet*, Derrida provides an answer to our question, via one of his frequent meditations on death: 'one must stop believing that the dead are just departed and that the departed do nothing. One must stop pretending to know what is meant by "to die" and especially by "dying." One has, then, to talk about spectrality' (TOJ, 30). By spectrality Derrida means the rethinking of presence and absence that characterizes much of his work. Spectrality, haunting, differance, the trace, the supplement, these and the many similar terms we find articulated in Derrida's rigorous deconstructive readings, all function to respect singularity, and to consider the remains of an intellectual legacy. They all indicate that texts can bring forth readings – either in the present or the future – that their authors might never have imagined or thought possible. This book is an attempt to respect the singularity of Derrida's own unique contribution to modern thought, principally by examining the reception of deconstruction. As such the book serves as an introduction to Derrida, especially when 'introduction' is understood in Julian Wolfreys's terms as offering 'on the one hand a refamiliarization with what is unfamiliar, and, on the other, a defamiliarization with that which has been taken for granted, particularly with respect to specific

1

dimensions of the reception of Derrida and the motif of so-called deconstruction' (Wolfreys, 2004, 4–5). The reception of Derrida was and will continue to be an 'incalculable' reception that will come from the future perhaps as much as from the past or present.

Since the late 1960s a politics of deconstruction has been a frequent demand of Derrida's readers. One could also add, a demand of many who have never taken the trouble to read Derrida at all. The 'trouble' and 'difficulty' that some encounter in the act of reading Derrida goes against the grain of our times with its emphasis on easily accessible and digestible information. This book approaches the demand from a fresh perspective in that it examines the political resonance of deconstruction as a function of its cross-cultural translation. Such an approach stems in fact from one of Derrida's own discussions of translation, 'Letter to a Japanese Friend', in which he outlines the need for a study of the 'very different connotations, inflections, and emotional or affective values' of the word deconstruction (LJF, 1). In this short missive Derrida suggests that an analysis of the reception of deconstruction's multiple identity would offer an acute example of cross-cultural translation, transformation and resistance. Deconstruction does not correspond 'in French to some clear and univocal signification. There is already in "my" language', Derrida writes:

> a serious problem of translation between what here or there can be envisaged for the word, and the usage itself, the reserves of the word. And it is already clear that, even in French, things change from one context to another. More so in the German, English, and especially American contexts, where the same word is already attached to very different connotations, inflections, and emotional or affective values. Their analysis would be interesting and warrants a study of its own. (LJF, 1)

Derrida's interest in such a study is also matched by Richard Wolin, who speculates that:

> It would ... be fruitful to subject deconstruction's impact as a mode of literary criticism itself to a deconstructive analysis. For after all, does not its 'transformation via reception' in a North American context represent a paradigmatic instance of several pet deconstructive themes concerning textuality and repetition: translation, iterability and dissemination? Yet I know of no such efforts to understand the immense cultural influence of deconstruction along these lines. (Wolin, 1992, 194)

Wolin recognizes how Derrida's deconstructive themes can also be used to explain the cross-cultural dissemination and transformation of deconstruction itself. As both Derrida and Wolin suggest, then, a study of the reception of deconstruction would trace how the political implications of this key word of postmodern theory have been continually reinvented – transformed via reception – by the cultural, intellectual and disciplinary contexts in which it has been used.

For reasons of space and relevance it is not possible to focus on all of the disciplines and theoretical movements that deconstruction has affected during the history of its reception to date. Derrida's influence in Departments of Theology, Architecture, Fine Art and Law, as well as in the work of feminists, gay and lesbian literary critics, and post-colonialists, would all be fitting subjects for full-length books. Furthermore, in contrast to the meanings deconstruction has acquired in a literary context a series of other interpretations has emerged. Deconstruction is now commonly associated with a range of issues, from nationalism (Satzewich, 1992; Silverman, 1992) to nursing (Ramprogus, 1995), and a range of other disciplines, from Architecture (Benedikt, 1991) to Social Psychology (Parker and Shotter, 1990). It is also possible to find critical studies claiming to deconstruct major thinkers such as Durkheim (Lehmann, 1993), as well as icons of classical and popular culture, from Macbeth (Fawkner, 1990) to Madonna (Lloyd, 1993). Deconstruction has been subject to cross-cultural and cross-disciplinary appropriation that has not been limited to the Liberal Arts. Nevertheless, by examining the reception of deconstruction in Anglo-American culture, it will be possible to analyse and to contextualize the first and perhaps most important wave of critical work on Derridean deconstruction, and to show how it has been a powerful political strategy in the work of many minority movements. Consequently, it will be evident that deconstruction has played a role in some of the most prominent struggles in the American and French academies: from the emergence of the Yale School to the 'de Man affair', and from Derrida's institutional concern with the reform of teaching and philosophy in the organization GREPH and the International College of Philosophy, to the publication of *Specters of Marx*.

Derrida remarks in the above passage from 'Letter to a Japanese Friend' that deconstruction has acquired a profoundly different meaning in the French, German, American and British academies. In responding to this idea what follows will be concerned with two main questions that arise from deconstruction's reception: Why has deconstruction been identified, as Derrida himself asks, with a modern form of immorality, amorality, or irresponsibility? (PA, 15). And how has deconstruction been associated with numerous political strategies, from anarchism to left-reformism, from totalitarianism to fascism? As Derrida recognizes in *Specters of Marx*, deconstruction has been removed from its politico-institutional context in the postwar French academy and inserted into a range of other ideological and pedagogical conflicts. In particular, Derrida's thought has been distorted by a number of postmodern currents that emerged at the same time in the Anglo-American academy. Derrida's initial reception, especially in American and British literary criticism, as Terry Eagleton argues:

> reminds us forcibly of just what deliberate blindness and amnesia, what violence, suppression and marginalisation have been active in the effort to make Derrida's thought serve the cause of an elitist rhetoric. (Eagleton, 1986, 87)

This misreading ventriloquizes Derrida's interest in how intellectual movements and ideas can be taken over and used for a different political and cultural agenda. The reception of deconstruction performs what Norris identifies as Derrida's own 'preoccupation with proper names (for instance, the name "Jacques Derrida"), and the way that these attach to a body of writing whose fate at the hands of readers and exegetes can never be controlled or kept within bounds by any power of authorial command' (Norris, 1987, 195). Perhaps the best evidence of Derrida's understanding of misreading – and by implication, of dissemination, iterability and translation – is provided by the reception of deconstruction's ambiguous political implications.

The argument of this book has two main aspects. On the one hand, Derridean deconstruction represents a challenge to all forms of philosophical and political authenticity. In the 'Afterword' to *Limited Inc* Derrida neatly rehearses this aspect of my argument:

> There is no one, single deconstruction. Were there only one, were it homogeneous, it would not be inherently either conservative or revolutionary, or determinable within the code of such oppositions ... Deconstruction, in the singular, is not 'inherently' anything at all that might be determinable on the basis of this code and of its criteria. It is 'inherently' nothing at all; the logic of essence ... is precisely what all deconstruction has from the start called into question ... Deconstruction does not exist somewhere, pure, proper, self-identical, outside of its inscriptions in conflictual and differentiated contexts; it 'is' only what it does and what is done with it, there where it takes place. (LINC, 141)

Deconstruction attacks all forms of the proper including its own. It is an interminable critique of totalizing modes of thought.

On the other hand, this is not to say that deconstruction is opposed to or negates political thinking. In fact many of Derrida's texts describe how deconstruction is strongly committed to rethinking the enlightenment tradition of rationality, justice, international law and democracy: deconstruction 'respectfully pays homage to a new, very new *Aufklärung*' (LINC, 141). Deconstruction is best thought of as an attempt to rethink existing forms of the political, especially in the domain of institutions and the subject. Consequently, in order to understand these dual aspects of deconstruction – Derrida's rejection of authenticity and his conception of justice and democracy – one must understand Derrida's thinking of temporality as *differance* and *alterity*. This conception of time as repetition and alteration – as opposed to the metaphysical idea of repetition as sameness – underpins Derrida's understanding of deconstruction in the above passage. In the following extract from *Specters of Marx* it is also possible to see the clear connection between Derrida's deconstruction of authenticity with his non-horizal understanding of undeconstructible justice and the promise of democracy:

> Even beyond the regulating idea in its classic form, the idea, if that is still what it is, of democracy to come, its 'idea' as event of a pledged injunction that orders one to summon the very thing that will never present itself in the form of full presence, is the opening of this gap between an infinite promise ... and the determined, necessary, but also necessarily inadequate forms of what has to be measured against this promise. (SM, 65)

The logic that binds the 'pledged injunction' and 'what has to be measured against this promise' is the logic of originary repetition (Beardsworth, 1996, 18). The temporal logic that underpins Derrida's notion of originary repetition is also the very logic that underpins this book's study of the historical reception of deconstruction and Derrida's legacy.

The reading of Derrida's reception advanced in what follows will be based on the premise that his work has been received in three waves in the Anglo-American academy. First, in the early to mid-1970s, deconstruction was transformed via its reception in American literary studies. This translation of Derrida has been most often identified with the so-called Yale School critics (de Man, Hartman, Hillis Miller and Bloom) and the book, *Deconstruction and Criticism* (Hartman, 1979). Derrida's early influence was in actual fact determined by the need to find a formalist successor to the

American New Criticism. The politico-institutional context of deconstruction was profoundly underestimated as a result. As Beardsworth points out, 'the literary reception of Derrida's thought overplayed its rhetorical side and, at its institutional worst, made it into a practice of literary criticism, the political orientation of which was easily advertised but poorly elaborated' (Beardsworth, 1996, 3).

Following Alan Bass's English translation of *Positions* (1981), the early 1980s saw a number of readings of deconstruction by Marxist literary critics (Ryan, 1982; Eagleton, 1983, 1984). Michael Ryan's study of *Marxism and Deconstruction*, for instance, focused on deconstruction as a form of ideology-critique, arguing that deconstruction could provide a democratic and anti-hierarchical supplement to critical as opposed to scientific Marxism. A common complaint of many of these readings was that deconstruction had been stripped of its left-wing sympathies by American literary critics. Terry Eagleton, for example, argued that 'the Yale deconstructionists have been able to effect a more fruitful commerce between North American bourgeois liberalism and a certain selective reading of Derrida – one which, most glaringly, eradicates all traces of the political from his work' (Eagleton, 1984, 101).

Secondly, since the mid-1980s, there has been a series of more conventional philosophical readings of Derrida (Gasché, 1986; Harvey, 1986; Llewelyn, 1986). The purpose of these readings was also essentially corrective. They challenged the idea that Derrida's work has been used by literary critics to bolster their discipline's argumentative rigour and rejected by philosophers precisely because it was too literary. Nevertheless, in correcting the literary reading, Harvey and Gasché are often guilty of underplaying the significance of literature in Derrida's work.

And thirdly, since the early 1990s, there has been an effort to foreground the ethico-political dimensions of Derrida's thought (Critchley, 1992; Bennington, 1994; Royle, 1995; Beardsworth, 1996). My reading of Derrida's reception is largely seen through the lens of these studies, as well as that of an earlier essay by Bill Readings (1989), in which he turned the question of the politics of deconstruction into that of the deconstruction of the political, without signalling an avoidance of the former. Of particular importance in this respect is Critchley's *The Ethics of Deconstruction* (1992), in which he established Derrida's indebtedness to Levinas's understanding of ethics. The ethical relation is shown to be the basis of Derrida's thinking of community and of his notion of a 'democracy to come' in *The Other Heading* (1992).

Both Bennington (1994) and Beardsworth (1996), who write in the wake of Derrida's *Specters of Marx* and its extended account of justice and the promise of democracy, develop Derrida's resistance to metaphysical notions of politics and temporality. In these readings, the abandonment of any totalizing notion of the political (Bennington, 1994, 97) emerges as a prerequisite of the attempt to come to terms with the political implications of deconstruction. The same can be said for the notion of an autonomous and transcendent political subject. Beardsworth's reading begins with these assumptions in mind and develops Derrida's thinking of justice and the 'promise of democracy' via the organizing principle of the aporia and originary repetition (Beardsworth, 1996, 18).

Rather than beginning by offering a definition of deconstruction, the overall effect of the following chapters will be to allow a number of conflicting and differentiated readings of deconstruction to emerge prior to a fuller elaboration of Derrida's account of deconstruction as justice and democracy in *Specters of Marx*. In what follows, each chapter will focus successively on the reinvention – the repetition and alteration – of deconstruction's political implications and Derrida's resistance to these readings.

Chapter 1 discusses Derrida's understanding of 'translation as transformation' in *Limited Inc* (1988) and 'Des Tours de Babel' (1991). The second part of the chapter examines the implications of deconstruction for translation theory as a preface to the translation of deconstruction in the pages that follow.

Chapter 2 considers the translation of deconstruction in American literary criticism, focusing in particular on some of Paul de Man's major essays from *Allegories of Reading* and *Blindness and Insight*, especially 'Semiology and Rhetoric' (1979) and 'The Rhetoric of Temporality' (1988a). Having established similarities between Derrida's and de Man's style of reading, Part Two will consider the political implications of de Man's deconstruction of aesthetic ideology as an anti-totalitarian strategy by looking at his essays on 'Wordsworth and Hölderlin' (1984), 'Heidegger's Exegeses of Hölderlin' (1988a) and 'The Temptation of Permanence' (1983). Next I turn to Derrida's discussion of the originary violence of law in 'Declarations of Independence' (1986), an essay that directly confronted the political implications of deconstruction, but was nevertheless overlooked by many American readers of his work.

Part Three focuses on Derrida's reading of phallogocentrism in *Spurs: Nietzsche's Styles* (1979) that serves as a preface to my discussion of feminism. Via Barbara Johnson's feminist reading of abortion in 'Apostrophe, Animation, and Abortion' (1987), I will argue that it is possible to link deconstruction with questions of gender and race in ways which sharply contrast with the literary readings of Derrida's thought that emerged at the beginning of the 1980s. In conclusion, Readings's (1989) and Elam's (1994) discussion of the deconstruction of the subject in relation to feminism will be foregrounded.

Chapter 3 examines how Derrida's involvement with GREPH, the International College of Philosophy, and the essays, 'The Principle of Reason: the University in the Eyes of Its Pupils' (1983), 'Languages and Institutions of Philosophy' (1984), 'Sendoffs' (1990) and 'Mochlos: or The Conflict of the Faculties' (1992), challenged the literary reading of deconstruction throughout the early 1980s. As the pivotal centre of the book, this chapter defines deconstruction as a responsible interrogation of the legacy of the post-Kantian critical tradition, rather than of its abandonment.

Chapter 4 considers the reinvention of deconstruction as a neoconservative strategy of postmodernism by examining Habermas's discussion of deconstruction in *The Philosophical Discourse of Modernity* (1987). In spite of Derrida's concern with political and pedagogical reform, it was still possible for Habermas to claim that deconstruction was akin to a type of neoconservatism. Rejecting Habermas's reading, Derridean deconstruction emerges as a form of post-Kantian enlightenment critique, evident in Derrida's essay 'Of an Apocalyptic Tone Recently Adopted in Philosophy' (1984).

Chapter 5 looks at the politics of reading an intellectual legacy, focusing on Derrida's reading of Nietzsche in *The Ear of the Other* (1985) and Paul de Man in 'Like the Sound of the Sea Deep within a Shell' (1988) and 'Biodegradables' (1989). This chapter explores how the de Man affair came to light, de Man's deconstruction of aesthetic ideology, and how it was possible to read Derrida's work as a form of totalitarianism or as a rejection of historical context. In conclusion, Derrida's *The Other Heading* (1992) provides further evidence of his deconstruction of the discourse of European exemplarity, which underpinned the antisemitism and xenophobia of National Socialism.

Finally, Chapter 6 considers Derrida's *Specters of Marx* (1994) as a rejection of Francis Fukuyama's 'end of history' thesis and as a further elaboration of the 'promise of democracy'. Returning to Beardsworth's (1996) argument, the themes of spectrality, inheritance and indebtedness will be discussed alongside Derrida's major concern with the law and justice. Beardsworth's discussion of the 'aporia of time' is further elaborated via Derrida's essays, 'Before the Law' (1992) and 'Force of Law: the "Mystical Foundation of Authority" ' (1992). In conclusion I will examine how Derrida's thinking of justice and the aporia allow him to develop his commitment to the promise of democracy and the New International.

The format of these six chapters demonstrates that any attempt to consider the debate about the political implications of Derrida's thought, its legacy and future, must come to terms with the cross-cultural reception of deconstruction – a process underpinned by the concept of translation as transformation.

1

The Task of the Translator: Translation as Transformation

Since his earliest essays, Derrida has been aware of the implications of the deconstruction of metaphysics for translation theory. In an interview in *Positions*, Derrida clearly outlines how metaphysics supports a particular understanding of translation based on univocity. The deconstruction of meaning as intention leads Derrida to question the successful transportation of meaning from source to target text in this notable section:

> [F]or the notion of translation we would have to substitute a notion of *transformation*: a regulated transformation of one language by another, of one text by another. We will never have, and in fact have never had, to do with some 'transport' of pure signifieds from one language to another, or within one and the same language, that the signifying instrument would leave virgin and untouched. (POS, 20)

Derrida's comments on translation theory add an important new dimension to the translation and transformation of his own work, and to the conflict between the positive and negative understandings of deconstruction that have been mixed up in the process.

The exchanges with Searle about deconstruction and speech act theory in 'Signature, Event, Context' (*Sec*) clarify Derrida's main concerns with the question of translation still further. The function of *iterability* in particular illuminates the repetition and alteration of deconstruction itself, that is to say, its re-mark in a number of intellectual and cultural contexts. Iterability describes the process of alteration, the logic that ties repetition to alterity. One of the main theses of 'Signature, Event, Context' is that 'Iteration alters, something new takes place' (LINC, 40) – a process that inevitably courts misinterpretation and challenges the naive belief in the transport or expression of pure intentions or transcendental signifieds. Derrida's use of iterability in the 'Afterword' to the later edition of *Limited Inc* clarifies the formation of deconstruction's political implications during the following chapters in this book. Here, Derrida challenges the traditional oppositions of political thought, and all forms of authenticity: deconstruction is not 'conservative or revolutionary, or determinable within the code of such oppositions' (LINC, 141). Deconstruction is owned by no one and is not determined by any horizonal form of political thought: 'Deconstruction does not exist somewhere, pure, proper, self-identical, outside of its inscriptions in conflictual and differentiated contexts' (LINC, 141).

In 'Signature, Event, Context' Derrida picks up many of the themes of his earlier work in *Speech and Phenomena* and *Of Grammatology*, principally those related to metaphysics as a system of privilege based on exclusion and essential distinctions. In the context of Anglo-American speech act theory, Derrida is concerned with the problematical notion of literal meaning; the inadequacy of the current concept of context; and the displacement of the notion of writing that has been dominant throughout the history of western philosophy. In order to examine the classical concept of writing – the idea that, while writing is secondary to the plenitude of full speech, it is still a medium through which the unity and wholeness of meaning would not be affected in its essence – Derrida focuses on Condillac's notion of meaning.

The form of writing, organized throughout the history of western philosophy, 'presupposes the simplicity of the origin, the continuity of all derivation, of all production, of all analysis, and the homogeneity of all dimensions' (LINC, 4). Derrida examines Condillac's genealogy of writing as an example of these themes. According to Condillac, writing was invented as a vehicle of communication in a progressive movement beyond speech, which enabled human beings to perpetuate their thoughts to people who are absent. Derrida, however, is critical of Condillac's insistence that writing can unproblematically convey an authorial intention to absent readers, and, by implication, 'writing will never have the slightest effect on either the structure or the contents of the meaning (the ideas) that it is supposed to transmit' (LINC, 4). Condillac forms an uncritical relationship between writing as a type of representation, communication and expression. It is this triad of terms that underpins all of the species of writing, from pictographic to alphabetic, from Egyptian hieroglyphics to the ideographic writing of Chinese. But the question of the absence of an addressee, the idea that writing will continue to convey authorial intentions independently of an author's presence, even after his/her death, raises profound questions about writing's ability merely to represent rather than to transform what it transports. To a certain extent Condillac's discourse even acknowledges this, as Derrida points out: 'The absence of which Condillac speaks is determined in the most classic manner as a continuous modification and progressive extenuation of presence' (LINC, 5). Nevertheless, the process of 'supplementation is not exhibited as a break in presence but rather as a continuous and homogeneous reparation and modification of presence in the representation' (LINC, 5).

These aspects of Condillac's thought are also evident in the work of the French ideologues that followed him, principally gathered around the notion of the 'theory of the sign as representation of the idea which itself represented the object perceived. From that point on, communication is that which circulates a representation as an ideal content (meaning); and writing is a species of this general communication' (LINC, 6). Derrida is concerned, then, with the absence that intervenes in the classical functioning of writing. It is not a complete absence – but the oscillation between presence and absence. In this context it is referred to as the *trace* – later it will be called *spectrality*.

This classical conception also posits that the intention of the author is always effectively transmitted to an absent receiver. For Derrida, however, 'To be what it is, all writing must … be capable of functioning in the radical absence of every empirically determined receiver in general' (LINC, 8). Rather than be a mere modification of presence, as Condillac's understanding of the supplement suggested, 'absence is not a continuous modification of presence, it is a rupture in presence, the "death" or the possibility of the "death" of the receiver inscribed in the structure of the mark' (LINC, 8). The same logic of iterability applies to the sender also. Writing functions in this fashion regardless of the intentions of the sender, producer or author:

> For a writing to be a writing it must continue to 'act' and to be readable even when what is called the author of the writing no longer answers for what he has written, for what he seems to have signed, be it because of a temporary absence, because he is dead or, more generally, because he has not employed his absolutely actual and present intention or attention, the plenitude of his desire to say what he means, in order to sustain what seems to be written 'in his name.' (LINC, 8)

Derrida lists a number of areas where his criticism of this concept of writing emerge: (1) there is a 'break' with the idea that writing is a faithful communication of consciousness and thus of authorial intentions; (2) the emergence of the idea of writing as dissemination; and (3) the disqualification of the limiting concept of context. These aspects are not restricted to the narrow conception of writing, Derrida contends, as they are to be found in all language, in spoken languages and in the totality of experience: the 'unity of the signifying form only constitutes itself by virtue of its iterability, by the possibility of its being repeated in the absence not only of its "referent" ... but in the absence of a determinate signified or of the intention of actual signification, as well as of all intention of present communication' (LINC, 10). Moreover, these traits are generalizable beyond the scope of the classical concept of writing. This leads Derrida toward a different understanding of context:

> Every sign, linguistic or nonlinguistic, spoken or written ... can be *cited*, put between quotation marks; in so doing it can break with every given context, engendering an infinity of new contexts in a manner which is absolutely illimitable. This does not imply that the mark is valid outside of a context, but on the contrary, that there are only contexts without any center or absolute anchoring. (LINC, 12)

In 'Reiterating the Differences', Searle's response to 'Signature, Event, Context', he disputes Derrida's main arguments: the idea that oral speech is opposed to writing; Derrida's challenge to Austin's distinctions between normal and serious speech acts; his apparent undermining of the intentional understanding of meaning; and the consequences of iterability for the metaphysical concept of intentionality and context. Searle's arguments, however, seem to ignore key aspects of Derrida's thought. In *Of Grammatology*, for example, it is evident that Derrida does not simply *oppose* writing to speech, as is so often suggested. The same misunderstandings also inform Searle's second and third points of contention. Searle fails to understand that Derrida refuses to establish any kind of authenticity. This effectively means that Searle is led – certainly in the case of his interpretation of the opposition between writing and speech – to seriously underestimate Derrida's notion of originary repetition.

Rather than provide an overview of *Limited Inc* in its entirety, I will focus on those elements which are most apposite to my discussion of the translation of deconstruction, that is to say, Searle's rejection of Derrida's argument that *iterability* conflicts with his notion of authorial intentionality and the idea that the repeatability or survival of a text entails its reproduction. In this respect, Searle claims that Derrida's argument is that:

> somehow the iterability of linguistic forms (together with the citationality of linguistic forms and the existence of writing) militates against the idea that intention is the heart of meaning and communication, that indeed, an understanding of iteration will show the 'essential absence of intention to the actuality of the utterance.' (Searle, 1977, 207)

For Searle, the 'iterability of linguistic forms facilitates and is a necessary condition of the particular forms of intentionality that are characteristic of speech acts', rejecting what he takes to be Derrida's general argument, namely, that speech acts are *not* 'single events in particular historical contexts' (1977, 208).

Derrida returns to the issue of iterability in relation to the central object of the debate with Searle – the propriety of the *signature* – cleverly using the occasion to voice the struggle for the propriety of his own signature. Underneath his article Searle has written 'Copyright © 1977 by John R. Searle'. Derrida asks why Searle should claim copyright on an article if he believes in the successful transportation of authorial intention? If this is so, then everyone 'will in advance *have been able*, to reproduce what he says' (LINC, 30). The copyright reveals Searle's 'anxiety and compulsion to stamp and to seal the truth' (LINC, 31), thus indicating to Derrida that his signature is always already 'divided, multiplied, conjugated, shared' (LINC, 31). In fact, Searle acknowledges this in his preface where he states his indebtedness to H. Dreyfus and D. Searle. Derrida's title, *Limited Inc* – from the French, *Société à responsabilitié limitée*, meaning 'Society with Limited Responsibility' or 'Limited Liability' – attempts to convey the divisions within Searle's (or for that matter any) proper name. This idea is represented by Derrida's use of the mnemonic *Sarl* throughout his text to refer to Searle.

The question of propriety is linked by Searle to Derrida's misreading of Austin – as Derrida indicates, Searle accuses him of misunderstanding and misinterpretation throughout his rejoinder – and this raises the question about the very structure of speech acts. This question returns Derrida to the themes of re-production, iterability, citation and translation, all of which are neutralized by metaphysics' linear conception of time. Searle's emphasis on Derrida's *mis*reading of Austin is one reason why he takes obvious pleasure in citing Searle's rejoinder at great length. Derrida's point of course is to emphasize that a 'certain practice of citation, and also of iteration ... is at work, constantly *altering*, at once and without delay ... whatever it seems to reproduce. This is one of the theses of *Sec*. Iteration alters, something new takes place' (LINC, 40). Searle's repeated identification of such misreadings and mistakes thus proves Derrida's point about the logic of iterability and challenges the assumption that communication is *simply* the communication of an intentional meaning.

For Searle, however, the main argument of *Sec* is that writing continues to function in the absence of the sender, the receiver and even the context in which it is produced. Searle misunderstands Derrida's point once again. He implies that Derrida believes that this is always the case. In fact, Derrida is merely arguing that it is *possible* that writing can function in the absence of the sender: 'Such iterability is inseparable from the structural possibility in which it is necessarily inscribed' (LINC, 48). In familiar deconstructive style, Derrida challenges the essential distinctions and exclusions of Searle's discourse. Searle's example of a shopping list would not be what it is unless it combined the two aspects, which Derrida identifies through the logic of contamination. Whether this logic is identified as the 'remark' or the 'blinking-effect', it mounts the same attack on the idea that the survival of a text depends on its repeatability without alteration. Searle is guilty of confusing survival with permanence, and thus he cannot grasp that at the heart of Derrida's logic of contamination is his refusal to establish 'any kind of authenticity' (LINC, 55), whether it relates to a mode of thought, to politics or to a formerly marginal pole of a binary opposition such as speech and writing. This kind of thinking underpins his misreading of Derrida's notion of intentionality throughout his rejoinders. Derrida's rejoinder is consistent with the logic of contamination – the *trace* of nonpresence that disrupts the presence of the 'now'. What Derrida questions, then, is the teleology that 'orients and organizes the movement and the possibility of a fulfilment, realization, and *actualization* in a plenitude that would be *present* to and identical with itself' (LINC, 56). Here again the main point emerges. What is at stake for Derrida is an analysis that can 'account for *structural possibilities*' (LINC, 57). In the case of this book, this is an analysis of the *structural possibilities* – the translation as transformation, or iterability – of deconstruction on its passage away from Jacques Derrida as its author. In 'Des Tours de Babel' Derrida continues the implications of iterability via his detailed discussions of translation as transformation in the work of Walter Benjamin.

'Des Tours de Babel'

In 'Des Tours de Babel' Derrida discusses the biblical story of the tower of Babel alongside Benjamin's essay 'The Task of the Translator'.

Derrida's target is the traditional conception of translation, the idea that it is possible to achieve a 'transparent and adequate interexpression' (DTB, 3) between an original text and its translation. Deconstructing this notion leads Derrida to speculate on the interpretative afterlife or survival of a body of work. The first theme was evident in a number of Derrida's early works, from *Of Grammatology* to *Positions* and *Limited Inc*; the second theme is evident in *The Ear of the Other*, 'Biodegradables' and *Specters of Marx*, to name just some prominent examples. In what follows I am going to elaborate on the role that these two themes play in 'Des Tours de Babel', before turning to examine how these concerns – legacy, inheritance and indebtedness – can be used to describe the 'translation as transformation' of deconstruction itself.

Derrida's thesis is stated at the outset of 'Des Tours de Babel':

> The 'tower of Babel' does not merely figure the irreducible multiplicity of tongues; it exhibits an incompletion, the impossibility of finishing, of totalizing, of saturating, of completing something in the order of edification, architectural construction, system and architectonics. What the multiplicity of idioms actually limits is not only a 'true' translation, a transparent and adequate interexpression, it is also a structural order, a coherence of construct ... It would be easy and up to a certain point justified to see there the translation of a system in deconstruction. (DTB, 3–4)

Derrida's rejection of the coherence of construct and the incompleteness of the constructure echoes his analysis of the 'structurality of the structure' in 'Structure, Sign and Play in the Discourse of the Human Sciences'. Once again Derrida's reading turns on the undecidability of language. The word Babel, which functions in the story as a proper name and a pure signified, also refers to the word *confusion*. As Derrida's reference to Voltaire's *Dictionnaire philosophique* indicates, on the one hand, *Ba* derives from the word for father in Oriental tongues, whereas *Bel* signifies God. The word Babel, on the other hand, means both the city of God or the holy city and confusion. The latter mood is exacerbated, as Voltaire points out that there are two meanings of the word confusion: the 'confusion of tongues, but also the state of confusion in which the architects find themselves with the structure interrupted' (DTB, 4). To follow Voltaire's discussion, God names the origin of language as a proper name and, as a result of his anger at the Shemites' dream of a universal language and his destruction of their tower, the source of linguistic confusion. God's destruction of the

Shemites' tower is thus likened by Derrida to dissemination and deconstruction:

YHWH disperses them from here over the face of all the earth.
They cease to build the city.
Over which he proclaims his name Bavel, Confusion,
for there, YHWH confounds the lip of all the earth,
and from there YWHW disperses them over the face of all the
earth.

(DTB, 6–7)

Through God's anger, Derrida writes, 'he opens the deconstruction of the tower, as of the universal language; he scatters the genealogical filiation' (DTB, 7). The dissemination of the universal language marks the emergence of the necessary but impossible task of translation, a process Derrida likens to the struggle for the appropriation of a proper name. Babel restates Derrida's argument that the proper name is always already a common noun. In the biblical story, Babel refers to three different things: it is no longer merely the title given to the narrative, the name of a 'tower or a city but a tower or a city that receives its name from an event during which YHWH "proclaims his name" ' (DTB, 8). Derrida's point is that Babel's association with these meanings *and* the word confusion exemplifies how the proper name is also a common noun. No satisfactory solution is available to the translator because there can be no successful or pure transportation of the signified: 'At best it reproduces approximately and by dividing the equivocation into two words there where confusion gathered in potential, in all its potential, in the internal translation, if one can say that, which works the word in the so-called original tongue' (DTB, 8). The necessity and impossibility of translation is thus conveyed by the problems that plague the proper name effect: the proper name 'makes the language possible (what would a language be without the possibility of calling by a proper name?)' while at the same time 'it can properly inscribe itself in a language only by allowing itself to be translated therein, in other words, *interpreted* by its semantic equivalent: from this moment it can no longer be taken as proper name' (DTB, 8–9).

From this conclusion Derrida is able to reject the notion of transparent translation. The contamination of the proper name by the common noun is related to the theme of 'genealogical indebtedness' (DTB, 10) and an originary linguistic violence. The transparency of the human community reiterates Rousseau's and Lévi-Strauss's desire for a natural community. God's intervention, however, leads to the deconstruction of transparent translation:

> [W]hen God imposes and opposes his name, he ruptures the rational transparency but interrupts also the colonial violence or the linguistic imperialism. He destines them to translation, he subjects them to the law of a translation both necessary and impossible ... (DTB, 10)

God's name embodies a 'translatable-untranslatable' conflict, which makes univocity impossible. The significance of the story of Babel – what Derrida refers to as the Babelian performance – lies in the *aporia* or *double-bind* that bonds translatability with untranslatability. Translation emerges as a law, duty and debt that can never be discharged. Consequently, the word Babel once more marks the point at which Derrida identifies the undecidable relation between the proper name and the common noun.

It is at this juncture that Derrida turns to consider Maurice de Gandillac's French translation of Benjamin's 'The Task of the Translator', an essay that is itself a preface to a translation of Baudelaire's *Tableaux parisiens*. Derrida's notion of the *debt* is echoed by Benjamin's use of the word task in his title, as is the idea that pure translation is impossible. The translator, Derrida surmizes, 'is indebted, he appears to himself as translator in a situation of debt; and his task is to *render*, to render that which must have been given' (DTB, 11). Derrida's main focus concerns how this restitution is to be achieved and the elaboration of Benjamin's conception of meaning in this context.

Benjamin's discussion of an important passage from Mallarmé makes Derrida's points well. Reinforced by Benjamin's naturalistic metaphors, translation is located *between* literary creation and theory. Although it has 'lower relief', its impact on history is arguably just as significant. Benjamin challenges the ordinary concept of translation and the restitution of meaning upon which it depends. Derrida's point about the contamination of the proper name is reiterated: the 'proper name is not totally insignificant; it is merely welded to that whose meaning does not allow transport without damage into another language or into another tongue' (DTB, 12).

Benjamin's use of vitalist or geneticist metaphors enhances his concern with the 'sur-vival' (Derrida inserts the hyphen) or afterlife of the original text. The task of the translator is to insure that the original survives. Benjamin's main point is that there can be no access to pure translation. For Derrida, this point emphasizes Benjamin's concern with the history of texts, their interpretative afterlife, which succeeds their biological life and death. Here begins the task of the translator: the 'indebted subject, obligated by a duty, already in the position of heir, entered as a survivor in a genealogy, as survivor or agent of sur-vival. The sur-vival of works, not authors. Perhaps the sur-vival of authors' names and of signatures, but not of authors' (DTB, 13). Benjamin confirms Derrida's challenge to the notion of pure translation and its guarantee that it will always ensure the 'sur-vival' of the source text as a copy or image of the original. The translation does not guarantee the restitution of the original.

Translation ceases to be viewed as an operation between two languages that can eschew the process of transformation. On the contrary, texts are continually in the process of interpretation, translation and transformation; the original text is always intercepted and renarrated. In Benjamin's terms, the original source text gives itself to be modified, hence it survives as a consequence of its life-giving transformation. The process of growth via translation responds to the structure of the original text, that presents resources for further interpretation. Lovingly and with a sensitive attention to detail, the translation attempts to convey the intentions of the original in its own language. In this fashion both become elements of a larger, more integrated language. For Benjamin, then, translation does not restore the original meaning of the text; rather it enlarges it by placing the original alongside an aggregate of existing and potential meanings. When the translation is placed alongside the original, they complete each other by transforming each other. Through its survival the original has been renewed by its modification, demonstrating that the apparent solidification of words is still open to a process of 'postmaturation'. The original text is always subject to change, Derrida summarizes, 'it gives itself in modifying itself ... it lives and lives on in mutation' (DTB, 16). This does not mean, however, that the translator bears no responsibility for his translation. On the contrary, Derrida is very careful to establish the responsibility, duty or task of the translator, and, by implication, of the deconstructor. Reminding readers that his reading is itself a translation of Maurice de Gandillac's French translation of Benjamin's German text, itself a preface to a translation, Derrida is keen to articulate the nature of his role, not as a 'passer' or 'passerby', but as one who is aware of the process of indebtedness that is implicit in the act of translation. The original pleads for translation in order to fulfil its lack of completion. At the same time, it is also constrained; the translation cannot be universalized. God's intervention is similarly understood by Derrida as an example of the *double-bind*: the demand of the proper name to request translation is accompanied by its simultaneous dissemination. What Derrida identifies as a double indebtedness moves between the names of the author and the translator. In turn this notion disrupts the traditional idea that translation depends on a principle of transferability among languages without remainder. While not adhering to this classical view of translation, Benjamin states that the final goal of translation is to articulate the close proximity between languages. Derrida interprets this line as a strategy of the double-bind: 'A translation would not seek to say this or that, to transport this or that content, to communicate such a charge of meaning, but to re-mark the affinity among the languages, to exhibit its own possibility' (DTB, 19). While it is not simply possible to re-present the original, the translator is indebted to it, and 'renders *present* an affinity that is never present in ... [the] presentation' (DTB, 19).

Though the translation is an entirely original mode of representation, the relationship between the source and the target text is that of an original convergence. The source text lives on by transforming itself. Picking up on Benjamin's organic metaphors, Derrida writes that, 'The translation will truly be a moment in the growth of the original, which will complete itself *in* enlarging itself' (DTB, 20). The translation marks a moment in the growth of the original, but such a growth that does '*not give rise to just any form in just any direction*' (DTB, 20; my italics). Derrida is careful here to align deconstruction with Benjamin's understanding of translation, but at the same time to forcefully echo a passage from the 'Exorbitant Question of Method' section in *Of Grammatology*, where he reflects on his strategy of reading: 'Without this recognition and this respect, critical production would risk developing in any direction at all and authorize itself to say almost anything' (OG, 158). The original calls for a translation because it was never complete to begin with: it was never an origin of pure self-presence. Benjamin's language at this point is fittingly described by Derrida's *supplement*: the translation liberates itself from the pure language of the source text, but in such a way that represents its growth and enlargement, both adjoining it and adding to it. The translation obeys what Benjamin calls a law of fidelity or movement of love, even though the translation touches the original in a fleeting manner and only at a small point of meaning. The metaphysical notion of truth is questioned by this movement, even as it attempts to be faithful to its restitution. It is no longer, Derrida suggests, 'a matter, either for the original or even for the translation, of some adequation of the language to meaning or to reality, nor indeed of the representation to something' (DTB, 22). The original translation, Benjamin argues, never fully reaches the kingdom of full presence. In apparently rejecting the metaphysical notion of truth Benjamin is committed to maintaining a harmony between the original and the translation, which he expresses in a mixture of organicist and quasi-religious language: 'This perpetual reviviscence, this constant regeneration ... by translation is less a revelation, revelation itself, than an annunciation, an alliance and a promise' (DTB, 31). This entails, as Derrida recognized in the passage from *Positions* quoted at the beginning of this chapter, a notion of transformation. Like the concept of differance, translation is not a pure process. In place of translation Derrida substitutes what he calls a process of 'regulated transformation' (POS, 20), thereby challenging the pure transport of meaning from original to translation, both within or between languages. Importantly, Derrida qualifies his use of the term transformation: he writes of a 'regulated transformation' rather than of a form of 'unfettered transformation'. Let me, in closing, reiterate Derrida's summary of Benjamin's essay: 'a translation espouses the original when the two adjoined fragments, as different as they can be, complete each other so as to form a larger tongue in the course of a sur-vival that changes them both' (DTB, 22). The point of my reading of this text was to identify how Derrida's understanding of translation can be used to describe the cross-cultural translation of deconstruction.

In order to focus on the transformations of deconstruction the following chapters will reconstruct a series of intellectual contexts – deconstruction in America (Chapter 2), the politics of pedagogical institutions (Chapter 3), postmodernism (Chapter 4), the de Man affair (Chapter 5), and deconstruction's relationship with Marxism (Chapter 6) – in which its meaning has been transformed and resisted. Consequently, it will be possible to show how the meaning of deconstruction has been constantly modified by its *articulation*, by the pedagogical and historical contexts in which it is used. Deconstruction implies that institutions, practices, texts and so on do not have a determinate or self-present meaning and that meaning is always 'to come'. Every attempt to stabilize its meaning fails as it is always being reinvented. With this understanding of 'translation as transformation' in mind, let us now turn to the literary reception of deconstruction in America.

2
Interpretation and Overinterpretation: Deconstruction in America

From the early 1970s to the early 1980s deconstruction was a prominent form of textual exegesis in departments of Comparative Literature in the elite American universities where it was strongly identified with the work of Paul de Man, J. Hillis Miller, Geoffrey Hartman and, to a lesser extent, Harold Bloom. Aided by Derrida's regular visits to Yale beginning in the early 1970s, these critics were frequently associated with a school of literary criticism, now commonly known as the Yale School or Yale Derrideans. Though this name seemed to provide a sense of homogeneity, their understanding and application of deconstruction was often strikingly different, and this is especially true of their relationship with the tenor of Derrida's own thinking, where significant differences existed. Many who assumed a strict correspondence between these literary critics forget Geoffrey Hartman's frank assessment in the Preface to *Deconstruction and Criticism*:

> Derrida, de Man, and Miller are certainly boa-deconstructors, merciless and consequent, though each enjoys his own style of disclosing again and again the 'abysm' of words. But Bloom and Hartman are barely deconstructionists. They even write against it on occasion. (Hartman, 1979, ix)

Unfortunately, this did not prevent literary critics from assuming that their work maintained a strict adherence to the Yale Party line. Though deconstruction was first used as a literary methodology from the early 1970s onwards, many of Derrida's own readings of literary texts were in fact published for the first time in English translation during the mid-1980s, and thus the literary translation largely derived its emphasis on *play* and *mis en abyme* from Derrida's philosophical readings of Saussure and structuralism, though in ways which seriously underestimated them. Readings from the first wave tended to be highly selective, and there is a profound discrepancy between the early essays of the American deconstructionists and Derrida's own philosophical readings from this period. The work of the early deconstructionists is primarily based on such essays as 'Structure, Sign and Play in the Discourse of the Human Sciences', 'Différance' and 'The Ends of Man', as the books from which they were taken were not available in English translation until the mid- to late 1970s, or even the early 1980s, in some cases. In his discussion of the literary reception of Derrida's works in *After the New Criticism*, Frank Lentricchia argues that the closing lines of 'Structure, Sign and Play in the Discourse of the Human Sciences' mark the source of the Yale critics' 'new hedonism' and concern with *mis en abyme*:

> The fundamental aspects of Derrida's writings plainly do not sanction a new formalism or a new hedonism, but the Yale appropriation of him ... is just as plainly an ultimate formalism, a New Criticism denied its ontological supports and cultural goals ... (Lentricchia, 1980, 169)

The literary reception of deconstruction, then, was neither philosophical, political nor institutional in orientation. In 'Declarations of Independence', originally delivered as a paper in 1976 to mark the bicentennial of the American Declaration of Independence, a strong case can be made for the argument that Derrida *was* overtly concerned with a politics of reading, representation and the law, rather than the 'abysm of words'.

The reception of Derrida's early works by this group of American literary critics has attracted a number of notable studies. Principally critics have concentrated on the relationship between particular members of the Yale School and deconstruction (Lentricchia, 1980; Norris, 1981; Abrams, 1989) or on the movement of 'deconstruction in America' as a whole (Norris, 1987; Berman, 1988). In the literary left's critical histories of the period, the American deconstructionists have been typically associated with the continuation of the formalism of the New Criticism at the expense of a more historical or politically committed form of criticism (Lentricchia, 1980; Eagleton, 1984). While the left argued that deconstruction had not gone far enough in the direction of radical politics, traditionalists accused deconstruction of going too far. In both instances, literary critics' views were far removed from the original intention behind the first serialization of *Of Grammatology* in the American journal *Glyph* beginning in 1974, prior to the publication of Gayatri Spivak's English translation in 1976. The editor of *Glyph* at the time, Samuel Weber, points out that the actual intention behind his foregrounding of Derrida's thought was firstly institutional. If there was an overall impetus behind the importation of Derrida's thought at that time, Weber writes:

> it was designated not by the term 'deconstruction' but by that of 'transformation,' entailing not merely the alteration of the prevailing conceptual schemes and interpretive practices of Anglo-American criticism and thought, but also the concomitant alteration of the specific concerns and procedures, largely continental in origin, that *Glyph* sought to 'graft' onto the Anglo-American scene. (Weber, 1981, 233)

Evidently there are a number of complex reasons behind the marginalization of the politico-institutional aspects of Derrida's thinking. It is tempting to interpret this process in terms of Tony Judt's rather generalized understanding of the cross-cultural translation of intellectual thought. 'The passage to Britain, the USA, and beyond', Judt writes:

> usually entails some desiccation of the original; what was political in Paris became theoretical in London, before being reduced to the merely academic in its final resting place further afield. (Judt, 1992, 169)

Judt is persuasive in describing the marginalization of Marxist and left-of-centre thought in the American academy. But his passage returns to one of the key points of my earlier discussion of Derrida's debate with Anglo-American speech act theory. Recalling Derrida's understanding of *iterability* in *Limited Inc*, it is precisely the 'desiccation of the original' that cannot be avoided as deconstruction is re-cited and re-inscribed in 'conflictual and differentiated contexts' (LINC, 141).

Alongside Judt's understanding of the *iterability* of writing, to which the reception of deconstruction is also prone, Steven Helmling offers one other potential source of the problem. Helmling identifies the idea of temporal discontinuity that inevitably contributed to the mistranslation of deconstruction:

> a historically informed awareness of Derrida has been further hindered for us [in America] because Derrida's work became available in translation here only in the late '70s, so pre-'68 work mingled with post- in ways that blurred the differences between them. (Helmling, 1994, 1)

This view is equally persuasive. While in France deconstruction emerged as a challenge to Husserlian phenomenology and structuralism, as Derrida's readings of Husserl and Saussure indicate, in America, post-structuralism emerged without a prominent structuralist movement. American critics, as Helmling implies, interpreted deconstruction as a more generalized attack on western metaphysics. Such confusion led literary critics to neglect Derrida's concern with political and institutional questions at the expense of unstable processes of signification – what de Man refers to as the 'vertiginous possibilities of referential aberrations' in *Allegories of Reading* (1979, 10). In this fashion Derrida's essay, 'Structure, Sign and Play in the Discourse of the Human Sciences' took precedence over the ethico-political tenor of his reading of Saussure in *Of Grammatology*, his understanding of the inheritance of Marx in the interview in *Positions*, and that on the formation of GREPH, and 'Declarations of Independence'. As Vincent Leitch summarizes:

> By 1972, when Derrida published *Positions, Margins of Philosophy*, and *Dissemination*, deconstruction had attained widespread, often reluctant, recognition as the newest avant-garde intellectual movement in France and America. It remained steadfastly post-structuralist and postphenomenological. And it seemed still Freudian and Nietzschean. In France it was vaguely Marxist, although not in Derrida's hands; in America, it was non-Marxist, if not silently anti-Marxist. (Leitch, 1983, 259)

This passage acutely condenses some of the main problems associated with the cross-cultural translation of deconstruction's political implications. The main question of this chapter concerns the political status of deconstruction once it has been cut free from its Marxist sympathies in the French academy and inserted into the intellectual context of American literary criticism.

In *After the New Criticism*, Frank Lentricchia argues that while the American deconstructionists have misread Derrida's work by misplacing an emphasis on freeplay, deconstruction remains an ultimate model of formalist criticism. The first section of this chapter will examine Lentricchia's distinction between Derrida and the Yale School critics, focusing in particular on a number of essays by Paul de Man. In the second section, which turns to consider the political implications of de Man's work in more detail, it will be necessary to take issue with Lentricchia's metaphysical conception of the political. Lentricchia's accusation that both Derrida and de Man are in flight from questions of politics and history is based on his nostalgia for a totalizing Marxist politics. If

Derrida and de Man do not subscribe to Marxist categories of political thought, Lentricchia's arguments run, then they do not engage with substantive political questions at all. It is worth recalling Beardsworth's point again in this context. Detractors of Derrida's politics, he argues, are frequently 'working with an explicit or hidden metaphysical understanding of the political which makes them quickly impatient with Derrida's investigations' (Beardsworth, 1996, 150). This is certainly true of Lentricchia, as my reading of 'Declarations of Independence' will show.

Although de Man's later work does exemplify a number of political concerns, deconstruction has also been effectively deployed as a powerful tool of political criticism in the hands of many minority movements. As an example of these developments, section 3 will discuss Barbara Johnson, an overlooked female member of Yale's English Department during the high point of de Manian deconstruction, who attempts to come to terms with deconstruction as a political strategy. By focusing on her essay, 'Apostrophe, Animation, and Abortion' (Johnson, 1987), I show how Johnson's concern with relating deconstruction to questions of gender and race emerges. In conclusion this theme will be developed by examining Diane Elam's reading of the deconstruction of the subject in *Feminism and Deconstruction* (1994).

Translating 'Structure, Sign and Play'

In *After the New Criticism* (1980) Lentricchia presents a wide-ranging discussion of the history of postwar American criticism between 1957 and the publication of Paul de Man's *Allegories of Reading* in 1979. Lentricchia's main analysis emerges from the chapter entitled, 'History of the Abyss', where he turns to consider the importance of 'Structure, Sign and Play' for the emergence of deconstructive modes of thinking among American literary critics at the end of the 1960s.

In 'Structure, Sign and Play' Derrida uses *deconstruction* in a very specific context. Deconstruction is bound up with the rethinking of metaphysics and its concept of the sign, and is connected with a *responsible* task that is at once both critical and traditional. In Derrida's hands, deconstruction illuminates his understanding of the logocentric assumptions of the philosophical tradition that he inherits:

> Here it is a question both of a critical relation to the language of the social sciences and a critical responsibility of the discourse itself. It is a question of explicitly and systematically posing the problem of the

status of a discourse which borrows from a heritage the resources necessary for the deconstruction of that heritage itself. A problem of *economy* and *strategy*. (WD, 282)

This important passage describes deconstruction as a critical responsibility rather than as a purely *destructive* force. While Derrida argues that there can be no question of choosing between the two types of interpretation that he outlines at the end of 'Structure, Sign and Play', it is evident that the literary translation of his work did identify deconstruction with an extreme form of Nietzschean play or epistemological scepticism that transformed undecidability into a notion of indeterminacy or freeplay.

In part, these misreadings developed because of the iconic prominence of 'Structure, Sign and Play', an essay that was collected in a volume along with the other papers from the 1966 conference at Johns Hopkins University, and then later published in *The Structuralist Controversy*. There followed during the early 1970s the appropriation and transformation of a number of key Derridean concepts, especially those associated with questions about the referential nature of language, largely inherited from the New Critics. Lentricchia usefully identifies a number of key areas: the translation of Derridean play into the idea of *freeplay* or *mis en abyme*; the idea that Derrida replaces the mimetic theory of linguistic reference with textual mysticism or an ultimate formalism; and the notion that Derrida institutes a form of hedonistic or joyful reading.

It is possible to follow Lentricchia and describe in general terms why the American translation of deconstruction was an appropriate successor to the New Criticism:

1. Deconstruction enabled the continuation of the New Critics' primary concern with the interpretation of Romantic poetry. The abiding interest of these critics in genre derived from their concern with a 'psychological poetics' rather than with a historical criticism (Berman, 1988, 104).
2. American deconstruction continued the erosion of a public audience and the common reader, and promoted the development of a professional academic culture of criticism during the mid-1970s.
3. American deconstruction continued the anti-Marxist drift of American New Criticism.
4. Deconstruction's relationship with other disciplines (the fact that Derrida was primarily a philosopher) strengthened professional

criticism's challenge to its traditional image as an unscientific and amateur pursuit.

All of these elements of Derridean deconstruction were amenable to the reinvention of deconstruction as a literary formalism. Even as this brief description of Lentricchia's arguments makes clear, his reading requires a more thorough critical engagement. In order to do this, the next section will examine Paul de Man's use of deconstructive themes before turning to the debate between Lentricchia and Norris about the political implications of de Manian deconstruction. While for Lentricchia de Man's translation of Derrida's work results in an ultimate 'idealism' that is bereft of political implications, Norris's more acute analysis suggests that de Man's thinking is better viewed in terms of a deconstruction of aesthetic ideology and the politics of representation. But first, let us turn to some of the main themes of de Man's work in order to provide a context for the debate.

De Man and deconstruction

Paul de Man is frequently credited with the role of translating Derrida's deconstruction of metaphysics into the mainstream of American literary criticism. The essays collected in *Blindness and Insight* exemplify the emergence of a Derridean vocabulary in his work, but many of their main themes predate the consolidation of Derrida's thought. In his earlier collection, *Allegories of Reading*, published in 1979, the distinctiveness of de Man's approach to Derridean deconstruction emerges. In what follows I will examine 'Semiology and Rhetoric' and 'The Rhetoric of Temporality' in order to introduce some of the main themes of de Manian deconstruction. Next, moving onto the political debate, I will consider 'Wordsworth and Hölderlin', 'Heidegger's Exegeses of Hölderlin' and 'The Temptation of Permanence', in order to examine whether de Man's work is tantamount to a type of 'apolitical formalism' (Lentricchia, 1980; Eagleton, 1984), or a form of criticism that 'lends itself to various, politically consequential forms of aesthetic ideology' (Norris, 1988, 16).

The relationship between grammar and rhetoric is one of the most important aspects of de Man's work. A prime example of de Man's illustration of the tension between grammar and rhetoric occurs in the first essay in *Allegories of Reading*, 'Semiology and Rhetoric'. Here, de Man is interested in the modern opposition between formalism and the 'authority of reference' (de Man, 1979, 5), an opposition which in 'opposing intrinsic to extrinsic criticism stands under the aegis of an inside/outside metaphor that ... [needs to be] seriously questioned' (1979, 5).

To demonstrate the existence of this opposition, de Man opposes rhetoric to grammar following Burke and C. S. Peirce, whom he names as significant intellectual precursors. De Man mentions Burke who argued that pure rhetoric represents the interpretative deflection of meaning, 'which he defines as any slight bias or even unintended error' (1979, 8). Deflection, in this sense, means the 'dialectical subversion of the consistent link between sign and meaning that operates within grammatical patterns' (1979, 8). A similar distinction between grammar and rhetoric is applied by Peirce, who inserts a notion of the interpretant between the sign and its object. The sign represents the object but not in a way that can be considered univocal. For Pierce, interpretation does not produce a meaning or an ultimate decoding; it gives rise to another sign that in turn must be interpreted ad infinitum. Peirce calls this process 'pure rhetoric' as opposed to 'pure grammar', which refers to the 'possibility of unproblematic, dyadic meaning' (1979, 9). De Man deconstructs this opposition, thus challenging the established notion that a text has a static meaning, in order to demonstrate how they assert quite different meanings. De Man shows that this discrepancy between meaning and assertion in the same text is a natural part of their logic. Though grammar and rhetoric are opposed, de Man describes how rhetoric *contaminates* grammar and leads to a form of suspension that is ultimately beyond oppositional thinking. De Man introduces his first example of this process via an anecdote from the American sitcom *All in the Family*:

> [A]sked by his wife whether he wants to have his bowling shoes laced over or under, Archie Bunker answers with a question: 'What's the difference?' Being a reader of sublime simplicity, his wife replies by patiently explaining the difference between lacing over and lacing under, whatever that may be, but provokes only ire. 'What's the difference' did not ask for difference but means instead 'I don't give a damn what the difference is.' (1979, 9)

De Man postulates that this confusion exemplifies how the grammatical pattern is able to generate two mutually exclusive readings. The literal meaning, namely, the difference between lacing under and lacing over, is refused by the figurative meaning. Punning on Derrida's concern with the deconstruction of origins (*arche*), de Man speculates that more is at stake when an 'archie Debunker such as Nietzsche or Jacques

Derrida ... asks the question "What is the difference" ' (1979, 9). The story demonstrates that rhetoric 'radically suspends logic and opens up vertiginous possibilities of referential aberration' (1979, 10). This is evident in that the:

> grammatical model of the question becomes rhetorical not when we have, on the one hand, a literal meaning and on the other hand a figural meaning, but when it is impossible to decide which of the two meanings (that can be entirely incompatible) prevails. (1979, 10)

De Man shows how a text swerves from meaning to assertion as a result of what he identifies as error, the dynamic process that is inherent in the text, rather than as a mistake, a term which relates more to the inaccuracy of the reader. The irony of the text is generated as a result of its inability to say what it does, and thus to unite saying and doing. What is significant for de Man at this point is the fact that these contradictory meanings make it impossible to choose between them. Rhetoric is no longer merely a duplicitous concept, but an event: 'the grammatical model ... becomes rhetorical ... when it is impossible to decide' (1979, 10). The two meanings show themselves to be dependent on an intentional act of persuasion. De Man is thus concerned with the fact that a text's literal structure is often taken to be identical with its author's meaning. De Man's reaction to this paradox confirms it; his reading performs it by losing control over the distinction that he makes.

Having just demonstrated how rhetoric consists of a form of undecidability that transcends the literal/figural opposition, de Man reintroduces this distinction on a much broader level by equating this rhetorical dimension with literature itself. De Man provides one further example of this tension in the closing lines of W. B. Yeats's poem, 'Among School Children'. Here, however, he demonstrates that the literal meaning 'leads to a greater complication of theme and statement than the figural reading' (1979, 11). The famous final line of the poem, 'How can we know the dancer from the dance?', is usually interpreted to emphazise the *union* of form and experience, creator and creation. But, for de Man, this figural reading gives way to a literal understanding. The line becomes an urgent question that challenges the experience of unity or, in Derridean terms, undifferentiated self-presence. The poem asks 'how we can possibly make the distinctions that would shelter us from the error of identifying what cannot be identified?' (1979, 11). De Man concludes that neither in fact has precedence over the other, nor can they be separated, since each depends on the horizon of the other for its impact.

The figural meaning is constituted by the very distinction it denies: we could not identify it as figural were there no literal horizon against which to distinguish it. Rhetoric emerges then not from the opposition of two categories, but from meaning's difference from itself. It is not possible simply to say that the poem has its own meanings that can be placed alongside one another, giving priority to one over the other. Neither can exist in the absence of the other, such that there can be no 'sign without a referent' (1979, 12). This means that our understanding of figural meaning must be redefined to encompass the point of decision between literal and figural that he identified.

Unlike the New Critics, then, de Man argues that it is impossible to draw firm or fixed boundaries between poetic and other forms of language. In fact it is these qualities that de Man sets out to challenge. This challenge is based on the acknowledgement that figural language not only applies to poetic language but to other forms of language as well. De Man, like Derrida, is intent on showing how figurative language contaminates writings which attempt to suppress them. Consequently, the traditional opposition between literature and philosophy in western metaphysics is one of the most important areas of his thought. Like Derrida, his thinking refuses to privilege literature or philosophy in this domain.

De Man's thought also concentrates on these internal contradictions, undermining the delusory character of any appeal to organic metaphors when dealing with poetry, language or representation. The second area concerns the idea that the reading of texts can only proceed by fastening onto these disparities and contradictions between meaning and intention. But de Man calls into question the idea that poetry could *unify* what he believes to be the disjunction between sensuous intuition and the concepts of pure understanding. It is a significant part of de Man's strategy of close reading to demonstrate how meaning cannot be reduced to sensory perception. De Man consistently refuses the idea that a privileged aesthetic realm, principally poetry, can resolve the inherent contradictions of language.

In the final part of 'Semiology and Rhetoric' on Proust, de Man explores the relationship between metaphor and metonymy. In a movement which is akin to the logic of the argument set out above, de Man demonstrates that 'the assertion of mastery of metaphor over metonymy owes its persuasive power to the use of metonymic structures' (1979, 15). Metaphor here corresponds to 'identity and total-ity' (1979, 14) while metonymy depends on a relational understanding of meaning. The passage by Proust that de Man examines 'shows that precisely when the highest claims are being made for the unifying power of metaphor, these very images rely in fact on the deceptive use of semi-automatic grammatical patterns' (1979, 16). De Man quotes a passage from *Swann's Way* which describes Marcel as a boy reading in an enclosed room. Proust advances reading as an experience that unites 'outer meaning with inner understanding, action with reflection' (1979, 13). Here is Marcel lying on his bed reading:

> It was barely light enough to read, and the sensation of the splendid brightness of the day came to me only from the blows struck in the rue de la Cure by Camus ... against some dusty crates, which, however, reverberating in the sonorous atmosphere peculiar to hot weather, seemed to send scarlet stars flying into the distance; and also by the horseflies that performed for me, in a little concert, a sort of chamber music of summer: this music does not evolve summer in the same way as a melody of human music ... it is connected to summer by a more necessary bond: born of fine days, born again only with them, containing a little of their essence, it not only awakens their image in our memory, it guarantees their return, their presence, actual, ambient, immediately accessible. (Proust, 2004, 84–5)

The passage is about the 'aesthetic superiority of metaphor over metonymy' (de Man, 1979, 14). Proust's invocation of the 'chamber music' of the flies is described in terms of the fulfilment of presence, 'permanently recurrent and unmediated by linguistic representations or figurations' (1979, 14). This theme is so strongly evident in the passage that de Man comments that 'it may seem sacrilegious to put it in question' (1979, 15). But that is precisely what he does. Once again de Man shows that the 'text does not practice what it preaches':

> A rhetorical reading of the passage reveals that the figural praxis and the metalingual theory do not converge and that the assertion of the mastery of metaphor over metonymy owes its persuasive power to the use of metonymic structures. (1979, 14)

The presence in Proust's passage of a metaphorical configuration of essence, action, truth and beauty, de Man points out, cannot remain unaffected by his figurative reading. Nietzsche's deconstruction of such metaphors – of causality, the subject and the referential view of meaning – thus serves as a significant precursor of de Man's own.

In this case, de Man's reading of Proust now moves from the 'self-willed and inventiveness of a subject' (1979, 16) to the subject's intention: 'our first examples dealing with the rhetorical questions were rhetorizations of grammar, figures generated by syntactical paradigms, whereas the Proust example could be better described as a grammatization of rhetoric' (1979, 15). The example of Proust 'shows that precisely when the highest claims are being made for the unifying power of metaphor, these very images rely in fact on the deceptive use of semi-automatic grammatical patterns' (1979, 16). Metaphors such as mimesis thus exist by effacing or disguising the operation of differences. As with Derrida, then, de Man's target is the 'whole series of concepts that underlie the value judgements of our critical discourse: the metaphors of primacy, of genetic history, and, most notably, of the autonomous power to will of the self' (1979, 16).

De Man argues that the two types of reading that he has outlined lead toward different points. Whereas the first of de Man's examples leads readers to 'end up in indetermination, in a suspended uncertainty that ... [is] unable to choose between two modes of reading', the example from Proust 'seems to reach a truth, albeit by a negative road of exposing an error, a false pretense' (1979, 16). As de Man writes:

> After the rhetorical reading of the Proust passage, we can no longer believe the assertion made in this passage about the intrinsic, metaphysical superiority of metaphor over metonymy. We seem to end up in a mood of negative assurance that is highly productive of critical discourse. (1979, 16)

The emphasis on the word *seem* in the final sentence of this passage is taken up in the last section of the essay where de Man turns to the implications for the subject. While de Man *seems* to pause at the point at which metonymy is shown to reverse its subordination to metaphor in his commentary on Proust, he continues to interrogate the assumptions of this reversal that in fact reinstates a metaphor of presence:

> For if we then ask the obvious and simple next question, whether the rhetorical mode of the text in question is that of metaphor or metonymy, it is impossible to give an answer ... The narrator who tells us about the impossibility of metaphor is himself, or at least, a metaphor ... (1979, 18)

In turn the narrator is subject to deconstruction. Consequently, the 'rhetorical grammatization of semiology' like 'grammatical rhetorization' ends up in the 'same state of suspended ignorance' (1979, 19).

De Man's closing lines skilfully merge and contrast his indebtedness to metaphysics *and* his deconstruction of its conceptual infrastructure:

> Literature as well as criticism – the difference between them being delusive – is condemned (or privileged) to be forever the most rigorous and, consequently, the most unreliable language in terms of which man names and transforms himself. (1979, 19)

It is impossible, de Man concludes, to know what language might be up to. Deconstruction is not done by the reader – 'deconstruction is not something we have added to the text', de Man writes, it was what 'constituted the text in the first place' (1979, 17).

'The Rhetoric of Temporality'

De Man's early work is frequently described in terms of its existentialist vocabulary, while his increasing reference to a Derridean terminology, as we saw in the previous section, is evident after the publication of 'The Rhetoric of Temporality' in 1969 (Lentricchia, 1980, 291). In de Man's early thought there is an emphasis on poetic language that is evident in the Romantics. This poetic aspect attempts to become entirely literal and thus to distance itself from all forms of figurative language. The dominance of literal language is manifested by the privileged role it ascribes to symbol rather than allegory. The symbol attempts to bridge the gap between sign and object, word and thing, thus naming the unmediated presence of reality. Such a romantic nostalgia, the desire to impose unity on an original division, remains self-delusive. As Lentricchia sees it, de Man challenges 'the tragic adventure of the nineteenth-century poet' with the understanding of a 'fully Husserlian imagination that does not yearn nostalgically for union with the natural object; by an imagination that looks with contempt upon nature as "blank abyss"; by an imagination that comes into play when the light of sense is extinguished' (Lentricchia, 1980, 289). 'The Rhetoric of Temporality' represents one of de Man's most striking attempts to examine the tension between symbolism and allegory, and is therefore a prime example of some of the main themes of his work.

In 'The Rhetoric of Temporality' de Man traces the fall of rhetorical criticism to the Romantic period. He positions these changes in the latter part of the eighteenth century, 'when the word "symbol" tends to supplant other denominations for figural language, including that of "allegory" ' (de Man, 1988a, 188). The origins of the supremacy of symbolism are located in the growth of an aesthetics in German literature where the world is no longer seen as a configuration of entities that designate a plurality of distinct and isolated meanings, but as a configuration of symbols ultimately leading to a total, single and universal meaning. This appeal to the infinity of totality constitutes the main attraction of the symbol as opposed to allegory, a sign that refers to one specific meaning and thus exhausts its suggestive potentialities once it has been deciphered. Other figures in German literature of this period, most notably Goethe, Schiller and Schelling, stand out from this general view of their relationship. Complex variations of this tension are also evident in the work of Hölderlin, Schlegel, Solger and Hoffman. Nonetheless this understanding of symbol and allegory still 'functions as the basis of recent French and English studies of the Romantic and post-Romantic eras, to such an extent that allegory is frequently considered an anachronism and dismissed as non-poetic' (1988a, 190).

Tracing the lineage of symbolism in Romantic thought, de Man next turns to Coleridge and then to French literature from the same period. In both instances de Man finds the main problem of Romantic Studies to be the subject–object tension. In English and French Romanticism, the unity between mind and nature and the predominance of the symbol are the fundamental characteristics of their diction. The emergence of both characteristics marks the origins of Romanticism. De Man's main argument derives from his attempt to show that critics of Romanticism have passed over the significant place that allegory has for the Romantics. In Rousseau's book, *La Nouvelle Héloïse*, de Man identifies how important the presence of allegorical elements were to the shaping of the novel's diction. The example of Rousseau shows that allegory has been a constant element in both pre- and Romantic literature.

The importance de Man attributed to allegory resides in its temporal dimension, a dimension that is effectively neutralized by the organic unity apparently conveyed by symbols. The 'prevalence of allegory', de Man writes, 'always corresponds to the unveiling of an authentically temporal destiny. This unveiling takes place in a subject that has sought refuge against the impact of time in a natural world to which, in truth, it bears no resemblance' (1988a, 206). Whereas symbolism is spatial in nature, 'in the world of allegory, time is the originary constitutive category' (1988a, 207). In a very important passage, in which Derrida's influence can be located, de Man refers to the slippage or deferral of meaning exemplified by allegory and thus also to the challenge to the ideality of meaning posited by symbolism:

The meaning constituted by the allegorical sign can then consist only in the *repetition* ... of a previous sign with which it can never coincide, since it is of the essence of this previous sign to be pure anteriority. (1988a, 207)

Derrida's influence in this area can be traced directly to his essay, 'Différance', which describes the familiar spatio-temporal challenge to ideality, notably in evidence in his idea of *iterability* and originary repetition.

So whereas symbols were primarily identified with the organic unity of sign and object, allegory represents the demystified state of language, and affirms the arbitrary and differential nature of the sign. Allegory conveys the separation of word and thing and the crucial importance of temporality for Derrida's deconstruction of ideal self-presence. It is allegory not symbolism that is a truly authentic discourse, and de Man argues that Romantic poets are at their most authentic when they are aware of the mystification of symbolist language:

> Whereas the symbol postulates the possibility of an identity or identification, allegory designates primarily a distance in relation to its own origin, and, renouncing the nostalgia and the desire to coincide, it establishes its language in the void of this temporal difference. (1988a, 207)

Such an understanding is couched in terms of the existentialist self coming to grips with self-mystification: such knowledge, de Man writes, 'prevents the self from an illusory identification with the non-self, which is now fully, though painfully, recognized as a non-self' (1988a, 207). The substitution of symbols for allegory is described in terms of an 'act of ontological bad faith' (1988a, 211). It is at this moment that Romantic literature discovers its authentic voice, that is to say, when it overcomes the 'tenacious self-mystification' that privileges symbolism over allegory (1988a, 208).

De Man next discerns a parallel in the tension between allegory and symbolism with the emergence of the problem of irony. The parallelism points to a structure shared by irony and allegory in that the relationship between 'sign and meaning is discontinuous ... In both cases, the sign points to something that differs from its literal meaning and has for its function the themetization of this difference' (1988a, 209). Allegory and irony are connected in their temporal aspect, and as they both participate in the demystification of an organic world of self-present representation. While there are evident similarities between de Man's and Derrida's understanding of metaphor and metonymy in 'The Rhetoric of

Temporality', in de Man's essay, 'The Rhetoric of Blindness: Jacques Derrida's Reading of Rousseau', he comes into direct conflict with Derrida's *Of Grammatology.*

'The Rhetoric of Blindness: Jacques Derrida's Reading of Rousseau'

One of de Man's main contentions is that Rousseau has always been systematically misread. Derrida's mistake in his reading of Rousseau in de Man's eyes is the idea that Rousseau is a partially mystified writer who is in need of deconstruction. De Man is therefore critical of Derrida's allegedly superior insight into the workings of Rousseau's text because he fails to grant him an unmystified, self-deconstructing consciousness.

De Man identifies a movement in critical thought of blindness and insight, in which insight proceeds from a:

> negative movement that animates the critic's thought, an unstated principle that leads his language away from its asserted stand, perverting and dissolving his stated commitment to the point where it becomes emptied of substance, as if the very possibility of assertion had been put into question. Yet it is this negative, apparently destructive labor that led to what could legitimately be called insight. (de Man, 1988a, 103)

The movement of blindness and insight is essentially based on the effacement of contradictory assertions. De Man cites the example of the New Critics' simultaneous 'description of literary language as a language of irony and ambiguity despite the fact that they remained committed to a Coleridgean notion of organic form' (1988a, 104). De Man's point here is once again the idea that 'critics seem curiously doomed to say something quite different from what they meant to say' (1988a, 105–6). Referring to a range of writers, from Poulet to Blanchot, de Man argues that insight proceeds from blindness:

> A penetrating but difficult insight into the nature of literary language ensues. It seems, however, that this insight could only be gained because the critics were in the grip of this peculiar blindness: their language could grope toward a certain degree of insight only because their method remained oblivious to the perception of this insight. (1988a, 106)

De Man's target here is clearly the transcendental conception of reading, the idea that a literary text *can* be granted a 'positive existence' (1988a, 107). This is because reading is never pure interpretation. In terms that recall Derrida's reading of Benjamin's 'The Task of the Translator', de Man contends that 'the work cannot be said to understand or to explain itself without the intervention of another language ... [because] interpretation is never mere duplication' (1988a, 108). De Man clearly draws on Derrida's idea of differance and iterability to describe the process of interpretation. Reading induces a process of violence and conflict with the original text, which does not leave it untouched: 'It can legitimately be called a "repetition," but this term is itself so rich and complex that it raises at once a host of theoretical problems. Repetition is a temporal process that assumes difference as well as resemblance. It functions as a regulative principle of rigor but asserts the impossibility of rigorous identity, etc.' (1988a, 108). The key idea here, recalling the passage about 'regulated transformation' in *Positions*, relates to de Man's rejection of the epistemological consistency of reading and the notion that by so doing reading becomes a merely arbitrary process of addition or subtraction. De Man reserves a special place for faulty readings, which he claims lead critics to achieve their greatest insights. The real purpose of de Man's analysis up to this point is his concern with the immanent as opposed to transcendental status of critical discourse:

> Since they are not scientific, critical texts have to be read with the same awareness of ambivalence that is brought to the study of non-critical texts, and since the rhetoric of their discourse depends on categorical statements, the discrepancy between meaning and assertion is a constitutive part of their logic. (1988a, 110)

De Man rejects transcendentalism, arguing that there can be no escape from immanentism, and reserves for Derrida a special place vis-à-vis the awareness of this movement of blindness and insight. Consequently, Derrida assumes a particular importance for de Man's attempt to 'restore the complexities of reading to the dignity of a philosophical question' (1988a, 110). Derrida's reading of Rousseau in *Of Grammatology* is de Man's example of the functioning of 'critical blindness and critical insight, no longer in the guise of a semiconscious duplicity but as a necessity dictated and controlled by the very nature of all critical language' (1988a, 111).

De Man's reference to the history of Rousseau's critical reception allows him to make the point that the ambivalence of his works have always been underestimated by his commentators, many of whom have systematically adopted a tone of moral superiority over the French philosopher, casting him as an 'interesting psychological case' (1988a, 113). This stance enables Rousseau's commentators to disregard what de Man sees as his own awareness of the functioning of the movement of blindness and insight. In de Man's eyes, Derrida's reading of Rousseau, especially his insistence on Rousseau's conception of original innocence and his simultaneous condemnation and dependence on the evil of writing, both departs from the history of Rousseau criticism while also confirming it. Derrida shows, for example, that Rousseau believes in speech as opposed to writing as the origin of language while at the same time relying on the logic of the 'dangerous supplement' that replaces the origin with an endless process of substitution. Derrida's reading assumes that Rousseau never acknowledges his complicity with these dual assumptions. On the contrary, Derrida describes Rousseau's attitude as deliberate, referring to him as a conjurer who consciously deceives himself, his aim being to subject Rousseau to deconstruction – that is to say, 'to bring to light what had remained unperceived by the author and his followers' (1988a, 116).

De Man takes issue with Derrida's accusation of duplicity, choosing in its place to argue that Rousseau merely reiterates one of Derrida's main theses: Rousseau's language confirms the priority of language over that of self-presence. De Man's critique of Derrida's reading is based on his assumption that 'Rousseau's text has no blind spots: it accounts at all moments for its own rhetorical mode' (1988a, 139). Derrida is guilty of confusing the functioning of the literal and the rhetorical in Rousseau's texts. 'There is', de Man writes, 'no need to deconstruct Rousseau' – but there is every need to deconstruct the 'tradition of Rousseau interpretation', which, like Derrida, insists on his duplicity (1988a, 139). For de Man, Rousseau is 'as clear-sighted as language lets him be', and he is an author who has been 'systematically misread' (1988a, 139). Derrida's misreading of Rousseau is an example of his own indictment of language and 'not somebody's [i.e. Rousseau's] philosophical error' (1988a, 140). Rousseau, de Man maintains, is a non-blind author who is aware of the fact that one can 'never escape from the regressive process of misunderstanding that he describes' (1988a, 140), rather than one who tries to ignore it. Thus the 'critical reading of Derrida's critical reading of Rousseau shows blindness to be the necessary correlative of the rhetorical nature of literary language' (1988a, 141). But in spite of this, de Man makes perhaps the most apposite point for my concern with the misreading of deconstruction by American literary critics:

> The existence of a particularly rich aberrant tradition in the case of the writers who can legitimately be called the most enlightened, is

therefore no accident, but a constitutive part of all literature, the basis, in fact, of literary history. (1988a, 141)

Reading or misreading leads de Man to confirm the 'absolute dependence of the interpretation on the text and of the text on the interpretation' (1988a, 141).

Having acquired this insight into de Man's critical practice, the next section will consider the political implications of his thinking. In this way it will be possible to disentangle Derrida from the notion that deconstruction is a form of nihilism or amounts to a withdrawal from politics.

De Man and politics

In *After the New Criticism* Lentricchia mounts a powerful critique of the political implications of de Man's work that is based on the charge that the Yale critic practises an ahistorical or formalist criticism. In a number of essays published since *Blindness and Insight*, Lentricchia argues that de Man 'reveal[s] a critical intention to place literary discourse in a realm where it can have no responsibility to historical life' (Lentricchia, 1980, 310). De Man's isolationism, Lentricchia points out, has led to an 'autonomous, closed, fortresslike world' for literary discourse that will:

countenance no conditioning by, no investment in, other kinds of discourses, unless those discourses can be robbed of their own determinative force as they are taken in by the self-deconstructing dynamics of what is called literary language. (1980, 310)

The early essays of de Man renounce the dream that language can reconcile mind and nature and subject and object in a moment of self-presence achieved through the power of the poetic imagination. Authentic reading would then depend on the courage to reject this temptation by confronting the contingency of language and the fact that privileged tropes such as symbol and metaphor must always depend, in the last resort, on undeluded figures like metonymy and allegory. The will to renounce this belief, however, still goes along with a certain attachment to the idea of renunciation itself as a measure of authentic misunderstanding. This view explains the marked existential-ist tone of de Man's early essays, the suggestion that authentic or undeluded reading is capable of rising above such forms of seductive or naive understanding. But this standpoint presupposes at least some residual notion of a subjectivity that becomes more authentic as it manages to renounce the illusions of premature meaning.

Norris argues that 'de Man's early essays are ... heavily "stacked" against Marxism and against any form of critical thinking that would privilege history as the ultimate ground of interpretative method' (Norris, 1988, 5), and are characterized by a 'radical disenchantment' (1988, 21) with political activism. For the early de Man, 'politics – or political activism – was a species of endlessly recurrent delusion for which poetry (or the depth of reflective self-knowledge that poetry required) was a kind of salutary antidote' (1988, 156). Norris outlines a biographical reading of de Man's uncle, Henrik de Man, a figure strongly identified with the failure of left-wing politics in pre-war Belgium, which attempts to account for his ironic and detached view of political activism. Whatever problems are normally associated with a biographical reading of this kind, Norris's account of the influence of Henrik de Man's political life, which 'was marked at every turn by an alternating cycle of activist zeal, followed by stages of intense disappointment, ironic resignation, and (ultimately) bleak despair' (1988, 24), persuasively underpins de Man's understanding of poetry as an allegory of political disenchantment and his warning against the confusion of temporal and ideal realms. So, Norris sees in the movement of de Man's early essays – most notably in his essay, 'Wordsworth and Hölderlin' – confirmation of Lentricchia's charge that he 'manifest[s] a strong mistrust of activist creeds, an insistence on the virtues of reflective non-involvement, and an ironic stance toward political beliefs that at times leans over into downright cynicism' (1988, 152). In the early essays, poetry is opposed to politics. What de Man 'always sets up in opposition to history', Norris writes, 'is a certain idea of the poetic, of poetry as a deeper, more authentic knowledge undeluded by the claims of merely secular understanding' (1988, 5). Lentricchia is therefore 'right to detect a mood of profound political disenchantment in de Man's early writings' (1988, 26), a mood which can easily be understood as a form of political quietism. De Man's early and middle-period essays do indeed exemplify trends of this kind, principally in three areas. First, truly 'authentic' poetry is the product of a continuous period of 'self-reflection'. Secondly, political acts, in contrast, follow from an impulsive drive that is not self-reflective. And thirdly, the purpose of criticism is to identify how poetry gives us a special insight into the failure that is an integral part of political events. These concerns are, however, gradually transformed by his later essays, where de Man is engaged with 'demystify[ing] those forms of false, premature, or totalizing thought which would seek to obliterate all traces of time, history, and difference' (1988, 152). De Man's thinking is traversed by such themes as the deconstruction of aesthetic ideology and the politics of representation. De Man's relocation in the American academy after the Second World War marked the transition as Norris contends, from 'a deep, if ambivalent regard for the writings of Husserl, Heidegger, and phenomenological criticism – to a stress on the virtues of textual close reading and on rhetoric as the chief and most reliable means of exposing the blind spots engendered by that same tradition' (1988, 174). In what follows I will examine de Man's essay on 'Wordsworth and Hölderlin', before turning to 'The Temptation of Permanence', which can be seen as an example of de Man's increasing concern with questions of history and politics.

'Wordsworth and Hölderlin'

According to Norris's reading of 'Wordsworth and Hölderlin', then, de Man 'raises questions of historical belatedness, of poetry's relation to politics, and specifically of the kind of revolutionary politics that preoccupies Wordsworth in *The Prelude*' (Norris, 1988, 5). This essay exemplifies de Man's opposition between the authentic and undeluded knowledge of poetry and the claims of reactionary politics. Norris focuses in particular on a sequence from Book VI of *The Prelude* that describes Wordsworth's reflections on his travels in post-revolutionary France in order to prove the point. Looking back on his journey through France in 1790 from the perspective of 1802, the date of composition, Wordsworth describes the conflict between the revolutionary spirit of his travel companions, two young representatives from the *états généraux*, and his own post-revolutionary scepticism. As de Man writes:

> This joy is spontaneous and sincere ... It is the joy in an active world in which the movement of our wishes appears to correspond to that of the age. But despite its doubtless healthy character, this joy conceals a danger which the continuation of the poem embodies in the threat posed to the cloister of the Grand Chartreuse in the wake of the revolutionary enthusiasm. (de Man, 1984, 55)

De Man's essay exemplifies the tension that I described earlier between two attitudes to political action, one which is based on the suppression of temporality and the inevitable disjunction between language and reality, and the other more zealous line which sees politics as a 'means of evading these ultimate issues' or as 'a premature escape from the concerns that characterize all true reflection on the nature and limits of human understanding' (1984, 6).

De Man quotes the following passage to capture Wordsworth's understanding of the tension between the two descriptions of nature that can be found in the poem. In the first instance, nature 'is the principle in which time finds itself preserved, without losing the movement of passing away' (1984, 56):

> ... these majestic floods – these shining cliffs
> The untransmuted shapes of many worlds,
> Cerulian ether's pure inhabitants,
> These forests unapproachable by death
> That shall endure as long as man endures,
>
> (Wordsworth, 1960, VI, 67–71)

In the second passage de Man quotes, Wordsworth's understanding of nature attempts to come to terms with the tension between the movement of passing away and the condition of remaining, a tension which de Man argues lies near the limit of comprehensible language:

> The immeasurable height
> Of woods decaying, never to be decay'd,
> The stationary blasts of water-falls, ...
> Were all like workings of one mind, the features
> Of the same face, blossoms upon one tree,
> Characters of the great Apocalypse,
> The types and symbols of Eternity,
> Of first and last, and midst, and without end.
>
> (Wordsworth, 1960, VI, 556–63)

Whereas the insurgents struggle to ignore the constraints of temporality, contingency and chance, de Man reads Wordsworth's reflections as a rejection of such a self-assured attempt to unify action and will. De Man praises the radicals' perspective and their attempts to avoid:

> the temporal nature of our existence. Their joy expresses itself with such self-assurance and lack of measure that it believes itself capable of reconciling the moment with eternity. They mean to possess something that endures which they fashion according to the intoxication of the act, and yet this thing that endures exists only in a

nature that endures precisely because it negates the instant, just as reflection must negate the act that nonetheless constitutes its origin. (de Man, 1984, 56)

As the radicals move toward the destruction of the cloister of the Grande Chartreuse, they are led by the 'naive influence of the poetic faculty' (1984, 58), which always leads them hopefully toward the future. Under this influence they have forgotten that the 'moment of active projection into the future ... lies for the imagination in a past from which it is separated by the experience of failure (*Scheitern*)' (1984, 58). This recurrent theme of failure is evident in Wordsworth's 'never-ending reflection upon an eschatological moment that has failed through the excess of its interiority' (1984, 59).

De Man's reading is underpinned by an existentialist rhetoric that is used to discredit the authenticity of the rebels' actions, and thus to support his own resistance to their bad faith, that is to say, their belief that their actions will lead to a transformation of history. De Man, in contrast, remains undeluded by this unmediated understanding of history which leads to moments in which mind and nature achieve a state of coexistence.

In Wordsworth's rejection of political action, de Man sees the rudiments of his own understanding of contemplative poetry. 'Poetry is seen as the source of an undeluded wisdom', Norris suggests, 'that can only look back on such moments of youthful abandon from a standpoint of "interiorized" reflection which contrasts with their naive, outgoing spontaneity' (Norris, 1988, 7). The rebels' outgoing spontaneity can lead to nothing but a spiral of violence and destruction. And though Norris admits that de Man does not 'side overtly with the older Wordsworth against his youthful alter ego, this is undoubtedly the tenor of ... [his] reading' (1988, 7). Norris's pinpointing of the 'very definite ideological ends' of de Man's reading of Wordsworth therefore confirms his thesis that in the early de Man poetic 'reflection must inevitably lead to a mood of political quietism' (1988, 9). The real point of de Man's analysis is to identify the correspondence between the thought of the radicals and the type of romantic thinking that, in relying on the imaginative powers accumulated from metaphor and symbolism, de Man attempts to deconstruct. This is where Norris's reading of the politics of de Manian deconstruction emerge. De Man is concerned, he argues, with undermining the aesthetic ideology that, in esteeming metaphor over metonymy and allegory, supports transcendental truth claims. De Man's deconstruction of this late-romantic ideology is also evident in his reading of Hölderlin later on in the same essay. Wordsworth's abandonment of the 'correspondence between nature and consciousness', which de Man traces to *The Prelude*, 'ensues at a highly advanced point in his thinking' (de Man, 1984, 59). Hölderlin, in contrast, suggests that, 'This overcoming ... belongs to ... [his] knowledge almost from the beginning' (1984, 59). Turning to Hölderlin's hymn, 'Mnemosyne', de Man takes up the theme of poetry and fulfilment, which he identified in Wordsworth. Whereas 'Mnemosyne' is normally interpreted as an 'eschatological poem in which Hölderlin, inspired by the memory of ancient heroism, decides to actively prepare the fulfilment of history' (1984, 60), de Man sets about reading it as a meditation on the 'gap that separates an act from its understanding' (1984, 64). Hölderlin surpasses Wordsworth because he achieves a more thorough understanding of the impossibility of immediate realization or plenitude. More precisely, action is shown to be dependent on inward reflection, rather than superior to and thus independent from it. This interdependence emerges from de Man's discussion of Titanism and poetry, in a mythical narrative about the power struggle between the traditional gods and the emerging divinities. Titanism, as Norris also notes, 'translates directly into power and performative deed, with no complicating detour through the mazy directions of human self-knowledge and doubt' (Norris, 1988, 15). Thus it corresponds to the role of the insurgents in *The Prelude*. Poetry, in contrast, de Man writes:

> never allows this power to rush blindly to meet the unknown future of death. It turns back upon itself and becomes part of a temporal dimension that strives to remain bound to the earth, and that replaces the violent temporality (*reissende Zeit*) of action with the sheltering temporality (*schützende Zeit*) of interpretation. (de Man, 1984, 63)

Titanism is not, however, opposed to poetry, then, but rather described as the prematurity of poetic consciousness. 'In reality', de Man writes, 'there is in Hölderlin not an oppositional relationship between the activity of the Titans and that of the poet, but rather one of prematurity' (1984, 61–2). Norris similarly reads this as an acknowledgement of the caution that constrains poetry from 'actively impinging on the world of historical events' (Norris, 1988, 16).

De Man reiterates this understanding of Hölderlin in 'Heidegger's Exegeses of Hölderlin'. His reading of Hölderlin sets out to challenge Heidegger's appropriation of the German poet as a precursor of his own attempt to recover the experience of Being that he traces to the pre-Socratic philosophers. Hölderlin, on the contrary, is frequently engaged in *denying* that poetry can have access to an unmediated concept of Being.

'Heidegger's Exegeses of Hölderlin'

In 'Heidegger's Exegeses of Hölderlin' de Man understands that Hölderlin occupies a special place for Heidegger:

> For Heidegger, Hölderlin is the greatest of poets ('the poet of poets') because he states the essence (*Wesen*) of poetry. The essence of poetry consists in stating the parousia, the absolute presence of Being. In this, Hölderlin differs from the metaphysicians Heidegger dismisses ... [as they merely] state their desire for the presence of Being ... (de Man, 1988a, 250)

The metaphysicians are thus 'the dupes of Being's subterfuge', de Man writes.

> [T]hey are naïve though they claim to be hyperconscious, for that which they name as the essential is nothing more than Being disguised, and that which they dismiss as the negation of the essential is, in fact, the authentic face of the very same Being. (1988a, 250)

Hölderlin's poetry on the contrary 'name[s] the immediate presence of Being' (1988a, 252). Heidegger requires Hölderlin as an example as his language preserves the knowledge of unmediated Being, the knowledge which has been lost to philosophy since the pre-Socratics. De Man actually acknowledges that Hölderlin exemplifies the same concern with the historical destiny of Germany that can be found in Heidegger prior to World War II, therefore connecting Heidegger's nostalgia for presence and his organic metaphors with an aesthetic ideology.

In order to pursue this theme, de Man examines Heidegger's understanding of Hölderlin's hymn, 'Wie wenn am Feiertage das Feld zu sehen' (Just as on a feast day, to see his field) written in 1800. His analysis of the line – 'Und was ich sah, das Heilige sei mein Wort' (And what I saw, the Holy be my word) – confirms his point that Heidegger has misread Hölderlin. Heidegger reads this line as a confirmation of Hölderlin's desire to reconcile such oppositions as subject and object, mind and nature, and thus as an instance of the immediate apprehension of Being. De Man, in contrast, interprets Heidegger as entirely *misreading*

Hölderlin, who in fact is engaged with saying '*exactly the opposite of what Heidegger makes him say*' (1988a, 254–5). Heidegger, de Man writes, 'reverse[s] his thought' (1988a, 255). Rather than confirming the reconciliation of such antinomies, de Man argues that Hölderlin resists the temptation of presence. In this line, Hölderlin does not:

> say: das Heilige *ist* mein Wort. The subjunctive is here really an optative; it indicates prayer, it marks desire, and these lines state the eternal poetic intention, but immediately state also that it can be no more than intention. It is not because he has seen Being that the poet is, therefore, capable of naming it; his word prays for the parousia, it does not establish it.
>
> It cannot establish it for as soon as the word is uttered, it destroys the immediate and discovers that instead of stating Being, it can only state mediation. (1988a, 258–9)

Heidegger's misreading of Hölderlin, in de Man's eyes, springs from his attempt to enlist Hölderlin in a 'quest for unmediated origins and presence which lies too close to Heidegger's central concerns for his readings to have followed any other path' (Norris, 1988, 13). Unlike de Man, Heidegger is unwilling to allow himself to dwell in the midst of the uncertainties of Hölderlin's discourse. De Man, however, resists the seductions of unmediated presence and he places himself in a superior cognitive position to Heidegger. For de Man, then, the difference between Being and beings is an irreducible problem of language:

> Their unity is ineffable and cannot be said, because it is language itself that introduces the distinction. Propelled by the appeal of parousia, it seeks to establish the absolute presence of immediate Being, but can do no more than pray or struggle, never found. (de Man, 1988a, 259)

Having taken a detour through Heidegger's understanding of Hölderlin, it is possible to return to de Man's 'Wordsworth and Hölderlin' with a clearer understanding of the political aspects of his deconstruction of organic ideology. The difference between Wordsworth and Hölderlin is that the latter displays the distrust of unmediated presence 'almost from the beginning' (de Man, 1984, 59). Glossing the special place that de Man reserves for Hölderlin, Norris argues that:

> Hölderlin is the poet in whom we can read the allegory of a consciousness that struggles to renounce all hope in immediate,

this-worldly fulfilment. What replaces that hope is a knowledge of the mind's self-conscious or reflective powers, its capacity to compensate the loss of heroic self-esteem through a sense of its own interior resources. (Norris, 1988, 15)

The movement from Wordsworth to Hölderlin is a movement that is distinguished by its increasing disenchantment with an activist politics. Nevertheless, it is possible to see an oscillation between these two sides of Hölderlin's thought – between the will to transcend the antinomies of subject and object, and the knowledge that resists such transcendence – rather than offer an interpretation that privileges a recurrent deconstructive drive. In the end, however, the argument in this essay confirms Lentricchia's interpretation of the underlying message of all de Man's work, that is to say:

the sheer impossibility of acting for the best in any political context, since actions can never know their ends and consciousness is always fated to a knowledge of its own incapacity to foretell safely the course of events. (Norris, 1988, 16)

This description only merits use in Norris's eyes, however, in relation to his early to middle period essays. In these essays, both Norris and Derrida argue that de Man is increasingly preoccupied with issues of aesthetic ideology and the politics of representation. This transitional stage can be traced to de Man's essay, 'The Temptation of Permanence', which first appeared in English translation in 1983.

'The Temptation of Permanence'

In de Man's resistance to Heidegger's readings of Hölderlin, Norris identifies the 'earliest signs of his own distinct "turn" toward a form of implicit ideological critique' (Norris, 1988, 158). Norris fastens onto moments in de Man's early essays which also resist the power of organicist ideologies, especially those represented by Heidegger's 'impulse to identify revealed poetic truth with the power of language – preëminently the German language – to articulate the nature of Being itself' (1988, 158). Crucially, Norris argues, it is de Man's resistance to this force in Heidegger's reading that enables us to make out the signs of de Man's transition.

Norris's reading of de Man was first published in 1987, the same year as researchers discovered the existence of an extensive number of book and music reviews written by de Man between 1939 and 1943 for *Jeudi: Hebdomadaire du Cercle 'Le Libre-Examen', Les Cahiers du Libre Examen,* the *Bibliographie Dechenne,* the pro-Nazi Belgian newspaper, *Le Soir,* and the Flemish newspaper, *Het Vlaamsche Land.* One of these articles in particular – 'Jews in Present-day Literature' – contained an openly antisemitic concluding paragraph, which extols the values of a western literary tradition, separated from Jewish influence, that has been able to protect its 'vitality' as a consequence. De Man goes on to suggest that a separate 'Jewish colony' set apart from Europe could be a possible solution to what he describes as the 'Jewish problem'. This 'solution' would not necessarily have any terrible implications for the vitality of the arts and literature in the west; at worst the European artistic tradition would only be deprived of a small group of 'mediocre' talents. In such a scenario, the great European traditions would continue to thrive as a result of its 'great evolutive laws' (LSS, 623).

While referring to this passage in this way lifts it out of its original context, it is necessary to let its meaning resonate in the context of my discussion of aesthetic ideology. Though Norris's book was written without the knowledge of these articles, his argument is acute enough to be able to withstand their emergence. The main impression left by de Man's wartime articles, Norris argues, 'is of just how remarkably little they have in common with the writings that began to appear some ten years later in *Critique* and other French-language journals' (Norris, 1988, 159). For in the academic articles that followed, de Man's work is characterized by a 'total rejection of organicist models and metaphors' (1988, 159). Heidegger's identification of authentic language with the redemption of mankind's fallen state, evident in his early reviews, is replaced by a type of thinking that exposes the dangerous ideological consequences of such undeconstructed ideas. This is one explanation for de Man's emphasis on the 'radical discontinuity between ... levels or modes of explanatory grasp' (1988, 162). De Man's attack on the hermeneutic violence that he associates with Heidegger is starkly at odds with the organicist creed that underpinned his reviews in *Het Vlammasche Land.*

'The Temptation of Permanence' reiterates de Man's opposition to the organic ideology that structured Heidegger's understanding of poetry, that is to say, as a form of language that resists the technologization of modern industrial society by enabling mankind to experience an authentic grasp of being-in-the-world. De Man is aware that Heidegger's theory of language and poetry is not merely limited to the aesthetic realm but can spill over in dangerous ways into politics and history.

De Man identifies how Heidegger's theory of language is underpinned by organic metaphors which thus describe what he calls the temptation of permanence: 'Relying on the relation, in the German language, between the word "destiny" (*Geschick*) and the word "history" (*Geschichte*) ... [Heidegger] affirmed in various ways that history is the concrete manifestation of the very movement of Being, a movement whose fundamental ambiguity is the origin of the historicity of our destiny' (de Man, 1983, 214–15). Heidegger's most frequently used metaphors – building and dwelling – attempt to unify those antinomies of western philosophical thought that lead to self-alienation. For de Man, however, such an attempt at transcendence is the temptation of permanence which his rigorous demystification of origins, truth and presence refuses. Heidegger's thought, he writes, 'is more dangerous than technical thinking since, instead of attacking an earth which is quite capable of defending itself, it betrays the movement of being' (1983, 220). Heidegger is guilty of an idealism that would seek to elevate itself over the contingencies of history, politics and reason. 'Far from being anti-historical', de Man writes, 'the poetic act ... is the quintessential historical act: that through which we become conscious of the divided character of our being, and consequently, of the necessity of fulfilling it, of accomplishing it in time, rather than undergoing it in eternity' (1983, 214). De Man clearly refuses the notion that European history is a 'process of predestined organic evolution' (1983, 172).

While in the context of de Man's work deconstruction is pushed to its most rigorous extremes of demystification, it is also evident that, like Derrida, de Man makes his understanding of writing the precondition of all thinking about history and politics. It is possible to concur with Derrida when he argues in *Memoires for Paul de Man* that in de Man's work ' "politics" cannot be separated, neither in its acts nor in what it leaves to be deciphered, from that thinking of the political and of law which traverses all of his writings' (MPD, 143). In fact Derrida provides crucial support for Norris's distinction between the early and late phases of de Man's work. Derrida's challenge to the common charge of political quietism, frequently levelled at himself because of his association with de Man, is clearly one target of his understanding of de Man's own politics. The main focus of Derrida's essay is his deconstruction of the 'mystique of origins'. What conventional readings ignore:

> is Derrida's argument that the repression of writing has always gone along with a certain mystique of origins that works to efface real history – the history of civil and political institutions – by evoking a

long-lost 'organic' community of souls where speech would suffice for all authentic social needs. (Norris, 1988, 153)

Derrida's discussion of Rousseau's simultaneous rejection and use of writing is clearly implicated in political thinking. His emphasis on writing, then, serves to resist the type of aesthetic idealization that attempts to overcome history and politics in order to preserve a mystical idealogy of pure origins.

To continue this theme – and to contrast Derrida's work with the emphasis on irresponsible freeplay – the next section will consider the deconstruction of origins in his short but profound essay, 'Declarations of Independence'. In this essay a clear argument can be made for the idea that deconstruction is profoundly antipathetic to the totalizing drive of aesthetic ideology.

'Declarations of Independence'

'Declarations of Independence' was delivered for the first time as a lecture in 1976 to mark the bicentennial of the American Revolution. Derrida returns to a number of his most important themes – the critical problematic of speech acts, specifically the relationship between the constative and the performative, the signature, the proper name and the founding act of institutions. These areas take on a more specific political dimension in relation to the origins and legitimacy of America's democratic institutions. His main question is *'who signs, and with what so-called proper name, the declarative act which founds an institution?'* (DOI, 8) – an act which institutes political and juridical authority prior to its formal acquisition. The other main questions Derrida confronts are stated clearly:

> How is a State made or founded, how does a State make or found itself? And an independence? And the autonomy of one which both gives itself, and signs, its own law? Who signs all these authorizations to sign? (DOI, 13)

Though the Declaration of Independence authorizes the representatives' signatures, the representatives were not democratically empowered with the authority prior to the act of signing. Thomas Jefferson is not the true signatory of the Declaration. True, he writes or draws up the document, but he is the representative of those other representatives, namely, those members of the United States' General Congress. 'These "representatives," of whom Jefferson represents a sort of advance-pen', Derrida writes, 'will have the right to revise, to correct and to ratify the project or draft of the Declaration' (DOI, 9). But these representatives remain the representatives of the people of the United States. As the Declaration puts it, the Congress is assembled in the name of all American citizens. Derrida's main argument is that the 'right is divided' at this point: 'It is the "good" people who declare themselves free and independent by the relay of their representatives of representatives' (DOI, 9). And Derrida's central theme emerges: one cannot decide, as he puts it, 'whether independence is stated or produced by this utterance' (DOI, 9). To quote Derrida:

> Is it that the good people have already freed themselves in fact and are only stating the fact of this emancipation in the Declaration? Or is it rather that they free themselves at the instant of and by the signature of this Declaration? (DOI, 9)

This choice, as always with Derrida, is offered as an undecidable relation between a performative and a constative structure. The Declaration denies the problem that Derrida raises by appealing to the idea of a transcendental signified or source of absolute authority:

> One can understand this Declaration as a vibrant act of faith, as a hypocrisy indispensable to a politico-military-economic, etc. coup of force, or, more simply, more economically, as the analytic and consequential deployment of a tautology: for this Declaration to have a meaning *and* an effect, there must be a last instance. (DOI, 12)

In the case of the Declaration, the last instance, the theological transcendental signified, is God. The representatives '*posit* their institutional laws on the foundation of natural laws and by the same coup ... in the name of God, creator of nature. He comes, in effect, to guarantee the rectitude of popular intentions, the unity and goodness of the people' (DOI, 11).

The main philosophical thrust of Derrida's reading emerges at this point. In the guise of a transcendental signified, God 'founds natural laws and thus the whole game which tends to present performative utterances as constative utterances' (DOI, 11). The familiar confusion that Derrida outlines between the performative and the constative marks once again a challenge to Searle's understanding of speech act theory. According to Searle, as we recall from his replies to Derrida's 'Signature, Event, Context', it is possible for an authoritative reader to understand the meaning of a text regardless of context. The problem that Derrida identifies, as we saw from his notion of iterability, is primarily a question of temporality – what in this context he refers to as overdetermined temporality or fabulous retroactivity. Here is Derrida again:

> The 'we' of the declaration speaks 'in the name of the people.'
> But this people does not exist. ... The signature invents the signer. The signer can only authorize him – or herself to sign once he or she has come to the end, if one can say this, of his or her own signature, in a sort of fabulous retroactivity. (DOI, 11)

The temporal discontinuity that Derrida reveals means that, 'There was no signer, by right, before the text of the Declaration which itself remains the producer and guarantor of its own signature' (DOI, 10). In his commentary, Norris makes this important point succinctly:

> What Derrida wants to bring out is the moment of authoritarian appeal – the recourse to an ultimate, legitimizing power – involved in all such fabulous myths of origin. And this means acknowledging the aporetic character – the root contradiction – of a liberal democracy founded on the 'representative' status of citizens who can only assume that title through a species of rhetorical imposition. (Norris, 1987, 198)

Norris continues by arguing that Derrida's reading of the Declaration of Independence raises important questions about the interpretation of legal documents. Unlike the British legal system that is based on case law, American law, though enshrined in a written constitution, is subject to State variations, particularly in relation to sensitive legislation about civil rights, the death penalty and abortion. The emphasis placed on interpretation is one reason behind the increasing influence of deconstruction in American legal studies.

In his reading of 'Declarations of Independence', Beardsworth also turns to the juridico-political implications of 'fabulous retroactivity' or the 'future anterior', particularly in relation to the concept of the *aporia*. Beardsworth argues that the temporal questions raised by the essay relate primarily to Derrida's concern with the originary violence of the law:

> The disjointure of the moment of invention is of a temporal nature. This disjointure of time remarks itself in the necessary violence of the

law invented: the invention of the United States must be violent since no previous law nor state can justify it. (Beardsworth, 1996, 99)

The temporal disjunction arises when Derrida fastens onto the relation between 'is' and 'ought' in the passage from the final paragraph of the Declaration already alluded to. Derrida's reading, Beardsworth writes:

> neatly catches the fact that it is the ellipsis of law *qua* time which institutions attempt to fill in by justifying the violence of the law. It also shows that the need to justify the law – to give it meaning, to conceal its violence and make it effective – is only derivatively a question of ideology or of power. It is, firstly, a question of disavowing time. The negation of the undecidability of the law ... translates as *denial of the relation between time and law.* (1996, 100)

The name for the concealment of undecidability is God. The use of the word God – the transcendental signified – serves to mask the originary violence of the law; God marks the desire to transcend the temporal discontinuity between 'is' and 'ought'. Derrida's deconstruction of the idealism of western metaphysics is, as Beardsworth concludes, 'the articulation of time in terms of the irreducibility of law and the articulation of law in terms of the irreducibility of time' (1996, 101).

'Declarations of Independence' is one of Derrida's most succinct and impressive discussions of temporality and the foundation of political institutions. Given that this essay was originally delivered as a paper in 1976 and was subsequently available in English translation in 1984, it has received remarkably little attention. Were it to have had the attention that it merited then discussions of the politics of deconstruction might have by-passed the unfortunate and profound misreadings that associated Derrida with a withdrawal from serious political thought. Continuing this emphasis, the final section of this chapter will turn to the use of deconstruction by feminist critics as a further example of its often ignored political dimension.

Deconstruction and feminist criticism

Discussions about deconstruction and feminist theory have led to an important debate in Gender Studies. Deconstruction has been simultaneously used to great effect by feminists as a political form of analysis and dismissed because it 'refuses to take gender differences seriously enough and does not provide a proper ground for political action' (Elam, 1994, 18). In conclusion to this chapter I propose to relate some of the important themes of Derrida's 'Declarations of Independence' to his discussion of the question of woman in *Spurs: Nietzsche's Styles*. Following this, it will be possible to see how deconstruction has been inscribed in the work of Barbara Johnson and Diane Elam. Johnson is a particularly apposite example of feminist analysis at this point because she attacks the Yale School as a predominantly Male School of literary criticism (Johnson, 1987, 32). Johnson's analysis of the politics of undecidability serves as a precursor of Elam's concern with the deconstruction of the subject in *Feminism and Deconstruction*. Here I will examine Elam's idea that the relation between deconstruction and feminism is one of 'groundless solidarity' rather than consensus (Elam, 1994, 25). The notion of groundless solidarity underpins her understanding of Kant's notion that the faculty of judgement is a bridge over an abyss (1994, 24). Deconstruction's interrogation of normative assumptions brings about an 'infinite displacement ... of the subject, of identity politics, [and] of the subject of feminism and deconstruction' (1994, 25). The contemplation of the incalculable abyss beneath the proper reinforces Elam's notion that deconstruction is an ethical duty that, without prior model or calculated mode of intervention, attempts to do justice to the singularity of the other. Deconstruction empowers women by unfixing their subject positions: 'Women are yet to be determined and so are their (political actions). We do not yet know what women *can* do' (1994, 27).

Spurs: Nietzsche's Styles

In *Spurs: Nietzsche's Styles* Derrida engages in an affirmative deconstructive reading of Nietzsche that raises questions of power, truth, textuality and gender. Derrida describes how Nietzsche's apparent misogyny is constantly made and unmade by his texts. On the one hand, Derrida identifies Nietzsche's argument that 'truth is like a woman' (SN, 51). On the other hand, 'Woman ... is scepticism and veiling dissimulation' (SN, 57). Derrida associates Nietzsche's conception of woman with his abyssal notion of writing. For Nietzsche, Derrida writes, 'Woman (truth) will not be pinned down' (SN, 55). *Spur*, the English translation of the French word, *éperon*, conveys this undecidability: spur means both the impress or mark of a stylate spur (evident, for example, in the German *Spur*, meaning trace or wake), and a rapier such as a stiletto which signifies a way of protecting truth or presence 'from the unveiling of ... difference' (SN, 39).

Derrida focuses on phallogocentrism, a term which associates logo-centrism with patriarchal power and specifically its symbolic represen-tation, the phallus. Phallogocentrism is determined by a masculine and therefore logocentric interpretation of self-present truth that erases the play of differance. While phallogocentrism attempts to impose a similar metaphysical understanding of truth on woman, for Derrida woman is an undecidable term: 'There is no such thing as the essence of woman because woman averts, she is averted of herself. Out of the depths, endless and unfathomable, she engulfs and distorts all vestige of essentiality, of identity, of property' (SN, 51). In other words, 'There is no such thing as a woman, as a truth in itself of woman in itself' (SN, 101). Here the other meaning of spur emerges: 'The stylate spur (*éperon stylé*) rips through the veil' (107). Like Derrida's other undecidable terms, woman destabilises the oppositions of logocentrism. This is particularly evident in relation to the opposition between truth and non-truth:

> The question of the woman suspends the decidable opposition of true and non-true and inaugurates the epochal regime of quotation marks which is to be enforced for every concept belonging to the ˙ system of philosophical decidability. The hermeneutic project which postulates a true sense of the text is disqualified under this regime. (SN, 107)

Woman thereby inaugurates an abyssal logic: 'There is no such thing as the truth of woman, but it is because of that abyssal divergence of the truth, because that untruth is "truth". Woman is but one name for that untruth of truth' (SN, 51). The complexity of Nietzsche's representation of woman places the metaphysical notion of truth under erasure: 'Nietzsche's writing is compelled to suspend truth between the tenter-hooks of quotation marks – and suspended there with truth is – all the rest' (SN, 57). As there is no truth in itself there is no self-present notion of truth: 'There is no such thing as a woman, as a truth in itself of woman in itself. That much, at least, Nietzsche has said' (SN, 101). Moreover, Derrida identifies how Nietzsche's style of writing is a type of feminine operation.

In order that metaphysics maintain its notion of self-present truth it attempts to efface the role of writing, woman and dissimulation. Female subjectivity cannot therefore be possessed or appropriated. Derrida symbolizes the status of the subject by associating 'woman' with play, negativity, seduction and otherness. These words resonate with the theme of resistance; 'woman' cannot be grasped: 'Truth, unveiling, illumination are no longer decided in the appropriation of the truth of being, but cast into its bottomless abyss as non-truth, veiling and dissimulation' (SN, 119). In place of the literality and the essence of 'woman' Derrida places an interminable movement of unveiling.

In the interview, 'Choreographies', Derrida relates Emma Goldman's statement – 'If I can't dance I don't want to be part of your revolution' – to his notion of truth. Goldman, something of a maverick feminist from the late nineteenth century, places an emphasis on dance that is similar to Derrida's mobile strategy of deconstruction. Goldman's figure of the dance fastens onto a completely other history of the women's movement – one that emphasizes its discontinuities and heterogenous particularities. The *dance* is therefore another term for a form of deconstructive activity which describes women who have always been concerned with inventing identities that are distanced from the main avenues of feminist thinking in a way that does not hinder them from becoming active when necessary. The affirmative notion of the dance produces the deconstruction or *displacement* of the metaphysical conception of women. The joyous disturbance of the dance describes neither a lack of power or fragility, but rather the need for a process of interminable negotiation that is always deprived of the security of closure. As the word choreographies suggests, deconstruction or the dance resists a mono-sexual discourse, affirming in its place the need for a group or chorus with multiple signatories. As Elam says, 'One important feature of the encounter between feminism and deconstruction is that it allows us to rethink the temporality of feminism's movement, perhaps as something closer to the dance than to Mao's long march' (Elam, 1994, 9). The political significance of undecidability and Derrida's undermining of literality is further taken up by Johnson and Elam in relation to the question of the subject.

Feminism and the politics of undecidability

Unlike a range of feminist critics who are antipathetic to deconstruction, Johnson interprets one of the main contentions of both de Man and Derrida – 'not that language is always absolutely random, but that we can never be sure that it isn't' – neither as a 'conservative plot to talk radicals out of social change' or as a 'nihilistic desire to cancel out human meaning altogether' (Johnson, 1987, 6). Johnson rejects both charges in her readings of gender in *A World of Difference*. This book, she writes, is concerned with 'transfer[ing] the analysis of difference ... out of the realm of linguistic universality or deconstructive allegory and into contexts in which difference is very much at issue in the "real" world' (1987, 2). Johnson attempts to challenge the popular idea that pedagogical institutions frequently maintain boundaries between inside and outside, the unreal and the real world. Whereas in her earlier study, *The Critical Difference* (1980), Johnson was motivated by the question, 'Here is a text; let me read it', the later book is predicated on questions such as, 'Why am I reading *this* text? What kind of act was the writing of it? What question about it does it itself *not* raise? What am I participating in when I read it?' (Johnson, 1987, 3–4). Johnson is concerned with challenging the boundaries between institutions and the real world, reading and politics, and showing how the 'constraints and opportunities afforded by gender, race, literary genre, or institutional context, for both writer and reader, can be located neither inside nor outside the texts but are rather effects of the complex dynamism of an interaction' (1987, 4). Johnson moves 'toward a critique of the fallacious naturalness and blindered focus of certain institutional boundaries ... concentrat[ing] on thresholds where an inside/outside opposition can be shown to be in a state of crisis, both within the text and between the text and the context of its reading or writing' (1987, 3). Most significantly, she attempts to interrogate the sexual and racial exclusions of the western literary canon. Her indebtedness to both de Man's and Derrida's understanding of differance is directly related to a number of political questions, frequently posed by the literary left:

> What are the political consequences of the fact that language is not a transparently expressive medium? What role does literature's radicalization of this fact play? How can the study of suppressed, disseminated, or marginalized messages within texts equip us to intervene against oppression and injustice in the world? Is a willingness to carry an inquiry to the point of undecidability necessarily at odds with political engagement? (1987, 7)

Such questions are not asked or addressed in such an explicit manner in the work of de Man or that of the other Yale critics, and it is interesting to pursue Johnson's answers in order to see how deconstruction can empower feminist analyses. First, it is necessary to understand her notion of deconstruction prior to an examination of her deployment of the term.

In 'Nothing Fails like Success' Johnson criticizes a number of arguments that have been levelled at deconstruction, focusing especially on the differences between the Yale critics and de Man's and Derrida's understanding of the word:

> As soon as any radically innovative thought becomes an *ism*, its specific groundbreaking force diminishes, its historical notoriety increases, and its disciples tend to become more simplistic, more dogmatic, and ultimately more conservative, at which time its power becomes institutional rather than analytical. (Johnson, 1987, 11)

Johnson sharply rebuts a number of obvious misreadings of Derrida's thinking – the idea that deconstruction attacks the logic of noncontradiction and the essence of western rational thought; that deconstruction relies on a limited understanding of textuality and applies 'its critical energy only within an institutional structure that does not question and therefore confirms' (1987, 14); and the mistaken notion that the phrase 'there is nothing outside the text' means that readers have no access to history or biography and so on. In place of these clichés, she outlines a notion of deconstruction as a form of strong reading that 'propagates the surprise of otherness' (1987, 15). Derrida brings to his reader the surprise of an undecidable logic that must never remain static or fixed. Such an idea is based on the assumption that, rather than taking knowledge for granted, the necessary task of readers should be to *surprise* one's ignorance:

> The surprise of otherness is that moment when a new form of ignorance is suddenly activated as an imperative. If the deconstructive impulse is to retain its vital, subversive power, we must therefore become ignorant of it again and again. It is only by forgetting what we know how to do, by setting aside the thoughts that have most changed us, that those thoughts and that knowledge can go on making accessible to us the surprise of an otherness we can only encounter in the moment of suddenly discovering we are ignorant of it. (1987, 16)

Johnson firmly rejects the idea that deconstruction should become a repeatable literary methodology. Once more deconstruction is wrestled free from this reading. How then does Johnson use deconstruction in her politically committed readings of gender and race?

As an example of Johnson's indebtedness to deconstruction, let's examine her essay, 'Apostrophe, Animation, and Abortion', where she is concerned with challenging the notion that 'to focus on undecidability is to be apolitical' (1987, 193). Johnson argues, 'on the contrary, [that] the undecidable *is* the political. There is politics precisely because there is undecidability' (1987, 194). Allied to this focus is her politicization of rhetoric, an area of literary study which is normally annexed from such discussions. 'What ... could seem more dry and apolitical than a rhetorical treatise?', Johnson asks, and 'What could seem farther away from budgets and guerrilla warfare than a discussion of anaphora, antithesis, prolepsis, and preterition?' (1987, 184). The CIA manual on psychological operations in guerrilla warfare, however, which came to light during the American campaign of propaganda in Nicaragua, contains an 'appendix on techniques of oratory which lists definitions and examples for these and many other rhetorical figures' (1987, 184). Defining rhetoric in terms of a 'language that says one thing and means another', Johnson argues that, 'Rhetoric clearly has everything to do with covert operations' (1987, 184).

Having established the political dimensions of rhetoric, however, the main focus of her analysis shifts to consider the debate about abortion, and the role that rhetoric plays in the politics of the debate. Are the 'politics of violence', she asks, 'already encoded in rhetorical figures as such? In other words, can the very essence of a political issue – an issue like, say, abortion – hinge on the structure of a figure? Is there any *inherent* connection between figurative language and questions of life and death, of who will wield and who will receive violence in a given human society?' (1987, 184).

Johnson begins her discussion of these issues by outlining her understanding of the figure of apostrophe, a common figure of lyric poetry. Apostrophe functions as a 'direct address of an absent, dead, or inanimate being by a first-person speaker' (1987, 185). It is based on the 'notion of turning aside, of digressing from straight speech, it manipulates the I/thou structure of direct address in an indirect, fictionalized way. The absent, dead, or inanimate entity addressed is thereby made present, animate, and anthropomorphic' (1987, 185). Johnson cites Baudelaire's 'Moesta et Errabunda' and Shelley's 'Ode to the West Wind', but it is the latter which she argues is perhaps the ultimate example of an apostrophaic poem.

In the first three sections of the poem, Shelley invokes the wind as a figure of animation, describing it as the 'breath of being', 'moving everywhere', 'blowing movement and energy through the world' (1987, 187). Conversely, the wind has a violent underside: it is destructive and brings death and winter in its wake. Johnson traces the evolution of the poem in terms of the birth or reanimation of the speaker's lost or former self. In the first three sections, the poem moves from the speaker's attempts to make the wind listen to him, to the fourth where he begins to inscribe his own identity – his own 'I' – in place of the wind's 'thou'. Through time, Johnson argues, a loss of animation and similarity between speaker and wind has occurred. The final section continues this tension by reversing the structure of apostrophe, as the speaker attempts to reanimate the lost sense of proximity to the wind as inspiration, muse or authentic former self. The possibility of achieving reanimation, however, is precisely what is placed in doubt. The speaker's hope of achieving this depends on the notion that the wind is the giver of death and also of life. This rhetorical question – does life entail rebirth, regeneration, reanimation? – remains unanswered. 'The rhetorical question', Johnson writes, 'in a sense, leaves the poem in a state of suspended animation', a state which, for the poem, is one of 'maximum potential' (1987, 188). This phrase recalls de Man's conclusion to the Proust section of 'Semiology and Rhetoric': 'We seem to end up in a mood of negative assurance that is highly productive of critical discourse' (de Man, 1979, 16).

Turning to Gwendolyn Brooks's poem, 'The Mother', Johnson describes how apostrophe can be linked, through the theme of abortion, to the lost life of another person. Reading the first line of the poem, 'Abortions will not let you forget', Johnson argues that, unlike Shelley, who sought to reanimate his lost self, Brooks 'represents the self as eternally addressed and possessed by the lost, anthropomorphised other' (Johnson, 1987, 189). The 'you' of the first line shows that the 'I' is already 'alienated, distanced from itself, and combined with a generalized other' (1987, 189). This confusion blurs the traditional boundaries between subject and object, agent and victim.

In the second section, Brooks replaces the first word abortion, with an 'I' and the first line reads: 'I have heard the voices in the voices of the wind the voices of my dim killed children'. Brooks's use of apostrophe moves from the inanimate concern evident in Shelley to the boundary between animate and inanimate life. The boundary here, which is a major element in the abortion debate, concerns the point at which an unborn foetus achieves personhood. For Johnson, however, the stakes are even higher. The transition signalled by Brooks concerns the:

> rewriting [of] the male lyric tradition, textually placing aborted children in the spot formerly occupied by all the dead, inanimate, or absent entities previously addressed by the lyric. (1987, 189).

In line 14 of the poem – 'I have said, Sweets, if I sinned' – Brooks's speaker suffers from an inability to forget rather than the desire for union, that was the case with Shelley. The poem dramatizes the attempt to clarify the tension between 'I' and 'you' – a conflict which, for Johnson, 'succeeds only in expressing the inability of its language to do so' (1987, 190). The 'I' here is always conditioned by the memory of the other – the 'you'. Though the poem is frequently interpreted as 'an argument against abortion' (1987, 191), Johnson argues that its complex use of apostrophe is in fact a powerful example of undecidability:

> [T]he poem makes no such claim [against abortion]: it attempts the impossible task of humanizing both the mother and the aborted children while presenting the inadequacy to resolve the dilemma without violence. (1987, 191)

Drawing on Carol Gilligan's discussion of the ethics of abortion in her book, *In a Different Voice* (1982), Johnson understands that the choice of whether or not to have an abortion cannot efface violence: 'The choice is not between violence and nonviolence, but between simple violence to a fetus and complex, less determinate violence to an involuntary mother and/or an unwanted child' (1987, 191). The figure of apostrophe plays an important role in the structure of the abortion debate. 'What I would like to emphasize', she writes:

> is the way in which the poem suggests that the arguments for and against abortion are structured through and through by the rhetorical limits and possibilities of something akin to apostrophe. (1987, 191)

The complexity of the speaker's role derives from her knowledge that she cannot escape without violence. Apostrophe makes the children she addresses human and she is unable to forget her role in their death. By reanimating them she can attempt to stave off the final act of abortion. Johnson accepts that this undecidability is part of language itself: 'It becomes impossible to tell whether language is what gives life or what kills' (1987, 191).

The same problems arise in juridical debates about the point at which a foetus achieves personhood. Johnson's discussion of the landmark US Supreme Court case about abortion, *Roe v. Wade*, leads her to agree with the argument that both pro-life and pro-choice activists fail to represent substantial proportions of Americans. Her point is that the debate depends on different understandings of the key terms involved, from motherhood to personhood. Johnson is led to reiterate the point, based on her discussion of Brooks's complex understanding of 'shifting address-structures', that there is 'politics precisely because there is undecidability' (1987, 194). In closing we once again return to Derrida's thinking of time and his argument that all decisions must pass via the trial of the undecidable.

In 'The Deconstruction of Politics' (1989) Bill Readings further refines deconstruction's relation to the political, principally by developing Johnson's understanding of the deconstructed subject. The main target of Readings's essay is Eagleton's and Said's charge that deconstruction erases the subject and therefore the chance of political agency. Readings recognizes that such critics misunderstand Derrida's notion of the deconstructed subject. Derrida has never said that there is no subject; merely that it is necessary to rethink the problem of subjectivity as it is produced by textuality. Readings's subsequent notion of the ethical subject is based on the rejection of this familiar misconception of deconstruction, as well as the idea that Derrida rejects the real or literal world for an all-embracing notion of textuality.

The traditional metaphysical conception of the political relies on an opposition between the real (or literal) and the textual (or figural). Readings shows, however, that Derrida's argument that these realms cannot be opposed in this simplistic fashion often leads to the charge that deconstruction is not concerned with 'real people' and 'real struggles'. According to this idea, the literal grounds critical insight and political action as pure knowledge. Readings rejects deconstruction as a 'critical method *before* politics' because it is not a transcendental strategy that attempts to 'ground in some sense the insights that it offers as "real" ' (1989, 224–5). Readings is quite clear about his rejection of this strategy: 'The attempt to lend deconstruction the status of demystification and then to seek to empower it for social change in a literal sphere of agency is futile' (1989, 225). Readings emphasizes the literal sphere in this passage because Derrida rejects the idea that the literal can be detached from the rhetorical sphere of signifying practices. Consequently, Derrida's reconsideration of the opposition that grounds the metaphysical notion of the political is not tantamount to a withdrawal from political thinking. The strategic force of Readings's understanding of the contamination of the literal by the figural is to be found in his attempt to shift the emphasis of the debate from the question of deconstruction *and* politics to the deconstruction *of* politics. Importantly, Readings's lucid and intelligent intervention argues that the force of deconstruction is in fact to be found in 'the extent to which it forces a rethinking of the terms of the political' (1989, 225). The privilege normally reserved for the literal sphere sets up an opposition between textuality (or books in general when the argument is stated in its crudest terms) and exterior reality. According to this view, 'literature is political only to the extent that the political is in some sense the *referent* of the text, a referent that is conceived literally, as something exterior to the text' (1989, 227). At this point two of the main threads of the sustained misreading of deconstruction can be identified and – more to the point – firmly rejected. Derrida's rethinking of the question of reference, linked to the idea that he denies the existence of an extra-linguistic reality, are usually taken as evidence of his withdrawal from politics. Derrida's main point is not to deny reference or the existence of an extra-linguistic reality. Rather he acknowledges that there can be no referent that is not subject to textuality, no access to the real that is not textually mediated. Just like de Man, Readings argues that Derrida astutely 'avoids any easy deferral of the question of politics by the invocation of strategic claims that always tend toward transcendence' (1989, 228). The prime example of the figurative contamination of the literal is the idea that the literal is itself a metaphor: 'The referent is in the text in the sense that reference is a figural necessity of the fiction that language is the vehicle of a communication or an expression, a vehicle that can *transport*, can move outside itself to the properties of things ... can function *literally*' (1989, 229). In other words, the 'literal is a trope within rhetoric, rhetoric's trope of the absence of rhetoric' (1989, 230), and, in a similar way, 'The referent is the text's fiction of the absence of text, the text's fiction of its own outside' (1989, 230). The resulting failure to acknowledge the mutual contamination of the literal and the figural underpins the traditional empirical conception of the political in western metaphysics. The transparent notion of representation – which Derrida deconstructs in 'Declarations of Independence', for example – shows that 'domination works by denying its politics, by establishing its particular politics as an empirical or prepolitical real, so that domination is invisible in that it takes place before what is named as the political' (1989, 230). Derrida's emphasis on undecidability and mutual contamination is a direct attack on a totalitarian conception of the political.

Readings proposes to replace the 'traditional subject of politics' with the 'subject of a tradition of ethical thought' (1989, 234) in order to rethink the question of political agency altogether. For Readings, 'The tradition of ethical thought offers a displacement of the subject/object distinction that may produce a subject under deconstruction' (1989, 234). The ethical subject which emerges from the process is aligned with a conception of justice that derives from Levinas:

> The subject of ethics is the subject who judges without criteria, who practices a justice that cannot be justified. The just person cannot be described justly, since to describe his or her prescriptive function would be to fall in with the injustice of reality. (1989, 234)

In other words, judgements are made without reference to existing criteria and 'the process of judging can never reach the point where a final account can be given of it' (1989, 234). This is a notion of justice without present realization, of a justice to come. Readings's notion of the ethical subject or subject under deconstruction does not 'deny the possibility of agency but merely disrupts its status in ways that precisely allow the possibility of a political resistance that might escape confinement to the field of a political real, which is always already defined by the State as the state (of things)' (1989, 235).

In *Feminism and Deconstruction: Ms. en Abyme* (1994) Elam attempts to apply Readings's notion of the ethical subject in a feminist context. The pun in Elam's subtitle – 'Ms. en Abyme' rather than *mise en abyme* – gives us an immediate clue as to her concept of the deconstruction of the female subject. In poststructuralist writings the figure of *mise en abyme* derives from the heraldic effect of infinite regression whereby a shield contains representations of smaller shields. The strategic effect of *mise en abyme* relates to the structure of infinite deferral or 'a spiral of infinite regression in representation' (Elam, 1994, 27). Elam's argument is based on the notion that *mise en abyme* is the condition of women. Rather than provoke the familiar criticism that this effect would lead to paralysis or uncertainty, Elam sees it as an empowering strategy which 'upsets the assumed relationship between subject and object in the scene of representation' (1994, 28). It is possible for the subject and object to change positions therefore challenging stable representations of female identity, either in relation to the traditionally negative role of object or even as a potentially empowered or active subject. As Elam explains, 'the *mis en abyme* acknowledges the subject/object positions assumed by representation, but it also makes those positions infinite and ultimately incalculable. Women ultimately will never be determined as either subject or object' (1994, 29). Feminism must assimilate the notion of infinite deferral if it is to be just to the possibilities of female subjectivity. In other words, ' "women" is a *permanently contested site of meaning*' (1994, 32).

Elam seeks to develop Johnson's notion that undecidability is the condition of politics. In the context of my previous discussion, Elam outlines a 'politics which is not grounded by a notion of subjective experience' and is based on the assumption that, 'The political remains the realm of the undecidable, which will not yield a theory of what women should be' (1994, 66). By the same token Elam thinks of deconstruction in a similar way to Readings as 'a questioning of the terms in which we understand the political, rather than as a simple negation of the political' (1994, 67). In other words, deconstruction has much in 'common with the feminist refusal to accept the terms within and by which politics is conventionally practiced' (1994, 67). For Elam, then, deconstruction is not concerned with the 'working out of a particular politics but rather [with] the insistence that the nature of the political must remain open to question, to modification' (1994, 68). This understanding also applies to what counts as politics, and both feminism and deconstruction thus conceived do not stop asking this question; this constant questioning is part of their political force. Elam is not concerned with attempting to account for how deconstruction and feminism stand on certain political questions of everyday significance. Elam's attempt to rethink the political in this respect relates to her rethinking of the essentialist notions of identity that underpin traditional forms of feminist praxis. Elam tries to outline a notion of the subject that opens up difference within identity by:

> explor[ing] the political practices made possible by *solidarity* which is not based on identity. The solidarity to which I am referring would, in fact, be a coalition built around a suspicion of identity as the essential grounding for meaningful political action. (1994, 69)

The resulting notion of groundless solidarity springs from the deconstruction of the fixed subject. This is accompanied by a move from politics to ethics that also names a shift from politics conceived as a regime of truth.

In the modern era politics has been founded on the idea of a subject that is free to make its own laws. There can, however, be no subject prior to logocentrism: 'the subject is a logocentric Being' (EO, 16) as Derrida has frequently reminded readers. Derrida disputes the idea that the subject exists prior to the political realm in a stable and coherent form. The deconstruction of the subject amounts to the same problematization of the subject/object relation that I established when I discussed *mise en abyme*. Consequently, Elam argues that feminism must begin to consider the implications of doing politics without a stable subject and therefore redefine what 'might constitute politics' (Elam, 1994, 77).

At this point Elam turns to Johnson's discussion of abortion in 'Apostrophe, Animation, and Abortion'. In opposition to those feminist critics who remain resolutely opposed to Derrida's emphasis on undecidability, Elam shows that Johnson is acutely aware of the way undecidability can empower new political possibilities: 'The specificity of feminism is thus its insistence that the politics of undecidability (among multiple determinations) must be understood from a standpoint of indeterminacy, of political *possibilities*' (1994, 84). In the context of the abortion debate, Johnson's emphasis on undecidability 'stands to make clear ... that it is precisely feminists who wish to preserve abortion as a difficult decision, a decision that is a woman's choice, that is not decided in advance' (1994, 84). In order to do justice to the debate on abortion it is necessary to 'allow the *undecidable* in so far as abortion would be neither a decision which could be made in advance or made once and for all for all women' (1994, 84). The undecidable is related to Johnson's notion of the surprise of the other. Politics is reconfigured via this notion of the subject as 'an encounter with difference, the attempt to handle differences' (1994, 86). This reading returns us to the thesis that Derrida's understanding of the political derives from his notion of temporality. Politics lapses into totalitarianism when it forgets the undecidable and the ethical subject. For Derrida, then, 'the present does not *ground* a politics any more than do the past (conservatism) or the future (technocracy). The past can only be recalled as a promise (it still awaits fulfilment), and the future fulfilment is dependent upon a past promise' (1994, 86). Elam also forecefully makes a point later to be taken up by Beardsworth, that connects the notion of originary repetition to a non-horizonal concept of justice in this context: 'the understanding of politics as undecidable is not about refusing to make decisions: it is about refusing to ground decisions in universal laws' (1994, 87). Deconstruction and feminism are ethical activities that require judgements be made, yet which do not 'supply the means of legitimating those judgements' (1994, 87). There can be no simple access to 'self-present subjects, natural rights, or transcendental truths' (1994, 88). The politics of undecidability amounts to an 'insistence that we have to *make* a decision, each time, in each case – that we cannot avoid making a decision by just applying a pre-existing universal law' (1994, 87).

This chapter has argued that the early institutionalization of deconstruction as a repeatable literary methodology drained Derridean deconstruction of its politico-institutional context. By focusing on such essays as 'Structure, Sign and Play in the Discourse of the Human

Sciences' and 'Différance', Derrida's emphasis on the dissemination of meaning took precedence over the ethico-political tenor of his reading of Saussure in *Of Grammatology*, his understanding of the inheritance of Marx in the interview in *Positions*, his work on the formation of GREPH, and 'Declarations of Independence'. Set against the background of these profound misreadings, the use of Derrida's work by de Man and Barbara Johnson is more attuned to the political resonance of Derridean deconstruction as a critique of aesthetic ideology and all forms of totalizing thought. Johnson's argument – that 'There is politics precisely because there is undecidabililty' – clarifies the main aspects of my reading of deconstruction thus far: (1) undecidability means that deconstruction is best understood as a questioning of the political and as an insistence that it remain open to negotiation and reinvention; (2) deconstruction proposes an ethical reading of the political; (3) deconstruction does not offer a single notion of political action; (4) political action is articulated in different ways at different times and in different contexts; and (5) deconstruction's questioning of the fixed subject leads to a self-differentiating notion of identity which is based on a bond of sameness and difference. The next chapter will continue to challenge the reading of deconstruction by the first wave of literary critics by turning to consider the pedagogical implications of Derrida's thought in more detail.

3
The Deconstruction of a Pedagogical Institution: Derrida and 'The Principle of Reason'

While generally overlooked by American literary critics during the mid-1970s and early 1980s, Derrida's work with GREPH and the International College of Philosophy has increasingly led a number of critics to consider what he describes as the 'deconstruction of a pedagogical institution and all that it implies' (LOB, 94). Margaret Rose, for instance, argues that, 'Deconstruction attacks not only the internal edifice ... but also its extrinsic conditions of practice: the historical forms of its pedagogy, the social, economic or political structures of this pedagogical institution' (1991, 41). Robert Young places a similar emphasis, arguing that deconstruction can be explained by its duty to question everything including the function of the university: 'There is ... a strategy for deconstruction and that strategy occurs within the institutions and institutional practices' (1981, 19). The views of these critics contrast sharply with Thomas McCarthy's (1989) argument that Derrida's work has not been supported by a significant critical engagement with historical or institutional questions.

Norris's more sustained reading of Derrida's essay, 'The Principle of Reason: the University in the Eyes of Its Pupils', develops the implications of Young's and Rose's points in more detail. Norris firmly locates Derrida in the tradition of post-Kantian critical thought and clearly challenges the charge that deconstruction is a form of textualist mystification or irrational nihilism. For Norris, 'Derrida thinks of philosophy, not only as a site of institutional struggle, but also as a highly specific discipline of thought whose central texts may indeed be "deconstructed" but *not* given up to any kind of intertextual or undifferentiated "freeplay" ' (1987, 26–7). Derrida's logic of contamination was never concerned with eroding the boundaries between disciplines, but with showing that they were always already eroded. 'We are deluded', Norris suggests, 'if we think that what goes on inside the university – whether in the depths of philosophy, literature or pure science – can ever be kept separate from what happens in the world outside' (1987, 139). Derrida relies on such assumptions to undermine the inside/outside oppositions of the Kantian model of philosophy, with its careful separation of faculties and the disinterested role that it attributes to philosophy – both of which have underpinned the development of western pedagogical institutions since the University of Berlin was founded in 1810. In 'The Principle of Reason: the University in the Eyes of Its Pupils', Derrida challenges the arguments of those critics who refuse to read him on account of his supposed irrationalism. In this major essay about the function of pure and applied research in the modern university, Derrida positions philosophy at the intersection of cultural memory and reflection so that the foundations of reason can be subjected to further rational critique. Derrida maintains the importance of 'philosophy's commitment to a *reasoned and responsible* critique of existing forms of institutionalised power/knowledge' (Norris, 1992c, 34).

Norris's 1987 study participates in this repositioning of deconstruction, emphasizing Derrida's overt statements on the role of the institution in his work as a 'distancing gesture with regard to the massive *institutional* success of deconstructive criticism in American departments of English and Comparative literature' and 'those forms of neo-pragmatist or "postmodern" thinking that renounce reason itself' (Norris, 1987, 14). Though Norris touches on Derrida's work with GREPH, the Etats Généraux de la Philosophie, the International College of Philosophy and 'The Principle of Reason: the University in the Eyes of Its Pupils' (1983), a number of other essays, not considered by him – 'Languages and Institutions of Philosophy' (1984); 'Otobiographies: the Teaching of Nietzsche and the Politics of the Proper Name' (1985); 'Sendoffs' (1990); and 'Mochlos, or The Conflict of the Faculties' (1992) – further develop Derrida's engagement with political issues in this area.

What follows will focus on Derrida's work with GREPH and the International College of Philosophy in the form of his essay, 'Sendoffs'. Part Two then turns to the philosophical underpinnings of Derrida's engagement with French pedagogical institutions, examining his discussion of Kant's *The Conflict of the Faculties* in 'Mochlos, or The Conflict of the Faculties', 'Languages and Institutions of Philosophy' and Nietzsche's little-known work, *On the Future of Our Educational Institutions*. The conclusion to this chapter explores one of Derrida's most acute and sustained engagements with the pedagogical implications of his thought in his seminal essay, 'The Principle of Reason: the

University in the Eyes of it Pupils', in which he brings to the fore the strategic political force of his rethinking of western rationality and its politico-institutional protocols.

The beginning of GREPH

Derrida's interest in the relationship between philosophy and the university has been evident since the mid-1970s, particularly as a result of his work with 'Group for the Research of the Teaching of Philosophy' [GREPH, Groupe de recherches sur l'enseignement philosophique], founded in 1975, and then subsequently with the Etats généraux de la Philosophie in 1979 and the International College of Philosophy, which was officially opened in Paris in 1983. This particular side of Derrida's work was largely ignored by his reception in the Anglo-American universities, where deconstruction was assimilated as a form of aggressive relativism or textual free-play. Derrida's contribution to these groups and movements expresses his resistance to the much-touted death of philosophy, and was particularly apposite at a time when the use value of humanistic, as opposed to scientific or ends-oriented, research was being questioned.

GREPH was formed by a group of prominent intellectuals (predominantly professors and teachers in the state sector) in response to what they viewed as a threat to the teaching of philosophy in French secondary schools. 'The Haby Reform', as this legislation was known, attempted to reduce the number of hours allocated to philosophy teaching in the curriculum and to limit final year students' access to the subject. The Haby Reform was interpreted as a major piece of post-1968 educational legislation, and even as a direct response to the events of May–June 1968, which sprang from student demonstrations about visiting rights in the University of Nanterre. For some of the key figures on the French left, the Haby Reform was interpreted as an attempt on behalf of the right to challenge the critical function of philosophy within the curriculum. The founding members of GREPH viewed the Haby Reform as a way of advancing a physiologically correct age for the study of philosophy. In 1979 GREPH's opposition to this aspect of the new educational reforms led to the formation of Etats généraux de la Philosophie, a larger national forum for the debate of these issues. With the exception of 'Sendoffs' (1990), none of the texts produced by GREPH had been published in full English translation before 1998. These significant elisions strengthened rather than questioned the misreading of Derrida's work, and determined its initial de-politicization in Anglo-American universities.

In a study of deconstruction and film theory, Brunette and Wills provide some interesting translations of Derrida's participation in the Etats généraux de la Philosophie, thus confirming the impact they would have had had they been available earlier. The translations indicate that Derrida's contribution was concerned above all with philosophy's ability to encourage the development of students' critical skills, as Derrida argues: 'the more that philosophical training is curtailed in this country [France], the less critical competence there will be outside of the educational institution' (Brunette and Wills, 1989, 26). This capacity, Derrida continues, can act as an 'arm of resistance (for example against all forms of violations of human rights, abuse of police power, and injustice)' (1989, 26).

Correspondingly, the published transcript of the Political Seminar in Cerisy in the early 1980s sheds some further light on Derrida's feelings at the time of the Haby Reform. According to Nancy Fraser, in her summary of the proceedings, Derrida referred to this pedagogical revisionism as a direct attack on Marxism, though he stressed that this association should not be used to indicate a simple form of political affiliation on his part (Fraser, 1984, 133). On the contrary, GREPH's intervention stemmed from the requirement to defend the freedom of critical enquiry in a way which questioned, rather than endorsed, the intervention of the state's political agenda into university life. As this GREPH text indicates, Derrida believed, 'that in a given historical, political situation of the University, it is necessary to fight so that something like philosophy remains possible' (1984, 141). Derrida's subsequent work on the relationship between pedagogical practices and the power of the state to intervene and delimit the production and dissemination of knowledge can be viewed as a long-term commitment, rather than as a passing fad to counter American deconstructionists.

In France, in contrast, Derrida continued to be concerned with pedagogical questions, most notably, through his involvement in the development of the International College of Philosophy following the election of the Mitterrand government in the early 1980s. This project has been engaged with the future of the university, combining Derrida's interest in the Kantian concern with the architectonics of the university with that of the metaphysical structures of western philosophy.

In a series of books published since the mid-1970s, then, Derrida sought to initiate discussion about what he refers to as the 'implacably political typography' of the university (POR, 18). In these texts Derrida recognizes that 'existing conventions of the university cannot be left out ... or withdrawn from the scene' of academic discussion (EO, 4).

Confirming Norris's argument that his work can be located in the post-Kantian tradition of representation and critique (Norris, 1987, 141), Derrida argues that deconstruction is intimately associated with engendering new forms of rationality.

In 'The Principle of Reason: the University in the Eyes of Its Pupils' above all, Derrida situates this new responsibility in relation to the requirement to rethink the university's model of community in terms of differance. While a number of critics have suggested that Derrida's work resists the ideal of community altogether, principally as an attempt to protect an ideal of singularity from the encroachment of totalitarianism, 'The Principle of Reason' challenges this assertion outright. The following passage exemplifies a strong undercurrent to Derrida's thinking about reason, the university and community. Derrida's understanding of community would speak of the 'responsibility of a community of thought'. He writes,

> for which the frontier between basic and oriented research would no longer be secured, or in any event not under the same conditions as before. I call it a community of thought in the broad sense – 'at large' – rather than a community of research, of science or philosophy, since these values are most often subjected to the unquestioned authority of a principle of reason. (POR, 16)

On the one hand, Derrida attempts to found a new form of community which is based on his understanding of differance rather than metaphysics, as was the case with Rousseau and Lévi-Strauss. On the other hand, at a deeper level, he is concerned with rethinking the very basis of community in western thought:

> It is not certain that such thinking can bring together a community or found an institution in the traditional sense of these words. What is meant by community and institution must be rethought ... I am defining the necessity for a new way of educating students that will prepare them to undertake new analyses in order to evaluate these ends and to choose, when possible, among them all. (POR, 16)

Evidently a series of threads runs throughout the following sections of this chapter on Derrida's engagement with the Kantian model of the university: (1) the harmful incursion of the state into the decision-making processes of the university, principally related to questions of censorship; (2) Derrida's critique of the Kantian model of the university that underpinned the foundation of the University of Berlin in 1810; (3) the significant place Derrida reserves for philosophy in the philosophical community, once again an important theme of Kant's thought; (4) the university as a model of a community based on the respect and tolerance of difference; and (5) Derrida's belief in an a priori form of radical questioning as opposed to the calculative logic of applied research.

The sections that follow intend to examine Derrida's analysis of the university more closely by placing his work in the context of philosophical responses to this area by Kant and Nietzsche, before returning to Derrida's 'The Principle of Reason' and 'Languages and Institutions of Philosophy', in more detail.

Kant and the limits of philosophy

Published in 1798, *The Conflict of the Faculties* was Kant's last major published work. Kant positions the philosopher in an intermediary position *between* the state and the public in the role of an educator who protects the principle of reason. This autonomous role frees philosophers from the influence and control of the state, and allows them to pursue the search for knowledge as an unquestionable end in itself. The existence of the philosophy faculty is absolutely essential because only it is free to evelute everything and to articulate its findings publicly. It is this understanding of philosophy, allied to the principle of reason, that founds the institution of the university; without it there can be no university in the Kantian sense. Philosophy, Kant contends, has the function of controlling the other faculties and subjecting them to an interrogation by reasoned critique. Within the university one would treat knowledge like an industry; the professors would be trustees of knowledge and together they would form a collective entity which would be entirely autonomous and subject only to laws given by reason, rather than by government. The word *conflict* in Kant's title relates to his discussion of the distinctions between the higher faculties (Medicine, Law and Theology) and the lower faculty (Philosophy). Insofar as the higher faculties are subject to the rule of law, they are bound by the power of the government of the day. They are higher faculties because they are inevitably much closer to the seat of power in the government. Kant's irony, however, is obvious – the higher faculties are concerned with the real work of inculcating vocational skills, while the academic freedom, enjoyed by the lower faculty of Philosophy, marks a questionable concession by the government.

Kant advocates a careful separation of the faculties that nevertheless attributes a special place to philosophy. The teaching of philosophy should be founded on the recognition that its main duty is toward the pursuit of truth, and its advocates should be allowed to speak the truth to the power of government without inhibition or loss of tenure. Ironically, as Kant points out, the philosophers do not speak directly to the people, but to the ministers of the state itself. The state, however, is in place to act on behalf of the people and to disregard the counsel of philosophy, if and when it decides to do so. Aware of the power of the state, Kant recommends a strategy of caution, arguing that the philosophers should not become politicians as the possession of power inevitably corrupts the free judgement of reason and the pursuit of truth. Philosophy cannot directly take a political position – it can only advise, or risk losing its right to immunity from the charge of interested enquiry. The power of the university, for Kant, is confined to a power to think and to say, though not necessarily in the public sphere, as this step would involve direct action, a form of power that he denies to the members of the university.

Nevertheless, conflict between the faculties, Kant writes, is inevitable, but also legal as well, as the lower faculty of philosophy has a duty to speak the whole truth and to ensure the veracity of everything articulated in public. Philosophy has the duty to investigate the rational origin and the rational basis of the proposals of the higher faculties, but the people will always side with the businessmen who represent the three higher faculties, and reject philosophy as it hinders their access to immediate enjoyment. Kant recognizes that the conflict of the faculties can never end and moreover that it is philosophy that must in fact be prepared to keep it going for as long as possible. Just as the three higher faculties will never renounce their desire for power, the faculty of philosophy must never concede its role as the protector of reason.

Kant's own political assessment of the relationship between the faculties is nevertheless strongly in evidence, notably in quasi-apocalyptic tones. It could well happen that one day the first shall become last and the last first and the government would realize that philosophy would be a more effective means of achieving its goals than the force of its authority alone. For the moment, however, philosophy's indeterminate use value and the conflict of the faculties which ensues is a luxury that enables the state to appear liberal.

'Mochlos, or The Conflict of the Faculties'

'Mochlos' was first delivered in 1980 at Columbia University to commemorate the centenary of the founding of its Graduate School.

Derrida describes how Kant's discussion of the function of the university, the purpose of philosophy and the nature of academic freedom served as a blueprint for Willhelm von Humboldt when he founded the University of Berlin in 1810, and thereafter for western pedagogical institutions. Kant's meditation establishes a natural link between the university, philosophy and the principle of reason as the court of the last resort. Seventy years after Humboldt's plan for Berlin, Kant's model was also particularly influential in the development of Columbia University in 1880; hence the significance of Derrida's lecture to the Graduate School one hundred years later.

In his discussion of Kant, Derrida reiterates the importance of the essay's historical and political context. One of the important dimensions of Kant's text relates to the question of state censorship, a theme that obviously preoccupied the members of GREPH. Thus an important configuration of themes in Derrida's discourse, though ones which were overlooked by literary deconstructionists at the time, is academic responsibility together with the self-legitimation and self-affirmation of the university. The opening questions of 'Mochlos' make these priorities explicitly clear:

> [W]ho are we in the university where apparently we are? *What* do we represent? *Whom* do we represent. Are we responsible? For what and to whom? If there is a university responsibility, it at least begins with the moment when a need to hear these questions, to take them upon oneself and respond, is imposed. This imperative for responding is the initial form and minimal requirement of responsibility. (MCF, 3)

All of these questions are touched on by Kant and it is Derrida's aim to recontextualize his assumptions in a modern setting. While Derrida does not answer these questions in definitive terms, he argues that it is part of the responsibility of those engaged in university teaching and research to determine the political implications and aporias of the academic community where one finds oneself engaged. Deconstruction should in fact be understood in terms of 'taking a position ... toward the politico-institutional structures that constitute and regulate our practice, our competences, and our performances' (MCF, 22–3). Moreover in terms which Derrida will later reiterate in 'The Principle of Reason', he positions deconstruction in relation to a rethinking of politics and responsibility in the university:

> Precisely because deconstruction has never been concerned with the contents alone of meaning, it must not be separable from this

politico-institutional problematic, and has to require a new questioning about responsibility, an inquiry which should no longer necessarily rely on codes inherited from politics or ethics. Which is why, though too political in the eyes of some, deconstruction can seem demobilizing in the eyes of those who recognize the political only with the help of prewar road signs. (MCF, 23)

Derrida's rethinking of the principle of reason that underpins the classical Kantian idea of the university is linked to a rethinking of all totalizing or global forms of the political, especially the exclusivist logic that opposes left and right.

The theme of academic responsibility is strongly allied in Kant to the question of autonomy as we have seen. A number of Kant's ideas are important for Derrida's reading: the autonomous status of the university is evident in its authority to create and award titles, and to pass judgement on the work of other scholars; knowledge is to be treated like an industry, the professors acting as trustees of knowledge; and the idea that the university is a collective organization that has autonomy from the state. Nevertheless, Kant's understanding of the university's autonomy is severely undermined by an unseen, non-university agency – the state.

In support of this argument, Derrida describes how the publication of Book 2 of Kant's *Religion Within the Limits of Reason* prior to the publication of *The Conflict of the Faculties* elicited a letter of disapproval from Friedrich Willhelm II, the King of Prussia. In the letter that Kant quotes at length in the Preface to his discussion of the university, the King questions Kant's responsibility and duty as a teacher of the young. The King's letter confronts Kant with a breach of his own understanding of a responsible university teacher. Though it is to be expected that Derrida highlights the power of state censorship in order to reject it, the purpose behind his quotation returns us to his opening questions about the responsibility of the university. Derrida in fact foregrounds this argument with a certain amount of nostalgia, for it shows that Kant, unlike many contemporary academics engaged in research and scholarly activity, was at least aware of where his responsibilities resided:

The agencies invoked – the state, the sovereign, the people, knowledge, action, truth, the university – held a place in discourse that was guaranteed, decidable, and, in every sense of the word, 'representable'; and a common code could guarantee, at least on faith, a minimum of translatability for any possible discourse in such a context. (MCF, 7)

Derrida finds it difficult to assume that he could be sure of as much in the modern university: 'For if a code guaranteed a problematic, then we in the university would feel better about ourselves, whatever the discord of the positions held, or the contradictions of the forces present. But we feel bad about ourselves, who would dare to say otherwise?' (MCF, 7). Derrida finds the King's intervention 'unimaginable today [1980] from the pen of a Carter, Brezhnev, Giscard, or Pinochet, or even, perhaps, from that of an ayatollah' (MCF, 6). Whereas for Kant responsibility and reason 'make an appeal ... to a pure ethico-juridical agency, to pure practical reason, to a pure idea of the law, and correlatively to the decision of a pure egological subject, of a consciousness, of an intention that has to respond, in decidable terms, from and before the law' (MCF, 11), Derrida is concerned with interrogating the assumed 'natural' status of these categories. He is led to question the meaning of responsibility as it functions in Kant's discourse, not in order to abandon reason, as so many critics have mistakenly argued, but so as to enable him to consider a 'new type of university responsibility' (MCF, 11). Derrida believes that by asking these questions he continues to act as a guardian of these traditional responsibilities.

In order to pursue this theme, it is necessary to take a further detour through another of Derrida's discussions of *The Conflict of the Faculties* – in this case, through the third of four lectures entitled, 'Unoccupied Chair: Censorship, Mastership and Magistrality', which was published under the main title of 'Languages and Institutions of Philosophy' (1984).

'Languages and Institutions of Philosophy'

In 'Languages and Institutions of Philosophy' Derrida returns to Kant's understanding of censorship in *The Conflict of the Faculties*, outlining his main questions at the outset:

> [C]an reason be censored? Should or must it be censored? Can reason, in its turn, censor? Or, can reason censor itself? Can reason discover good or bad reasons for censorship? In short, what is censorship as a question of reason? (LIP, 123)

Kant is important for the modern university vis-à-vis the question of censorship precisely because of the emergence of the philosopher teacher at the end of the eighteenth and beginning of the nineteenth century. Unlike Descartes, Spinoza, Leibniz and Hume, Kant was concerned with organizing the new space of the university. The changes that took place could not remain exterior to philosophical discourse itself, to its procedures and its content. The succession of Friedrich Willhelm II in August 1786 set in motion a train of events that Derrida describes as an 'offensive ... against the supporters of the *Aufklärung'* (LIP, 124). Derrida argues that the King's attempted censorship of Book 2 of Kant's *Religion Within the Limits of Reason Alone* must be read in the context of the Edict of Religion in July 1788 that prohibited everything that appears opposed to official religion. This decree was further strengthened in December 1788 following the emergence of the law against the freedom of the press.

As was evident in 'Mochlos', Kant responds to the King's letter in the Preface of *The Conflict of the Faculties*. Derrida's point is to explore Kant's understanding of censorship in greater depth. In Book 1 of Kant's treatise on religion, Derrida describes how he establishes the necessity and legitimacy of censorship and that the 'sanctity of the moral law should be the object of the greatest respect' (LIP, 124). At this time experts in theology were authorized by the state to act as censors within the university. According to Kant, the theologian must assume one of two functions: he is appointed as an ecclesiastic, to see the well-being of souls, or as a scholar where his function is the well-being of the sciences. Even if these roles are overseen by one person, the rule of bipartition should not be crossed. While such a concern with censorship was overtly evident in the late eighteenth century, Derrida warns against those who seem to believe that it is no longer active in the modern university:

> It would, however, be naive to conclude from this that censorship disappeared from that time on, even if one refers to Kant's definition of censorship, that is, 'a critique which has power'... and consequently prohibits, reduces to silence, or limits the manifestation of thought, the written or spoken word. What can have changed is the form which the use of this force takes; the place and apparatus of its application, of its distribution; the complexity, the diversification, and the overdetermination of its pathways. But how can one deny it? There are things that cannot be uttered in the university – or outside of the university. There are certain ways of saying things that are neither legitimate nor authorized. (LIP, 125)

Today, Derrida cautions, censorship does not derive in its modern form from a central authority, but rather from a 'highly differentiated, indeed contradictory, network' (LIP, 125). The fact that the modern university is always censured and censoring is evident in the restrictions placed on research projects and research funding. Derrida's involvement in the International College of Philosophy was directly motivated by the attempt to give precedence to research projects that are not currently considered legitimate, and it was concerned with focusing on those areas that are marginal to mainstream institutions. The College is committed to a 'theoretical-cum-institutional analysis (an auto- and hetero-analysis), in order to detect within itself the effects of censorship or of nonlegitimation of all kinds' (LIP, 126). Derrida returns to what constitutes the Kantian concept of censorship.

For Kant, then, censorship occurs at the intersection of pure reason and the force at the disposal of the state, and it is impossible to 'construct the concept of the state without inscribing the censoring function within it' (LIP, 127). The Kantian understanding of censorship is simple: it describes 'a *critique* which has force ("Gewalt") at its disposal' (LIP, 127). Kant's main example is the nexus of theological and state power that had been the official institution of censorship since the seventeenth century; the place of the theologian thus explains his role in the university. Derrida maintains that Kant's point is to 'take note of a censoring power and of a legitimacy of state reason as a censoring reason, the power of censorship, but also to delimit this power; not by opposing it with a counter-power, but with a sort of non-power, of heterogeneous reason opposed to power' (LIP, 127). Unsurprisingly Kant would like the Faculty of Philosophy to have the right of censorship but, because he defines philosophy in terms of *saying* rather than *doing*, he must also deny it the political force that it requires. Derrida states the conflict that arises in the following terms:

> Kant intends to legitimize reason of state as a censoring reason, which is supposed to have the right of censorship in certain condi- tions and within certain limits. But, on the other hand, he wants to protect pure reason itself from all censuring power. Pure reason should, by right, exercise no censorship and should be exempt from all censorship. (LIP, 128)

It is precisely this limit between reason that censors and reason that does not which interests Derrida – principally because it passes right through the institutional space of the university and through Kant's division of the faculties. As long as philosophy maintains its place in terms of *saying* rather than doing, staying strictly inside the university rather than outside, it should remain free of inspection by any external authority.

Kant wants to protect reason from censorship. Now, once again it is only the philosopher, as the guardian of truth and reason, who can determine who and what should be censored. Such power should not reside with the members of the Higher Faculties. As Kant establishes in the Preface to the Second Edition of Book 1 of *Religion Within the Limits of Reason Alone*, the philosopher not the theologian should be the 'master of pure reason' (LIP, 131). This leads to the unique position of the philosopher: 'The master of pure reason is simultaneously located in a department, in the outside space of the larger circle, which remains exterior to the circle of biblical theology, for example, and by the same token, is able to comprehend in his vision and his critical inspection the entire field of knowledge' (LIP, 132). While the philosopher is the legislator of reason he can only teach an action not a content. As a consequence the university and the Faculty of Philosophy, which provides it with meaning and truth, 'constitutes an institutional place for a master of pure reason who, in truth, remains an ideal and never takes place anywhere' (LIP, 133). Coupled with these two aspects – the philosopher as legislator and the non-place of the philosopher in the institution – is Kant's architectonic description of the university as a living organism, meaning that the university is regulated by its own internal rhythms and laws.

A challenge to this commitment to reason is evident in Kant's distinction between technique and architectonics. The former applies to what today would be called ends-oriented research, that is, research that is regulated by industry and business. Kant's concern with architectonics similarly corresponds to the modern notion of pure or fundamental research. For Kant, the latter should prevail. When Kant argues as Derrida maintains that 'we cannot learn philosophy, we can only learn to philosophize' (LIP, 137), he emphasizes that the philosopher is above all 'the legislator of human reason' (LIP, 138). In the face of state censorship, Derrida describes deconstruction as a 'principle of disturbance' or 'counterforce which permits the utterance and even the deciphering of the forbidden sentence' (LIP, 130).

If we now return to 'Mochlos', we can place Derrida's critique of Kant's understanding of the university in the context of two recent developments in the politico-epistemological space. The first relates to the 'border-conflicts' between centres of research and those engaged with producing and reproducing knowledge. Whereas for Kant, the outside of the university could be confined to the margin, in the modern university, the 'state no longer entrusts certain investigations to a university that cannot accept the structures or control the techno-political stakes' (MCF, 14). The relationship between the modern state and modern university, where some universities merely function as teaching or research-based institutions, means that the 'whole architectonics of *The Conflict of the Faculties* finds itself menaced, and with it a model regulated by the happy concord between royal power and pure reason' (MCF, 14). New technological developments, especially in the retrieval and storage of information, threaten the centrality of the university as the centre of knowledge. The power of transnational corporations means that it is no longer possible to 'separate knowledge from power, reason from performativity, metaphysics from technical mastery' (MCF, 15). In the modern setting, Derrida contends, 'It is not ... for reasons involving the structure of knowledge, especially impossible to distinguish rigorously between scholars and technicians of science' (MCF, 16). Such ideas mean that the university has to forsake its role as a guardian or trustee of knowledge, that Kant suggested it possess.

Of course, for Kant, the management of the outside was fundamental, as Derrida points out: 'In tracing the system of the pure limits of the university, Kant wants to track any possible parasiting. He wants the power to exclude it – legitimately, legally' (MCF, 15). One such area of exclusion is that of the lettered class, students trained by the universities, who go on to become 'government agents, diplomatic aides, instruments of power' (MCF, 15). Kant calls them businessmen or technicians of learning, as they undoubtedly represent the power and interests of the state as opposed to the exercise of responsible and free judgement that resides with the Lower Faculty of Philosophy. Kant calls on the government to institute a law that will put before the university all statements issuing from the lettered class of clerics, magistrates and doctors, therefore requiring that they submit all 'statements of a constative type (those claiming to tell the truth), or indeed of a "practical" type' (MCF, 16). Kant's decree embodies his classical understanding of the pure function of the university, as Derrida writes:

> The university is there to *tell the truth*, to judge and to criticize in the most rigorous sense of the term, namely to discern and decide between the true and the false; and when it is also entitled to decide between the just and unjust, the moral and the immoral ... (MCF, 17)

No state bureaucrat 'would have the authority to use his or her knowledge *publicly* without being subject, by law, to the control of the faculties, "to the censorship of the faculties," as Kant literally says' (MCF, 17).

Kant's understanding of pure philosophy is underpinned by a familiar target of Derrida's thought: the attempt to distinguish between *constative* and *performative* utterances, which, as we saw in 'Declarations of Independence', 'tries to limit the effects of confusion, simulacrum, parasiting, equivocality and undecidability produced by language' (MCF, 18). To reduce the inherent instability of language, Kant's response to the King of Prussia's letter argues that philosophy is a quasi-private language, which, by circulating only within the university, diminishes the risk of flaunting its equivocal status. The concept of the university is underpinned by a pure concept of philosophy and the separation of constative and performative utterances.

Derrida's deconstruction of the constative/performative opposition attacks the Kantian idea of pure philosophy. Focusing on the inescapability of equivocation in any speech act, Derrida confronts Kant's attempt to reconcile or disavow the conflicts that inevitably arise between the faculties. Though Kant proposes various ways of interiorizing the conflicts within the university, thus protecting the disputes from the ears of the public, whom he castigates as idiots and incompetent, he recognizes that such conflicts are interminable and insoluble. In order to ameliorate such internal strife, however, Kant proposes a parliamentary solution. Here the Higher Faculties are aligned with the state, and according to the traditional conception of parliamentary conflict, occupy a position on the right. Philosophy, on the other hand, is aligned with the forces of change, or the left. Because the Higher Faculties will never renounce the desire to govern or dominate, Kant argues that philosophy must remain a vigilant protector of reason and truth. While the Higher Faculties take up the right side of the parliament of learning, supporting the government, philosophy acts as an opposition party, seated to the left. Like Kant, Derrida does not outline a way of ending the conflict between philosophy as an organ of truth and the faculties of the state. He refuses to align himself with the left or the right in Kant's model, and to resist the description of a 'tireless parasite moving in random agitation, passing over the boundary and back again' (MCF, 29). Derrida *is* concerned, however, with the transformation of the university and with the attempt to found a modern institution based on a new charter and a new constitution. Such a new institution is connected in Derrida's mind with a new kind of responsibility. This new law and new responsibility finally lead Derrida to outline the meaning of the curious word, *mochlos*, in his title. Mochlos is a Greek word meaning the 'best lever' (MCF, 31): 'A *mochlos* could be a wooden beam, a lever for displacing a boat, a wedge for opening or closing a door, something, in short, to lean on for forcing and displacing' (MCF, 31). By deploying this metaphor, Derrida indicates that he chooses the middle way, adopting the law of contamination to describe a strategy that encompasses both left *and* right. Alluding to another of Kant's marginal works, *How to be Oriented in Thinking*, published in 1786, Derrida describes Kant's idea that the 'university will have to go on two feet, left and right, each foot having to support the other as it rises with each step to make a leap' (MCF, 31).

In summary, then, Kant's understanding of philosophy's role vis-à-vis the state in *The Conflict of the Faculties* has a number of shortcomings. Philosophy's access to forums of popular debate is limited by the influence of the state, which may or may not take heed of its voice. The marginal position from which Kant attempts to protect the free functioning of reason also limits the scope of its social and political effectiveness. Derrida's readings of Kant attempt to bring his discussion up-to-date and to clarify the political role that a deconstructive strategy can have in this area. Nevertheless, Kant's position seriously fails to take into account how philosophy's position *outside* of the polis is 'always already' *inside* and thus always contaminated by questions of politics. Many of the theoretical proposals that Derrida outlines in 'Mochlos' are evident in his work with the International College of Philosophy to which I shall now turn.

The International College of Philosophy

We can perhaps understand Derrida's model of an academic community founded on differance if we turn to his comments on the foundation of the International College of Philosophy which was officially opened on 10 October 1983 in Paris. Derrida played a prominent role in the emergence of the College. It was Derrida who disseminated a letter on behalf of the other main organizers – François Châtelet, Jean-Pierre Faye and Dominique Lecourt – to the academic community in May 1982, requesting proposals for potential research projects. Derrida's letter led to much discussion and prompted the organizers to outline their recommendations in an official report. The first section of the report was taken up by the main proposals, centring on the College's academic autonomy from but financial dependence on the state, followed by a personal statement by each of the main organizers. 'Sendoffs' is the title of Derrida's individual contribution to the report.

In the 'Foreword' to 'Sendoffs' Derrida renounces the idea that his proposals take the form of a system, method, or programme thus reiterating his objection to predetermined forms of thinking; but this is not to say that his discourse lacks coherence or purpose. Derrida takes for granted that the College is concerned with the mission of questioning and dislodging the ontological model of the university that has guided thinking about pedagogical institutions for the last two centuries. Derrida is engaged here with speculating on the *raison d'être* of the first four years of the College's life – what he refers to as a 'four year sendoff' – in which he is preoccupied with coordinating all of the College's activities by adopting a mobile strategy that challenges rather than feels constrained by existing models of planning and authority. The College is for sure a *pathbreaking* and even trailblazing institution that is linked in his mind with instigating new forms and avenues of pedagogical research. But the most significant aspect of these inaugural incursions is the interrogation of a number of keywords, such as philosophy, science, art, research, technique, theory, practice, problem, law, legitimacy, title, production, culture and so on. The commitment to interrogate these foundational and ontological terms is necessarily inscribed in the charter of the institution. Derrida attempts to bring all of these themes together by focusing on one of his familiar preocuppations: the question of destination or *sendoff*, which he refers to as a strategic *lever*, a term that he also uses, as we have seen, in 'Mochlos'. The same logic of thought is embodied elsewhere in his thought, as Derrida points out, by differance, the trace, writing and undecidability, to name a few of his familiar figures. Derrida is interested in outlining how these principles structure the *destination* and operation of the College, by focusing especially on its function. His aim is to embody the political implications of deconstruction in the College's infrastructure, declaring that the critical debates will operate in a non-hierarchical fashion. As such the College's agenda and how it effectively formulates its agenda challenge Derrida's familiar target of onto-theology and its investment in philosophical discourse. But once again Derrida is not concerned with establishing his protocols as a new form of legitimation. The formulation of the instituting contract should never be left out of the College's discussions. The target of Derrida's self-reflexive understanding of the College's instituting contract is therefore the totalizing model of the university established by Humboldt in Berlin, a uni-totalizing organization that precisely rejects Derrida's emphasis on the compatibility of pauses, different rhythms, accents and phases.

The opposition between fundamental or pure and ends-oriented research is a major part of Derrida's discussion of the destination of the College. The predominance of ends-oriented research has led to renewed criticism of fundamentalist thought (or pure research), particularly since the late 1960s in the Human and Social Sciences. Derrida's defence of fundamental research is allied to the affirmation of the free functioning of philosophy, which he sees as one of the main aims of the College. The defence of pure or fundamental philosophical research underpins Derrida's conception of the university as a site of vigilant reflection. The understanding of destination that is embodied in the College's instituting contract is seen as a way of interrogating prevailing concepts of power and legitimation. By challenging the prevailing conception of reason, Derrida argues that the College emphasizes research whose legitimacy is yet to be recognized. This strategy itself attempts to recognize that while the College can never escape the networks of legitimation, it can attempt to be highly conscious of them. The main problem for Derrida in pursuing this strategy is the opposition between ends-oriented research and fundamental research, an opposition which in his view has always been naive. Derrida is challenging those critics who valorize ends-oriented over fundamental research. In the Human and Social Sciences fundamental research finds itself undermined when confronted with the practical value of ends-oriented research. Inevitably Derrida is concerned with replacing this binary logic with the logic of contamination: ends-oriented research is always based on fundamental research projects, and so-called fundamental research can always be harnessed by ends-oriented programmes. In order to redress this imbalance, Derrida argues that the College must reelaborate this opposition from its base and insist on the acceptability and necessity of fundamentalist research in a number of areas which he outlines in minute detail.

Derrida describes a range of research groups and elaborates upon their themes and destination: the questions of metaphysics and of ontotheology; the problematic of the completion or of the limit of philosophy; the philosophy of Heidegger; the need for the College to inaugurate a women's studies programme, often missing from the French academy; the philosophical implications of the life sciences; the philosophical, ethico-political, juridical problems posed by the new medical technologies; psychiatry and psychoanalysis; law and the philosophy of law; the police, the army and warfare. To this list he also adds linguistics, semiotics, pragmatics, the technology of telecommunications, archiving, the mass media, poietics, and the central theme of translation, transfer(ence) and transversality. In all of these areas Derrida is concerned with establishing a new configuration and another style of posing questions as to how and under what conditions philosophical movements assert their influence and become dominant.

In the section on Heidegger, for example, Derrida outlines the need for research on the question of Heidegger and politics in great detail, refuting those critics who argue that he attempts to avoid such questions. In relation to the '*Law and the Philosophy of Law*', Derrida calls for the College to enact a significant reappraisal of the axiomatics of all areas of the law, focusing especially on the development of human rights. In the section on '*The police and the army, warfare*', Derrida argues against the idea, prominent in the French academy at the time, that philosophical reflection is keeping too great a distance from research into the problematics of the police, the army, biocybernetics, so-called smart weapons, as well as ideological, economic and broadcast warfare.

In the penultimate section of Derrida's contribution to the report, 'Translation, Transfer(ence), Transversality', he turns to the principle task of an International College of Philosophy. The emphasis of Derrida's research guidelines is firmly placed on the word *international* as he considers how the College should engage in a questioning of the concept of translation. Among the numerous areas that Derrida sketches – from setting up specialized centres for linguistic training and international working groups on translation to examining the modern technology of translation – Derrida considers the important theme of 'philosophical transcontinentality'. The International College of Philosophy should examine the differences within and between philosophical traditions or philosophical continents. Derrida sees the College as attacking the fixed borderlines of such traditions – the French, Anglo-Saxon and German traditions – thus making it possible to understand that these traditions have borders that are constituted in each national tradition. One prior example of this challenge is Derrida's resistance to the idea that Searle and Austin are the prime examples of 'Anglo-Saxon' philosophy while his work is thoroughly 'continental'.

In summary, then, Derrida's contribution to the College's report reiterates a number of key themes which we have also seen in his reading of Kant: the politics of translation, the reflection on western rationality, and the deconstruction of the classical conception of the university. His submission is a powerful and detailed commentary which effectively refutes many critics who have confused Derridean deconstruction with more damaging interpretations. By implication, one of the main targets of 'Sendoffs' is the College's understanding of the state and its role as it was in 'Mochlos'. This argument is also an important constituent theme of his reading of Nietzsche's lecture series, *On the Future of Our Educational Institutions*, to which he turns in 'Otobiographies'.

Nietzsche and *On the Future of Our Educational Institutions*

In his discussion of the inheritance of Nietzsche's work in 'Otobiographies' in *The Ear of the Other*, Derrida describes one of the German philosopher's most marginal works, *On the Future of Our Educational Institutions*. Published posthumously in 1909, *On the Future of Our Educational Institutions* consists of a series of lectures that Nietzsche delivered for the first time in 1872, in his capacity as Professor of Classical Philology at the University of Bâsle. Not unrelatedly perhaps, Nietzsche resigned his chair seven years after delivering the lectures. It would not be entirely misleading to argue that the dissatisfaction with the state of Germany's educational institutions, which Nietzsche forcefully expresses in this series of lectures, may prove to have been near the source of his discontent. Derrida's discussion of the book indicates how the final contribution of the 'midnight philosopher', with whom he associates Nietzsche throughout, suggests that the philosopher believed that the irrevocable disintegration of the university was at hand.

On the Future of Our Educational Institutions focuses on two aspects of the German state's engagement with educational institutions during the 1870s. On the one hand, Nietzsche identifies the attempt to 'achieve the greatest possible *extension of education*'. On the other hand, this is coupled with a 'drive after the *dimunition and weakening*' of educational independence (Nietzsche, 2004, 17). While the first of these drives, Nietzsche writes, wants to extend education to an 'ever wider circle; in the mind of the other tendency it will be expected of education that it give up its highest claim to self-mastery and subordinate itself serving another form of life, namely that of the state' (2004, 17). Nietzsche raises a series of questions similar to those that have subsequently preoccupied Derrida, principally those which engage with the *raison d'être* of the university, and the function of the Human and Social Sciences. Nietzsche's criticisms target two clear areas of the German state's education policy in the latter half of the nineteenth century: (1) the expansion of higher education to include the masses; and (2) the implied subordination of the university's independent claims to the service of the state. In place of these measures, Nietzsche would like to see limitations placed on the momentum of mass expansion and a movement towards the strengthening of the independence of educational institutions vis-à-vis their relations with the state. It is the second part of his argument, however, that is more interesting in the context of this chapter.

This aspect of his argument issues a dramatic warning about the power of scientific technology and the marginalization of the critical power of the social sciences – a theme that is developed by Derrida in his response to Kant both in 'Mochlos' and in 'The Principle of Reason'. The emphasis that Nietzsche places on the role the state plays in the production and delimitation of knowledge, particularly the cultural knowledge of the humanities, and its role in the determination of the use-value of a cultural education, finds a number of parallels in Derrida's institutional critique.

Derrida describes Nietzsche's understanding of the state in the closing pages of 'Otobiographies', and it is worth taking a detour through this text before returning to *On the Future of Our Educational Institutions*. Derrida reads Nietzsche's lecture series as a 'modern critique of the cultural machinery of State and educational system that was, even in yesterday's industrial society, a fundamental part of the State apparatus' (EO, 33). Behind the state's use of the phrase academic freedom, according to Derrida, Nietzsche 'discern[s] the silhouette of a constraint which is all the more ferocious and implacable because it conceals and disguises itself in the form of laissez-faire. Through the said "academic freedom", it is the State that controls everything' (EO, 33). The autonomy that Kant attributes to philosophy is thus rejected by Nietzsche as an insidious 'ruse of the State', that enables it to 'attract docile and unquestioning functionaries to itself' (EO, 33). Derrida refers to Nietzsche's description of the state in *Thus Spoke Zarathustra* in which the German philosopher berates the state as a wicked and insidious force. Nietzsche's portrayal of the state presents a rather simplified idea of indoctrination that is based on a vehement disregard for the critical power of the masses, similar in fact to Kant's description of the public as idiots and incompetents in *The Conflict of the Faculties*. Nietzsche conveys his understanding of ideological indoctrination via the metaphor of the ear, as Derrida quotes:

> If a foreigner wants to become familiar with our university system, thus he first asks with emphasis: how is the student connected with the university with you? We answer: through the ear, as listener. – The foreigner is astounded. 'Only through the ear?' he asks again. 'Only through the ear,' we answer again. The student listens. When he speaks, when he sees, when he walks, when he is sociable, when he practices the arts, in short, when he lives, he is independent, i.e., not dependent on the educational institution. Very frequently the student immediately writes something as he hears it. These are the

moments in which he hangs on the umbilical cord of the university.
(Nietzsche, 2004, 106)

Derrida picks up on Nietzsche's use of the phrase 'umbilical cord',
arguing that, 'It is an ear … that dictates to you what you are writing at
this moment when you write in the mode of what is called "taking
notes" ' (EO, 35). Derrida sees Nietzsche's views as a forerunner of
modern-day concerns with the power of the media, describing the link
between student and institution in graphic terms: 'This writing links
you, like a leash in the form of an umbilical cord, to the paternal belly
of the State. Your pen is its pen, you hold its teleprinter like one of those
Bic ballpoints attached by a little chain in the post office' (EO, 36).

If we now return to *On the Future of Our Educational Institutions*, I will
argue that Nietzsche's real emphasis on access to education is coupled
with the more important imperative to foreground philosophy as a mode
of cultural and critical enquiry that *resists* the interests and short-term
politics of the state or higher faculties in Kant's terms. By attempting to
strengthen the independence of education from the pernicious influence
of the state, Nietzsche advocates a special place for philosophical enquiry
that takes him beyond Kant's position. Nietzsche's argument serves as a
precursor of Derrida's concern with the relationship between the modern
state and the function of the cultural disciplines *in* and *outside* the university. Nietzsche's own response to Germany's modernization programme enables him to confront the apparent harmony of the present
state of affairs that he significantly refers to as *selbstverständliches*, which
literally means something granted or self-understood. Nietzsche's main
targets are a number of naturalized assumptions which have been disen-
tangled from all traces of historical, cultural and political conflict.
Nietzsche's genealogical method attempts to recover this presence of the
past in the present, and thus acts as an early precursor of Derrida's own
concepts such as the *trace* and *cinders*. This particular emphasis, evident
in both Derrida and Nietzsche, attempts to recover an awareness of the
discontinuous conflicts that have led to the ascendancy of normative or
taken-for-granted assumptions. For Nietzsche, then, this process replaces
the idea that knowledge is transparently learned or natural with the
notion that it is *produced* or *constructed* and thus embedded in history and
subject to interpretative violence.

In one other key area, Nietzsche's reflections on the university
strikingly preempt those of Derrida. Nietzsche's discussion takes
the form of a *polylogue* – a method that Derrida has deployed in a
number of his own texts – between two representatives of contemporary

students, a philosopher and his companion. The philosopher confronts what he views as the harmful consequences of the expansion in the number of students undertaking a cultural education. This, Nietzsche argues, is an attempt to prepare students for a vocation in some part of the civil service and to undermine the true concept of cultural education:

> We were conscious that at that time we had never altogether thought about a so-called profession, thanks to our union. The ever-so-frequent exploitation of these years by the state, which as soon as possible enlists useful officials and wants to secure their unconditioned obedience through excessively exhausting examinations, had remained in the furthest distance throughout our educations ... (Nietzsche, 2004, 33)

The state, for Nietzsche, ignores the requirement to educate the few in the interests of educating the masses. This process has led to the marginalization or even banishment of philosophy and the faculty of disinterested critical enquiry. This occurrence is equated with the diminishing of the real or true educational institution. The only hope of rectifying this situation lies in the possibility of returning the university to its concern with fundamental or pure knowledge.

Derrida's purpose in his reading of Nietzsche is to outline a key advocate of the post-Kantian idea of the university. In 'The Principle of Reason' Derrida brings a number of these themes together in a discussion of the modern role of the state and pedagogical institutions.

Reflecting on 'The Principle of Reason'

During the 1980s, then, Derrida responded to the misreadings of American literary critics by attempting to foreground his work on pedagogical institutions and to make it relevant to an American context. A major part of this venture also entailed a challenge to the idea that deconstruction was apolitical, that it was unconcerned with or withdrew from questions about the responsible control and exercise of power. Perhaps Derrida's most sustained and successful attempt to grapple with these questions emerges from his discussion of the *raison d'être* of philosophy in 'The Principle of Reason'. The essay was first presented on the occasion of Derrida's inaugural address as Andrew Dickson White Professor-at-large at Cornell University. In what is clearly a response to the shortcomings of the American translation of his work, the essay

begins with the following imperative to reflect upon the political function of the human sciences – especially the teaching of literature,
linguistics, literary theory and philosophy – in the modern university.
'Today, how can we not speak of the university?', Derrida writes:

> I put my question in the negative, for two reasons. On the one hand,
> as we all know, it is impossible, now more than ever, to dissociate the
> work we do, within one discipline or several, from a reflection on the
> political and institutional conditions of that work. Such a reflection
> is unavoidable. It is no longer an *external* complement to teaching
> and research; it must make its way through the very objects we work
> with, shaping them as it goes, along with our norms, procedures, and
> aims. We cannot not speak of such things. (POR, 3)

This opening paragraph announces the urgency of Derrida's discussion
of the politics of knowledge. In contrast, it is also concerned with teasing
out the *limits* which impede such a discussion: how can we *not* speak of
the university, Derrida writes, implying that the liberal ideal of academic
freedom must also entail an understanding of its own internal barriers. In
this respect, critics or philosophers always-already find themselves *within*
institutions, and thus there can be no pure or unmediated pursuit of
truth as Kant argues in *The Conflict of the Faculties*. Having established
this understanding of the complicity between pedagogical institutions
and the state, the purpose of Derrida's essay is to question the 'cause, purpose, direction, necessity, justification, meaning and mission of the
University; in a word, its destination' (POR, 3). Derrida's concern with
the twin themes of the principles of reason and reflection are associated
with the idea that deconstruction grapples with 'turning back upon the
very conditions of reflection' itself (POR, 3). Though Derrida acknowledges that this form of questioning – what he once more describes as a
new responsibility – is profoundly important to his project, he does not
name this process deconstruction, nor, in fact, does he use this word at
any point in this important statement on the pedagogical implications
of his thinking. This is striking evidence of Johnson's understanding of
Derrida's attack on rigid modes of thought, but especially of her argument that the institutionalization of deconstruction in American literary
studies made it 'more simplistic, more dogmatic, and ultimately more
conservative' (Johnson, 1987, 11) than it is in Derrida's hands.

   This is not to say that Derrida's thought is uncritically aligned with the
traditional left. Nevertheless, 'The Principle of Reason' performs a series
of familiar movements of Derrida's thought, and thus his analysis combines both radical and conservative implications. Derrida challenges

fixed conceptualizations of reason and truth, but he is also deeply committed to maintaining critically traditional forms of thought. In response to his own question, 'what is the *raison d'être* of the university?', Derrida responds with a two-pronged analysis of 'ends-oriented' (or applied) and 'pure' research that challenges the increasing primacy of the former. For Derrida, oriented research is 'organized in an authoritarian fashion *in view of* its utilization ... whether we are talking about technology, economy, medicine, psychosociology, or military power' (POR, 11). Derrida describes the deliberate change of terminology that attempts to disguise the change of direction: 'We speak of "oriented" research where, not so long ago, we spoke ... of "application" ' (POR, 12). It is growing increasingly obvious, Derrida argues, that such research has to be seen to pay-off or yield results. Research is not merely undertaken in what 'used to be called the techno-economic, medical, or military' areas of the university (POR, 12). Other disciplines such as linguistics and even literary studies can be appropriated by this technocratic ethic:

> Once upon a time it was possible to believe that pure mathematics, theoretical physics, philosophy (and, within philosophy, especially metaphysics and ontology) were basic disciplines shielded from power, inaccessible to programming by the pressures of the State or, under cover of the State, by civil society or capital interests. The sole concern of such basic research would be knowledge, truth, the disinterested exercise of reason, under the sole authority of the principle of reason. (POR, 12)

Thus to reflect these changes a term like orient is preferred to applied, because the word is less utilitarian, and because it 'leaves open the possibility that noble aims may be written into the program' (POR, 12). Derrida's point is confirmed by the term techno-science, which ties together objective knowledge, the principle of reason and a certain metaphysical determination of the relation to truth that inextricably links the principle of reason with the technology of modernity.

Given Derrida's understanding of the complicity between the state and research activity, he is led to argue that it is difficult to maintain the boundary between basic and oriented research. In advanced technological societies the state 'orients, orders, and finances, directly or indirectly ... the front-line research that is apparently the least "end oriented" of all' (POR, 13). This is particularly evident in relation to the military-industrial complex. 'At the service of war, of national and international security,' Derrida continues:

research programs have to encompass the entire field of information, the stockpiling of knowledge, the workings and thus also the essence of language and of all semiotic systems, translation, coding and decoding, the play of presence and absence, hermeneutics, semantics, structural and generative linguistics, pragmatics, rhetoric. I am accumulating all these disciplines in a haphazard way, on purpose, but I shall end with literature, poetry, the arts and fiction in general ... (POR, 13)

Never before has so-called basic or pure scientific research been so deeply committed to aims that are also military and political aims. Correspondingly, oriented research also depends on non-scientific disciplines which are normally thought to be excluded from such areas: 'From now on, so long as it has the means, a military budget can invest in anything at all, in view of deferred profits: "basic" scientific theory, the humanities, literary theory and philosophy' (POR, 13). Derrida's enquiry into the foundations or architectonics of the university takes advantage of a remarkable metaphor. Derrida compares the topography of the Cornell university campus – where the buildings of the humanities are protected from a gorge by protective railings – to the relationship between the eye and its protective diaphragm. The eye of the humanities in turn signifies the ideal and unrestricted vision of philosophy (the gorge) negotiating with the ends-oriented programmes of the state (the protectionist barrier/the eye's diaphragm). Derrida does not propose that it is possible for the critical function of philosophy – or the humanities in general – to function independently of the state, as Kant wrongly believed in *The Conflict of the Faculties*. In his figurative description of Cornell, Derrida draws on the etymology of the word diaphragm meaning 'partitioning fence' to indicate the motion of opening and closing which divides the university from the outside, and which would, for a prominent faculty member, literally destroy the essence of the university. In the context of Derrida's metaphor of the eye, the community of the university functions by way of the familiar rhythm of a *supplementary* logic: the continual opening and closing of insides and outsides. Derrida exploits the metaphor of the 'Cornell' (*Cornea lens*: a contact lens covering the transparent part of the eye) campus to suggest that the function of the university, and of philosophy in particular, is to reflect upon reflection itself; hence the potentially infinite regression of the subtitle of the essay which plays on the theme of reflection and vocation, the university in the eyes of its pupils. With the aid of this complex metaphor, Derrida strategically positions the university at the nodal point – in *between*, as it were – society *and* the site of reflection, applied and pure research, memory and critique. Derrida's point here concerns the possibility of maintaining, 'in the *same* instant the desire for memory and exposure to the future, the fidelity of a guardian faithful enough to want to keep even the chance of a future' (POR, 20). In other words, the university must maintain this dual function, acting as a site of cultural memory *and* cultural critique. The institutional site of philosophy or what is now called theory challenges the values of technocracy, professionalism and the emerging ethic of excellence, by subjecting them to the double movement of the principle of reason. 'The time for reflection, here signifies', Derrida writes:

> not only that the internal rhythm of the university apparatus is relatively independent of social time and relaxes the urgency of command, ensures for it a great and precious freedom of play. (POR, 19)

It is also a time for critique, for reflecting on reflection itself, and for questioning the role of the state:

> The time for reflection is also the chance for turning back on the very conditions of reflection, in all the senses of that word, as if with the help of a new optical device one could finally see sight, could not only view the natural landscape, the city, the bridge and the abyss, but could view viewing. (POR, 19)

Derrida's idea that the university is concerned with the relaxation of social time is an obviously important determinant of the temporality of his own work, its resistance to existing political protocols, whether of the left or the right, and existing modes of political intervention. The politics of Derrida's thought emerges precisely at this point. Deconstruction is concerned with the abandonment of any global and totalizing notion of the political. Derrida advances the idea that deconstruction, to reiterate Bennington's point, 'can name "the political" only improperly or, better, can name the impropriety of the political in its dispersion' (Bennington, 1994, 97).

This chapter has described how Derrida sought to *reinvent* the meaning of deconstruction for an American audience, following the marginalization of his involvement with GREPH and the International College of Philosophy during the mid-1970s and early 1980s. Derrida's work is deeply implicated in what he refers to in 'Mochlos' as the taking of a position toward the politico-institutional structures that constitute and regulate the 'practice', 'competences' and 'performances' of universities (MCF, 23).

4
The Postmodern Political Condition: Deconstruction and Enlightenment

Regardless of Derrida's politico-institutional thinking deconstruction has often been approached as a form of postmodern neoconservatism or anarchism (Habermas, 1987). Over the course of the previous chapters we have seen how this postmodern reading was indebted to the literary translation of deconstruction which drained Derrida's work of its politico-institutional context and emphasized indeterminacy over a specific understanding of undecidability. Such interpretations have been based on a metaphysical conception of the political that fails to come to terms with the political implications of Derrida's notion of originary repetition and the aporia of time.

In *The Philosophical Discourse of Modernity* (1987), for example, Habermas outlined a strong misreading of deconstruction as a mystical or apocalyptic philosophy that remains caught up in Heidegger's thinking. Habermas identifies Derrida with a range of neoconservative poststructuralist thinkers whom he assimilates to the counter-enlightenment drift of postmodernism. While Derrida's metaphysical critique leads him to abandon Heidegger's totalizing metaphors, Habermas argues that his levelling of the 'genre distinction' between philosophy and literature, coupled with his inflation of rhetoric over logic, leads towards a politics of nihilism. Like Heidegger, Habermas writes, Derrida:

> degrades politics and contemporary history to the status of the ontic and the foreground, so as to romp all the more freely, and with a greater wealth of associations, in the sphere of the ontological and the archewriting. (Habermas, 1987, 181)

Habermas accuses Derrida of focusing exclusively on the *ontological* – that is, purely philosophical questions – at the expense of the *ontic* – questions concerned with social and political problems. It is clear that Habermas's reading of Derrida strongly influenced critics such as McCarthy (1989) and there is a direct line between the accusation that deconstruction amounts to a 'politics of the ineffable' and the charge that it degrades politics. In 'Before the Law' (1992), 'Force of Law: the "Mystical Foundation of Authority" ' (1992) and *Specters of Marx* (1994), Derrida provides much evidence to reject this reading. Chapter 6 will discuss these texts at greater length but it is necessary to point out now that Derrida responds to a new *Aufklärung* rather than attempts to abandon the heritage of enlightenment rationality. In *Specters of Marx* in particular Derrida challenges the idea that in rejecting the text of Marx he embraces postmodern irrationalism. In fact Derrida does neither. In a series of unambiguous passages, Derrida dates the decline of Marxism to the end of the 1950s in the French academy (rather than the early 1990s in Fukuyama's text) and describes the importance of the Stalinist atrocities for the formation of his political thinking. Deconstruction emerged from 'the historical entanglement' (SM, 15) of Marxism in the Soviet Union during the postwar years. The 'totalitarian terror in all the Eastern countries' and the 'socio-economic disasters of Soviet Bureaucracy' was the 'element in which what is called deconstruction developed' (SM, 15). In sharp contrast to critics such as McCarthy, Derrida explains that his understanding of deconstruction as a critique of totalitarian thinking:

> would have been impossible and unthinkable in a pre-Marxist space. Deconstruction has never had any sense or interest, in my view at least, except as a radicalization, which is to say also *in the tradition* of a certain Marxism, in a certain *spirit of Marxism*. (SM, 92)

Unlike the vast majority of readings of deconstruction and postmodernism, then, Derrida describes deconstruction as a positive attempt to come to terms with the intellectual inheritance of modernity; 'one *must*', he writes, '*assume the inheritance* of Marxism' (SM, 54). In this respect, the arguments of *Specters of Marx* are entirely consistent with the views Derrida expressed in *Positions* and powerfully refute Habermas's reading.

This chapter begins with an examination of Stephen Helmling's discussion of the historical reception of deconstruction, 'Historicizing Derrida' (1994), an essay that relies on an understanding of postmodernism as a withdrawal from politics, in order to establish a pre- and post-1968 division in Derrida's corpus. While I will argue that no such break exists in Derrida's published works, Helmling's rejection of postmodernism brings out a constant theme of Derrida's critics: because they rely on a metaphysical understanding of the political, Derrida's politics are dismissed as evasive, obscurantist or mystical.

This chapter will argue against Habermas's discussion of deconstruction in *The Philosophical Discourse of Modernity* as a postmodern strategy that flirts with the neo-fascist politics of Heidegger, and in support of the argument that Derridean deconstruction is a form of post-Kantian enlightenment critique (Norris, 1987, 1989). Derrida is post-metaphysical in the sense that he challenges metaphysics from within, but this does not mean that he is post-rational. As my reading of 'Of an Apocalyptic Tone Recently Adopted in Philosophy' (1984) will argue, Derrida's thought is closely connected with a form of Kantian respect for the *Aufklärung* – though one that is based on an interrogation of the limits of what is admissible philosophy. This reading is supported by my previous discussion of 'Declarations of Independence' (Chapter 2), and 'The Principle of Reason: the University in the Eyes of Its Pupils' (Chapter 3).

Deconstruction and the events of May 1968

Invoking the idea that postmodernism is concerned with a withdrawal from politics, a number of cultural commentators have argued that 1968 marks a division between a positive and a negative response to political questions by cultural theorists on the left (Callinicos, 1990; Helmling, 1994). Prior to 1968 writers and philosophers such as Barthes and Foucault espoused a politics of commitment. In the aftermath of 1968, in contrast, these theorists develop a response to political questions which, if identified with a strategy of resistance at all, is qualified by caution, failure and pessimism.

One such reading is outlined by Callinicos in 'Reactionary Postmodernism', where deconstruction and postmodernism emerge as a similar kind of response to the failure of the post-1968 cul de sac of avant-garde theory. 'There has emerged from the ruins a generation', Callinicos writes:

> now in its thirties and forties, of intellectuals and quasi-intellectuals who derive from their past leftist sympathies and present experience considerable scepticism about the rationality and justice of the existing order, but who have lost any belief in a desirable and feasible alternative. (1990, 113)

This understanding of the decline of radical politics has been unable to deal effectively with the enduring social and economic inequalities of capitalism. For Callinicos, capitalism has adapted not only to the aspirations of the revolutionary proletariat but also to the career aspirations of a generation of former left-wing activists:

> At the same time, the rapid expansion of posts in the new middle class of highly-paid professional, managerial, and administrative employees, a social layer that in America and Britain has done well out of the Reagan–Thatcher era, has offered the disillusioned children of '68 the prospect of social and political mobility and constantly increased consumption. (1990, 113–14)

The disillusionment of postmodernist politics is a direct product of the class location of its agents. For Callinicos, postmodernism mistakenly sees itself as an avant-garde theory raised to the level of a legitimate form of politics:

> The discourse of postmodernism is therefore best seen as the product of a socially mobile intelligentsia in a climate dominated by a retreat of the Western labour movement and the consumptionist dynamic of capitalism in the Reagan–Thatcher era. From this perspective, the term 'postmodernism' would seem to be a floating signifier by means of which the intelligentsia has sought to articulate its political disillusionment and its aspiration to a consumption-oriented lifestyle. (1990, 115)

So, on the one hand, Callinicos positions Derrida alongside Foucault and Deleuze, as representatives of a:

> somewhat heterogeneous group of French thinkers who have ... participated in the common effort of subverting the notions of truth, meaning and subjectivity held to be the defining features of Western metaphysics. (1990, 100)

On the other hand, he provides a detailed rejection of the political implications of a metaphysical critique, arguing, in fact, that they have rejected reality for language (1990, 101), a notion of truth for a Nietzschean conception of power, and failed to grant any coherence or agency to the subject (1990, 102). In place of 'real politics', these thinkers have fallen back upon a diluted and limited form of political resistance. As Callinicos's views suggest, Derrida has attracted a lot of criticism as a result of his apparent proximity to postmodern thought and its embrace of textualism, evident in the post-Marxist (or ex-Marxist) phases of other French theorists such as Baudrillard and Lyotard.

The previous three chapters distanced Derridean deconstruction from the reading of textuality, the subject and politics outlined in this context by Callinicos. While a similar misreading is outlined by Helmling in his essay, 'Historicizing Derrida' (1994), it is worth following his argument in more detail in order to focus on a particular understanding of post-modernism. Helmling argues that prior to 1968 deconstruction is tied to an optimistic belief in the possibility of social and political change. Thereafter, however, deconstruction becomes a postmodern strategy that signifies the disillusionment of post-1968 critical theory.

In the light of this distinction Helmling considers that it is now appropriate to provide a 'historically informed awareness' (1994, 1) of Derrida's reception. Helmling describes the break between Derrida's pre- and post-1968 texts in terms of a 'hopeful (even apocalyptic) sense of possibility' and the following awareness of despair and entrapment:

> Constrained and conditioned by the 'closures' of 'system,' we find ourselves 'inside' a vast social-historical-sexual-economic construct we cannot escape, cannot get 'outside' of. (1994, 4)

This break is distinguished by a different understanding of writing that Derrida deploys either side of this divide. Prior to 1968 Derrida is concerned with a 'grammatological *theme*' and thereafter with what Helmling calls a 'perverformative *practice*', with the latter working to 'confirm rather than to rupture the closure of logocentrism' (1994, 24).

Helmling returns to the theoretical analysis of Derrida's early texts in order to identify the characteristics of postmodern despair. He describes one of the most salient political problems that confronted intellectuals in the late 1960s in the following terms:

> if our language, our belief systems, our very subjectivities, are constructed by social forces, is it possible to get *outside* them, *outside* their system (or 'economy'), to escape their constraints, to glimpse possibilities they exclude, foreclose, repress? (1994, 3)

In these books Helmling 'discerns a political prospect, a quasi-prophecy of imminent cultural and social change' (1994, 7). Prior to 1968, Derrida challenges the prevailing sense of totality or system, identified primarily with Hegel's absolute spirit, by positing the idea that differance is ineradicable and hence cannot be mastered by the system. For western philosophy, the totalizing system par excellence, the other is always perceived to be a threat which must be brought under control; this oppressive understanding of the inexorable reduction of sameness to difference and, by implication, its association with a totalitarian politics is exemplified above all by Hegel. For Derrida, in contrast, the disruption of the inexorable grasping of the other is connected to the attempted preservation of the internal play of differance. Given these assumptions, Helmling argues that deconstruction was first articulated as:

> a new and uniquely potent instrument for rending the veils of various kinds of (false) metaphysics, and hence, false consciousness ... all of which sustained the early excitement about Derrida, and still sustains those who would use deconstruction 'politically,' in the service of *Ideologiekritik*. (1994, 6)

After 1968, Helmling continues, this question receives a pessimistic answer: 'Much "theory" (though by no means all) answers this question in the negative, especially since the disillusion following the late '60s generally, and in France ... in particular. Despair is obligatory, a sign of political vigilance, when hope is constructed as "ideological", a false and politically pernicious consolation – "an imaginary solution to a real contradiction" ' (1994, 4). The events of May seem to precipitate at a historical level a mood of political despair that he describes as postmodern:

> Derrida himself is one of the most potent enforcers of this (postmodern) sense of entrapment in a 'system' or 'economy' of semantemes enforced by the 'logocentrism' of 'Western metaphysics' since Plato. (1994, 4)

Though Helmling suggests that Derrida has deployed a number of strategies to deal with this sense of entrapment:

> Derrida more righteously 'deconstructs' the values or valorizations (the good/bad binaries) sustaining the exclusion, to suggest that the 'outside' does not exist, that 'the other' is only by way of ideological distortion projected as 'other,' and denied the status of 'the same.' This is, politically, a more hopeful operation, but its bottom line remains that there *is* no 'outside,' or if there were, it would only prove to be 'the inside' again, more of 'the same.' The 'outside' remains a construction, perhaps a delusion, but in any case inaccessible. (1994, 4)

Though the last of these strategies is a more hopeful operation, Derrida's work after 1970 has taken a less optimistic stance:

> since the early '70s, the point of Derrida's blueprint has been less to assist escape, than to demonstrate that escape is impossible. We're all lifers here in the prison-house of language: we may deconstruct, but we can never escape, its determinations, its reason(s), its meanings. (1994, 4)

In the aftermath of 1968, Derrida refashions deconstruction to take account of the changing fortunes of classical Marxism. Derrida's post-1968 work can be described as an entrapment model: differance, conflict and resistance are 'always-already' incorporated, assimilated and managed by the logocentrism they seek to undermine. Resistance is always-already being reappropriated. After 1968, Helmling continues, Derrida's work conformed to the 'sadder-but-wiser premise that those ideological programs had "always already" been "inscribed" in "writing" ' (1994, 14). After 1968, Derrida 'blows the whistle on all "ideological" hope as such' (1994, 17). Our postmodern despair is a product of the assimilation of the spirit of revolution: 'the potentially subversive is reinscribed within what it would subvert' (1994, 18). Derrida's optimism (and pessimism) is measured by Helmling's interpretation of his response to 'the question whether and how "escape" from a historically given "system" or "economy" of meanings might be possible' (1994, 18). Once again this tension is described as 'a thematic or problematic quite specific to our postmodern historical moment' or ' "postmodern" predicament' (1994, 5–6). The oscillation of 'liberation' and 'entrapment' is the 'spectacle our postmodern (i.e., post-'68) "libidinal economy" demands' (1994, 16).

Helmling's argument encounters a number of problems. These can best be highlighted if we return to his readings of those texts in which he finds evidence of the break in Derrida's corpus. Helmling supports his assertion about the political optimism of Derrida's pre-1968 work by turning to the 'Exergue' to *Of Grammatology*, an excerpt from *Positions* and the essay, 'Tympan', which functions as a preface to *Margins of Philosophy*. Let us take Helmling's example from *Of Grammatology* as an example of his argument. He is quoting Derrida:

> this exergue must not only announce that the science of writing – *grammatology* – shows signs of liberation all over the world, as a result of decisive efforts. These efforts are necessarily discreet, dispersed, almost imperceptible; that is a quality of their meaning and of the

milieu within which they produce their operation. I would like to suggest above all that, however fecund and necessary the undertaking might be, and even if, given the most favourable hypothesis, it did overcome all technical and epistemological obstacles as well as all the theological and metaphysical impediments that have limited it hitherto, such a science of writing runs the risk of never being established as such and with that name. (OG, 4)

Helmling continues so as to include Derrida's distinction between the closure and the end of metaphysics, and then concludes with what he refers to as the 'dark and ominous note' signalled by the final lines:

The future can only be anticipated in the form of an absolute danger. It is that which breaks absolutely with constituted normality and can only be proclaimed, *presented*, as a sort of monstrosity. For that future world and for that within it which will have put into question the values of sign, word, and writing, for that which guides our future anterior there is yet no exergue. (OG, 4–5)

Whereas these passages from *Of Grammatology* are supposed to confirm the distinction between pre- and post-1968, Helmling's own examples actually undermine his thesis. Prior to the quotation from Derrida's 'Exergue', Helmling refers to a passage from *Positions*, which, as he acknowledges, calls into question the simplicity of his before-and-after pattern. Helmling describes how he detects a 'powerful rhythm' (Helmling, 1994, 8) in these passages that oscillates between 'assertion and qualification, saying and unsaying' (1994, 9). Yet, more tellingly, 'in speaking of Derrida before and after 1968, I must seem to speak of "effects" as if they had "thetic" force or substance, and the inevitable binaries that will present themselves will overflow the temporal bar (1968) supposed to separate them' (1994, 10).

The remainder of Helmling's essay is full of further examples of this trend. Still insisting on the pre- and post-1968 schema, Helmling turns to the essays in *Margins of Philosophy* and acknowledges that some of the essays which prove his thesis about the 'massive ideological shift' (1994, 14) were in fact written *after* 1968 rather than before. Internal contradictions beset his whole argument in an extraordinary absence of consistency. His argument rests on the simplicity of the break while at the same time he understands that 'Derrida invests so much (and so effectively) in problematizing, sometimes altogether evading, the logic of "statement" ' (1994, 10). His distinction between grammatological writing – that is, the pre-1968 style of writing which is a 'sign of the revolution' – and perverformative writing – the post-1968 style which 'lowers, or registers a lowering, of the stakes for philosophy, and for "critique" at large' (1994, 26) – flounders on his notion of a simple break.

This can be seen finally in his flawed understanding of the *future anterior*. Rather than marking the repetition of the same, this concept, as this passage from Thwaites indicates, relates more to what I have described as iterability, differance and supplementarity:

> Invoking a past which has itself not yet arrived, or is always in the process of arriving, the future anterior not only describes the empirical delays attendant on any historicity, but also, in its complex textual folding, the very structure of historicity as perpetually renewed wager. (Thwaites, 1995b, 12)

The same, the now, is always-already contaminated by the presence of the other. Derrida's style of writing has always in fact been a merger of what Helmling awkwardly identifies as grammatological and perverformative. Helmling even acknowledges this in this self-contradictory passage:

> the tone of protest, continuous between early Derrida and late, has on the one hand kept Derrida's *fans* from seeing how Derrida's political import has been displaced after 1968, and on the other blinded his politically minded *critics* to such politics as his pre-'68 work did actually entertain. (Helmling, 1994, 29)

Helmling both affirms *and* denies that Derrida's work is and is not politically optimistic either side of the 1968 divide. As if to cover himself on all sides, he concludes that 'even granting that Derrida himself shies away from putting deconstruction to political use, it seems churlish not to acknowledge that his method, in other hands, has proved enormously useful for a variety of oppositional criticisms – feminist, gay/lesbian/queer, minority, postcolonialist, etc.' (1994, 29). While I disagree with the thesis that Derrida 'shies away from putting deconstruction to political use', Helmling is surely right to emphasize the political usefulness of deconstruction to a variety of marginal movements and critics, as my analysis of Johnson and Elam indicated in Chapter 2. But Helmling's general claim that Derrida's work is 'very much a "period" phenomenon, a sign of the postmodern times generally, and of the "emergence of that new type of discourse called theory" in particular' (1994, 34), cannot be supported if it is based solely on the idea of a pre- and post-1968 break in his corpus. Though Helmling does not offer a precise definition, his understanding of postmodernism is clear enough. The postmodern political condition began in the wake of the events of 1968.

Helmling's understanding finds a more detailed elaboration in Heller and Fehér's book *The Postmodern Political Condition* (1988). It is worth taking a detour through this text in order to flesh out the implications of Helmling's understanding of postmodernism. The implication of my reading is that where similarities exist between Derrida and postmodernism they do not mean, as we shall see when we turn to Habermas, that deconstruction is akin to a withdrawal from politics, a form of irrationalism or nihilism. Similarities exist because Derrida is concerned with rethinking the oppositions of modern political thought, not in order to abandon effective political action, but in order to reinvent existing modes of political analysis and transformation. Derrida's strategy predates the events of 1968, but was subsequently confirmed by them.

The Postmodern Political Condition

In *The Postmodern Political Condition* Heller and Fehér precisely locate the origins of postmodernism in a similar fashion to Helmling:

As a social theory, postmodernism was born in 1968. In a manner of its speaking, postmodernism was the creation of the alienation generation disillusioned with its own perception of the world. (Heller and Fehér, 1988, 138)

In this respect their thesis mirrors that of Helmling. The events of May–June 1968 became a touchstone for the postwar French left, disillusioned by the return of Gaullism in the July elections, and with what was interpreted by many to be the political failure of the French Communist Party. The events fuelled the demise of classical Marxism and the *engaged* intellectual – the transition from the intellectual as teacher to the less didactic role of a supporter in localized struggles. Explaining that postmodernism is 'fundamentally a European innovation and politico-cultural creation', Heller and Fehér argue that:

postmodernity may be understood as a private-collective time and space, within the wider time and space of modernity, delineated by those who have problems with and queries addressed to modernity, by those who want to take it to task, and by those who make an inventory of modernity's achievements as well as its unresolved dilemmas. (1988, 1)

Postmodernity is located within modernity, as their complex understanding of temporality suggests. Specifically, however, postmodernists are concerned with deconstructing the illusions of modernity, with addressing the unresolved dilemmas of enlightenment rationalism, as well as delineating its achievements. Postmodernism and modernism overlap in space and time, but in a way that makes them identifiable:

> Those who have chosen to dwell in postmodernity nevertheless live among moderns as well as postmoderns. For the very foundation of postmodernity consists of viewing the world as a plurality of heterogeneous spaces and temporalities. (1988, 1)

Postmodern society is directly related to the emergence of post-industrial consumer society. Consumerism acted as a celebration of difference, counteracting the gloomy understanding of the culture industry and the totally administered society. What emerged as postmodernism is 'the enormous pluralization of tastes, practices, enjoyments and needs' (1988, 142). Whereas the previous generation was led by its commitment to forms of grassroots politics based on collective action, postmodernists have pluralized ways of life and effectively induced the 'demise of self-complacent and ethnocentric class cultures' (1988, 142). Again there are similarities with Derrida's deconstruction of western ethnocentrism and logocentrism. Derrida's adoption of a more localized form of political intervention is not a withdrawal from politics, so much as a recognition that existing political strategies must be reconsidered in the light of the deconstruction of western metaphysics. It is not a failure of nerve or a withdrawal, then, but an attempt to come to terms with the changing reality of political theory and practice.

The emergence of this new type of politics is linked with the demise of the left's belief in solving the social question and of the perennial and uninterrupted existence of the affluent society. Postmodernism takes place after the demise of modernity's story of political emancipation, with its 'sacred and mythological origin, strict causality, secret teleology, omniscient and transcendent narrator and the promise of a happy ending' (1988, 2). The idea of a redemptive politics, normally based on the idea of the working class as the universal class, is incompatible with the postmodern political condition. Postmodernism cannot make guarantees about the future, nor can it attempt to describe accurately, as opposed to merely represent, the events of the past. Derrida's challenge to horizonal, teleological or messianic modes of thought is also in evidence here. It follows that like Derrida both Heller and Fehér reject the naivety of Fukuyama's end of history thesis.

There are some similarities between Helmling's and Heller and Fehér's understanding of postmodernism. Helmling does make the apposite point that while other critics subscribe to the attack on presence as a repudiation of the enlightenment project, this is 'staged less by Derrida than by those he has influenced' (Helmling, 1994, 22). Moreover, Helmling is right to interpret deconstruction as a strategy that faces up to the consequences of a changing political landscape rather than as a retreat to some kind of haven of silence or evasion. For Habermas, in contrast, to whom I shall now turn, Derrida's proximity to postmodernism confirms his rejection of enlightenment rationality and a progressive politics.

'Modernity – an Unfinished Project'

In his essay 'Modernity – an Unfinished Project', Habermas refers to the need to complete the enlightenment project – the process of rapid social, cultural and economic transformation that he traces to the eighteenth century – in the face of the emerging theories of antimodernity, whether they are called post-enlightenment, postmodernity or post-history. In short, all of these trends amount to a 'new kind of conservatism' (Habermas, 1996, 38).

In order to critique postmodernism and its related terms, Habermas first takes a detour through modernism and its related terms, modernity and modernization. The word modern emerges in the fifth century so as to distinguish the Christian present from the pagan and Roman past. Modernity, in contrast, describes the 'consciousness of an era that refers back to the past of classical antiquity precisely in order to comprehend itself as the result of a transition from the old to the new' (1996, 38). While the modern age began during the Renaissance, the definition Habermas describes is evident 'whenever the consciousness of a new era developed in Europe through a renewed relationship to classical antiquity' (1996, 38). It was not until the French Enlightenment and its emphasis on social and moral progress that the fascination with antiquity began to be lifted. Modernity represents an increasing concern with questions of human autonomy in a world now utterly changed by new technology and secularization. It was not until the nineteenth century when the classical and the romantic became opposed to one another that 'modernity ... detached itself solely in abstract opposition to tradition and history as a whole' (1996, 38). The modern came to signify the new, the style that in turn would be surpassed and devalued by the next in line. In art, the truly modern form 'no longer derives its power from the authority of a past age, but owes it solely to the authenticity of a contemporary relevance that has now become past' (1996, 40).

Aesthetic modernism refers to a movement (from the late nineteenth to the early twentieth century) in prose, poetry, painting and music that developed around a transformed consciousness of time, heavily influenced by Henri Bergson. Key figures for Habermas are obviously Joyce, Kafka and Henry James, poets such as Baudelaire, T. S. Eliot, Pound and Rilke, and painters such as Picasso and Matisse, all of whom are concerned with artistic production, the fragmentation of narrative and forms of representation in general.

Habermas's powerful critique of postmodern neoconservatism depends upon his understanding of the enlightenment project or the project of modernity. The development of this project by eighteenth-century philosophers is intimately connected with a 'differentiation of the value spheres of science and knowledge, of morality and art' (1996, 45). These areas have become the special preserve of experts:

> this professionalization treatment of the cultural heritage in terms of a single abstract consideration of validity in each case serves to bring to light the autonomous structures intrinsic to the cognitive-instrumental, the moral-practical and the aesthetic-expressive knowledge complexes. From now on there will also be *internal* histories of science and knowledge, of moral and legal theory, and of art. (1996, 45)

The enlightenment philosophers also sought to challenge the distance between expert cultures and the general public. This emphasis on the separation of science, law and art, Habermas writes:

> also results in releasing the cognitive potentials accumulated in the process from their esoteric high forms and attempting to apply them in the sphere of praxis, that is, to encourage the rational organization of social relations. Partisans of the Enlightenment such as Condorcet could still entertain the extravagant expectation that the arts and sciences would not merely promote the control of the forces of nature, but also further the understanding of self and world, the progress of

morality, justice in social relations, and even human happiness. (1996, 45)

The enlightenment philosophers wanted to utilize this accumulation of specialized culture for the enrichment and rational organization of everyday social life. Reason emerges as a universally valid concept and knowledge as the condition of individual freedom and self-realization. Truth, knowledge and rationality could be harnessed to control the development of society and to counter the uncritical inheritance of culture, traditions, customs and myths especially in order to curb the power of institutional religion. For Enlightenment philosophers, history moved forward in a progressive way toward the realization of human happiness.

What has been called postmodernism challenges the apparent optimism of this conception of the enlightenment project. Habermas's main question arises at this point: 'should we continue to hold fast to the intentions of the enlightenment, however fractured they might be, or should we rather relinquish the entire project of modernity?' (1996, 46). Even for those contemporary philosophers who have steadfastly refused to be appropriated by the neoconservatives or postmodernists, Habermas notes a fracturing of their approach. Popper, Lorenzen and Adorno all 'put their faith in only one of the moments into which reason has become differentiated' (1996, 46).

The failed attempt as Habermas sees it to *sublate* or reconnect these increasingly autonomous realms should not, as postmodernists mistakenly believe, 'mislead us into denouncing the intentions of an intransigent Enlightenment as the monstrous offspring of a "terroristic reason" ' (1996, 50). On the contrary, Habermas 'believe[s] that we should learn from the aberrations which have accompanied the project of modernity and from the mistakes of those extravagant proposals of sublation, rather than abandoning modernity and its project' (1996, 51). Habermas is concerned with embedding the insights of art, science and morality in the *lifeworld*, with incorporating them into the 'context of an individual life history or into a collective form of life' (1996, 51). Consequently, it is still possible and desirable to understand that:

the human, social and behavioural sciences have not been *entirely* divorced from the structure of practically orientated knowledge even now, and further that the concentration of universalistic ethics on questions of justice represents an abstraction which cries out to be connected to those problems concerning the good life that it initially excluded. (1996, 52)

Yet, in the face of this apparent optimism, Habermas understands all too well that:

> the prospects for this are not encouraging. Virtually throughout the Western world a climate of opinion has arisen which promotes tendencies highly critical of modernism. The disillusionment provoked by the failure of programmes for the false sublation of art and philosophy, and the openly visible aporias of cultural modernity, have served as a pretext for various conservative positions. (1996, 53)

Habermas delineates three types of conservative thinking in order to understand the union of antimodernist and postmodernist ideas that are gaining ground in the Green movement in particular. He identifies the *Young Conservatives* with a tradition of French thought that is influenced by Nietzsche and leads from Bataille to Foucault and Derrida. Members of this group are distinguished by an implacable opposition to modernism.

Unlike the Young Conservatives, the *Old Conservatives* – whom he identifies with Leo Strauss, Hans Jonas and Robert Spaemann – do not allow themselves to be contaminated by cultural modernity. Their mistrust of the differentiation of art, science and morality leads them to recommend a return to positions prior to modernity.

And finally it is the *New Conservatives* who affirm the success and achievements of modernity most vociferously. They welcome the differentiation of the spheres of knowledge, while acknowledging the 'development of modern science so long as it only oversteps its own sphere in order to promote technological advance, capitalist growth and a rational form of administration' (1996, 54). In all other cases their concept of politics is concerned with 'defusing the explosive elements of cultural modernity' (1996, 54).

Heirs of enlightenment: Derrida and Habermas

In his reading of Derrida in *The Philosophical Discourse of Modernity* Habermas positions himself as a modern and Derrida as a postmodern. Habermas's argument is based on three main assumptions about postmodernism: (1) postmodernism represents a profound break with the whole history of philosophical rationalism; (2) it is impossible and undesirable to break with either the rationality or universality that underpins enlightenment philosophy, and this is one reason why Derrida's attempt to do so frequently leads to unintelligible results; and

(3) though Derrida pretends to escape from foundationalist thought his use of concepts such as *archewriting* and his indebtedness to Levinas's Jewish mysticism are evidence of his inability to do so.

Habermas portrays Derrida as the authentic disciple of the Heidegger who wrote the 'Letter on Humanism' and was so influential in the intellectual life of postwar France. Heidegger's 'familiar melody of the self-overcoming of metaphysics also sets the tone for Derrida's enterprise' (1987, 161). It is no surprise, then, that Habermas sees a correspondence between Derridean deconstruction and Heideggerian *destruktion*. Derrida's understanding of deconstruction in *Of Grammatology*, which emphasizes his strategy of 'an oblique and perilous movement, constantly risking falling back within what is being deconstructed' (OG, 14), therefore seems to confirm Habermas's understanding that deconstruction is an antimodern form of irrationality that systematically attempts to undermine the conceptual infrastructure of western reason.

At the same time, however, Habermas acknowledges that Derrida effectively distances himself from Heidegger's later philosophy, rejecting his organic ideology, and its metaphors of presence and plenitude. In opposition to Heidegger's 'sentimental homely pictures of a preindustrial peasant counterworld' (Habermas, 1987, 162), Habermas places Derrida's subversive attitude toward Heidegger's configuration of organic metaphors. The focus of Habermas's discussion is whether Derrida's understanding of grammatology remains constrained by the metaphysics of presence that it seeks to overthrow. Habermas's point in this respect is that Derrida has nothing to put in the place of the metaphysics he deconstructs.

So, while Heidegger views language as the 'house of Being', Derrida takes language and linguistics as his starting point for the critique of metaphysics, thereby founding *grammatology* as the science of writing, with its emphasis on a text's detachment from context and author. Derrida's emphasis on his conception of writing allows him to connect Husserl's early philosophy of consciousness with Heidegger's philosophy of language. While Derrida has rejected the idea that his work is engaged in a positive or negative form of theology, his conception of writing is indebted, Habermas argues, to a Jewish understanding of interpretation that derives from Levinas:

> Within a traditional context marked by catastrophe, the substrate of written signs is the only thing that survives corruption. The text is often damaged and fragmented so that it denies any access to interpreters in succeeding generations. But the signification remains even

upon unintelligible texts, the signs last – matter survives as the trace of spirit that has vanished. (1987, 165)

While Derrida seeks to progress beyond Heidegger's inverted foundationalism he remains in its path. What emerges is a form of thinking that nevertheless seeks to ground itself by using mystical concepts such as *archewriting*. Derrida's anti-enlightenment stance returns him to the premodern lineage of Jewish mysticism.

Similarities with Heidegger's attitude to political thinking remain. Habermas argues that, in a way similar to Heidegger, Derrida:

> degrades politics and contemporary history to the status of the ontic and the foreground, so as to romp all the more freely, and with a greater wealth of associations, in the sphere of the ontological and the archewriting. (1987, 181)

A little further down the same page Habermas's rhetoric is once more in evidence as he distinguishes between Derrida's and Heidegger's politics:

> But the rhetoric that serves Heidegger for the initiation into the fate of Being, in Derrida comes to the aid of a different, rather more subversive orientation. Derrida stands closer to the anarchist wish to explode the continuum of history than to the authoritarian admonition to bend before destiny. (1987, 181–2)

Nevertheless, Habermas views Derrida's insistence on a Jewish understanding of interpretation as a major point of criticism: 'The labor of deconstruction lets the refuse heap of interpretations, which it wants to clear away in order to get at the buried foundations, mount even higher' (1987, 183). What emerges from Habermas, then, is a picture of Derrida as a postmodern nihilist or anarchist, the inheritor of Nietzsche, who attacks enlightenment rationality and universality and threatens the Kantian distinctions between truth, value and taste. Deconstruction amounts to a form of mysticism that rejects social practices and effaces the subject.

The same themes are developed in Habermas's second chapter on Derrida entitled, 'Excursus on Levelling the Genre Distinction between Philosophy and Literature'. As the title implies, Habermas accuses Derrida of levelling the Kantian distinctions between philosophy and literature, and of stripping philosophy of its critical potential: 'Derrida wants to expand the sovereignty of rhetoric over the realm of the logical in order to solve the problem confronting the totalizing critique of reason' (1987, 188). It follows therefore that 'the deconstruction of great philosophical texts, carried out as literary criticism in this broader sense, is not subject to the criteria of problem-solving' (1987, 188). Because deconstruction rejects the 'discursive obligations of philosophy and science' (1987, 189), Derrida rejects an analytical method for a critique of style. Consequently, it is Derrida's intention to treat philosophical texts as if they were literary texts and thus to show how 'the genre distinction between [them] ... dissolves upon closer examination' (1987, 189). Deconstruction shows the frailty of the genre distinction through its emphasis on rhetoric rather than logic:

> in the end, *all* genre distinctions are submerged in one comprehensive, all-embracing context of texts – Derrida talks in a hypostatizing manner about a 'universal text'. What remains is self-inscribing writing as the medium in which each text is woven together with everything else. Even before it makes its appearance, every text and every particular genre has already lost its autonomy to an all-devouring context and an uncontrollable happening of spontaneous text production. (1987, 190)

Habermas's understanding of the general text means that 'philosophy and science no more constitute their own proper universes than art and literature constitute a realm of fiction that could assert its autonomy vis-à-vis the universal text' (1987, 191).

The postmodern linguistic turn has led to a privileged position for literary as opposed to rigorous philosophical analyses. Against the manifest sense of philosophical texts, deconstruction unfolds the 'surpressed surpluses of rhetorical meaning' (1987, 191). By implication, 'philosophical texts can be rendered accessible in their essential contents by literary criticism' (1987, 191). If, following Derrida's recommendation, Habermas writes:

> philosophical thinking were to be relieved of the duty of solving problems and shifted over to the function of literary criticism, it would be robbed not merely of its seriousness, but of its productivity. (1987, 210)

According to Habermas deconstruction threatens the genre distinction between philosophy and literature, thereby reducing philosophy to another kind of writing, which gives up its privileged status as the language of truth. For Habermas, on the contrary, though rhetorical elements are present in all areas of language use they should not be overemphasized. Habermas argues that Derrida 'fails to recognize the special status that both philosophy and literary criticism, each in its own way, assume as mediators between expert cultures and the everyday world' (1987, 207). Both literary criticism and philosophy:

> have a family resemblance to literature – and to this extent to one another as well – in their rhetorical achievements. But their family relationship stops right there, for in each of these enterprises the tools of rhetoric are subordinated to the discipline of a *distinct* form of argumentation. (1987, 209–10)

Like Kant, Habermas is here concerned with separating the faculties, but in such a way that refuses to give philosophy a privileged understanding of truth. Nevertheless, the implications of the final sentence are clear enough. Unlike serious or rigorous philosophers, Derrida's work does not display the distinct form of argumentation that validates it in Habermas's eyes.

As my previous discussion of 'Declarations of Independence' and 'The Principle of Reason' indicated, Habermas has failed to come to terms with Derrida's understanding of originary repetition and his form of post-Kantian critique.

Derrida and the post-Kantian critical tradition

In the essay, 'Deconstruction, Postmodernism and Philosophy: Habermas on Derrida' (1996), Norris persuasively contests a number of Habermas's main arguments about the relationship between Derrida and postmodern neoconservatism. Norris restates his opposition to the arguments that mistakenly assimilate deconstruction to postmodern irrationalism. 'It seems to me', Norris writes:

> that he [Habermas] has misread Derrida's work, and done so moreover in a way that fits in all too readily with commonplace ideas about deconstruction as a species of latter-day Nietzschean irrationalism, one that rejects the whole legacy of post-Kantian enlightened thought. (Norris, 1996, 97)

Habermas has misread Derridean deconstruction precisely because he has failed to acknowledge those works 'in which Derrida has distanced his own thinking from a generalized "postmodern" or poststructuralist discourse' (1996, 97). Added to this is the idea that Derrida collapses all genre distinctions, especially those between philosophy and literature, reason and rhetoric and the constative and performative. Habermas seems to go along with the assumptions of the literary reception of Derrida's work. While supporting these elements, Norris is squarely opposed to the other aspects of Habermas's position. On the contrary, Norris is actually in broad agreement with his commitment to re-examine the 'character and historical antecedents of postmodernism' and for approaching the term not as a 'radical challenge to the outworn enlightenment paradigm, but rather as the upshot of a widespread failure to think through the problems bequeathed by that tradition' (1996, 97). Norris also concurs with Habermas's understanding that the 'post' in postmodernism is a 'delusive prefix' that actually effaces the fact that many so-called postmodernists 'are still caught up in problems that have plagued the discourse of philosophy since the parting of ways after Kant' (1996, 98). Although Habermas profoundly misreads Derrida, Norris gives his consent to Habermas's attempt in *The Philosophical Discourse of Modernity* to 'recall the present-day human sciences to a knowledge of their own formative prehistory' (1996, 98).

In rejecting Habermas's reading of Derrida, Norris advances the radical idea that Derrida's and Habermas's view of enlightenment rationality have a good deal in common. A key aspect of this argument is the assumption that deconstruction should not be regarded as an offshoot of a 'wider postmodernist or counter-enlightenment drift' (1996, 99–100). Norris returns to the argument that Derrida's work should be read within the context of the post-Kantian tradition of enlightenment critique. According to this reading, Derrida does not dispense with the regime of truth, reality, reference or representation. On the contrary, Derrida cannot be assimilated to a postmodernist pragmatist or irrationalist position because, when properly understood, deconstruction 'belongs within that same "philosophical discourse of modernity" that Habermas sets out to defend against its present-day detractors' (1996, 100).

Norris takes issue, then, with all the major points of Habermas's discussion of Derrida: principally the idea that deconstruction is an offshoot of the postmodern anti-enlightenment drift; and that Derrida levels the genre distinction between philosophy and literature, therefore effectively effacing the critical potential of philosophy. Habermas's reading of deconstruction as an essentially literary enterprise that attempts to colonize philosophy is firmly rejected. While it is possible to see the origins of this reading in a number of Derrida's texts – in *Limited Inc*, in the closing sections of 'Structure, Sign, and Play in the Discourse of the Human Sciences' and in the 'Envois' part of *The Post Card* – Habermas, like many critics from the literary reception of deconstruction, interpreted these as confirmation of the idea that Derrida treats philosophical texts as 'purely rhetorical constructs on a level with poems, novels, postcards or any other kind of writing' (1996, 100). This claim, however, is a misreading of Derrida's challenge to the traditional idea that philosophy has special access to 'an order of pure, unmediated, self-present truth' (1996, 102). Derrida is indeed concerned with the idea that philosophy is a kind of writing but not in the sense that Habermas means. Derrida, as he shows at length in *Limited Inc*, is concerned with attacking the exclusivist logic that maintains the border lines between serious and non-serious, normal and deviant speech acts. The nub of Habermas's argument is that Derrida is set upon eroding the careful distinctions between the faculties which history has evolved. Habermas thinks it necessary to disregard those texts, such as *The Post Card*, that confuse philosophy with metaphorical and stylistic attributes. Derrida, however, does not mix genres so as to betray the project of enlightenment reason. He identifies how they are already mixed. 'What Habermas fails to recognize', Norris argues, 'is the extent to which so-called "ordinary" language is in fact shot through with metaphors, nonce-usages, chance collocations, Freudian parapraxes and other such "accidental" features that cannot be reduced to any normative account' (1996, 114). Derrida pushes post-Kantian philosophy in the direction of realizing 'its own covert involvement in a general problematics of language, writing and representation' (1996, 115). All forms of logocentrism are thus embedded in processes of signification, though their emphasis on intuition, essence and truth are all attempts to escape this reality.

Derrida is concerned with showing how the rhetorical aspects of language, normally excluded from philosophical language because they are commonly held to be the sole preserve of literary language, contaminate philosophy: 'What Derrida has achieved ... is a striking reversal of the age-old prejudice that elevates philosophy over rhetoric, or right reason over the dissimulating arts of language' (1996, 102). Habermas mistakes the 'character of deconstruction when he treats it as having simply *given up* the kinds of argument specific to philosophy, and opted instead for the pleasures of a free-wheeling "literary" style' (1996, 111). As I pointed out in my discussion of 'The Principle of Reason', Derrida clearly argues that those who directly criticize the inheritance of post-Kantian philosophy 'need not set themselves up in opposition to the principle of reason, nor need they give way to "irrationalism" ' (POR, 17).

Habermas's attempt to assimilate Derrida to his understanding of postmodern neoconservatism fails to engage with those texts in which Derrida effectively restates his commitment to a reinscription of enlightenment rationality. In 'Of an Apocalyptic Tone Recently Adopted in Philosophy' (1984), Derrida cleverly voices the criticisms levelled at deconstruction by Habermas in *The Philosophical Discourse of Modernity*, underpinning the thrust of Norris's arguments in more detail.

Derrida and the 'apocalyptic tone recently adopted in philosophy'

Appropriately the title of Derrida's essay, 'Of an Apocalyptic Tone Recently Adopted in Philosophy', derives from Kant's 'Of an Overlordly Tone Recently Adopted in Philosophy' [*Von einem neuerdings erhobenen Vornehmen Ton in der Philosophie*] (1796), a pamphlet in which the German philosopher also mounted a powerful critique of the opponents of enlightenment thinking. Kant's essay specifically challenges the tone of some of his contemporaries that announced the death of philosophy and those advocates of mystified thought – the *mystagogues* – who attempted to undermine the status of reason and universality through an unintelligible discourse. The reference to Habermas's critique of Derrida in 'Modernity – an Unfinished Project', originally delivered in 1980, is clear; as Derrida writes, 'Each of us is the mystagogue *and* the *Aufklärer* of an other' (OAT, 18).

The moment the mystagogues concern themselves with philosophy is the moment that philosophy 'loses its signification or its original reference' (OAT, 18). The mystagogues are characterized by their 'claim to possess as if in private the privilege of a mysterious *secret*' and their disregard for 'the concept of schooling' as they acquire their knowledge 'effortlessly, gracefully, intuitively or through genius, outside of school' (OAT, 9). As such they 'never fail to take themselves for lords ... elite beings, distinguished subjects, superior and apart in society' (OAT, 9). Kant's protest against the mystagogues is based on a rejection of their arrogance and disregard for philosophical reason. Their discourse is based on a number of characteristics such as 'prediction and eschatological preaching, the fact of telling, foretelling, or preaching the ends, the extreme limit, the imminence of the last' (OAT, 20). Kant, as Derrida explains, responds to the mystagogues' attempt to pervert the 'voice of reason, by mixing ... the voice of reason and the voice of oracle' (OAT, 11). Because they claim that their insight relies on an intuitive mode of understanding the mystagogues can say whatever they want, thus distorting in Kant's eyes the voice of reason that 'speaks to each without equivocation, and ... gives access to scientific knowledge' (OAT, 12). Derrida like Kant seeks to preserve the critical vigilance of reason not renounce it:

> We cannot and we must not – this is a law and a destiny – forgo the *Aufklärung*, in other words, what imposes itself as the enigmatic desire for vigilance, for the lucid vigil, for elucidation, for critique and truth, but for a truth that at the same time keeps within itself some apocalyptic desire, this time as desire for clarity and revelation, in order to demystify or, if you prefer, to deconstruct apocalyptic discourse itself and with it everything that speculates on vision, the imminence of the end, theophany, parousia, the last judgement. (OAT, 22)

'The overlordly tone', Derrida writes, 'dominates and is dominated by the oracular voice that covers over the voice of reason, rather parasitises it, causes it to derail or become delirious' (OAT, 11). Indeed it is 'in the name of an *Aufklärung* that Kant ... undertakes to demystify the overlordly tone' (OAT, 22). The mystagogues' idea that they can 'believe they *know* what is solely *thinkable* and reach through feeling alone the universal laws of practical reason' (OAT, 12) leads Kant to unveil their reliance on 'poetic schemas' and their corruption of true philosophy (OAT, 16).

Derrida is concerned with recognizing certain similarities between Kant's critique of the mystagogues and the repetition of such ideas in the late 1970s and early 1980s. As such Derrida sees in Kant's discussion of the apocalyptic tone of the mystagogues an echo of the accusation that he too is engaged in a similar kind of mystical or eschatological thinking. There is a strong resonance in the following passage where Derrida is clearly identifying himself with what passes for obscurantism:

> we could even say that every discord or every tonal disorder, everything that detones and becomes inadmissible in general collocution, everything that is no longer identifiable starting from established codes, from both sides of a front, will necessarily pass for mystagogic, obscurantistic, and apocalyptic. It will be made to pass for such. (OAT, 30)

While Derrida recognizes that he is often accused of this type of thinking, now commonly associated with postmodernism, he points out that signs of this kind have been ever present during the twentieth century:

> the end of history, the end of the class struggle, the end of philosophy,
> the death of God, the end of religions, the end of Christianity and
> morals ... the end of the subject, the end of man, the end of the West,
> the end of Oedipus, the end of the earth, *Apocalypse Now*, I tell you, in
> the cataclysm, the fire, the blood, the fundamental earthquake, the
> napalm descending from the sky by helicopters, like prostitutes, and
> also the end of literature, the end of painting, art as a thing of the past,
> the end of psychoanalysis, the end of the university, the end of
> phallocentrism and phallogocentrism, and I don't know what else?
> (OAT, 20–1)

But what is particularly important here is the idea, as expressed by
Habermas, that Derrida's challenge to the genre distinction between
literature and philosophy is the source of Kant's attack on the mystagogues.
In Kant's time, as Derrida recognizes, this criticism derives from a fight:

> around poetics (between poetry and philosophy), around the death
> or the future of philosophy. The stake is the same. Kant does not
> doubt this: the new preachers need to pervert philosophy into poetry
> in order to give themselves grand airs, to occupy through simulacrum
> and mimicry the place of the great, to usurp thus an essentially
> symbolic power. (OAT, 17)

Derrida is interested in the contract that Kant strikes between himself
and the mystagogues as this reveals what is admissible and inadmissible
in philosophical discourse. Derrida fastens onto the fact that, by placing
such limits, an exclusion or excluded middle is presupposed. Derrida's
point is that both Kant and the mystagogues engage in an apocalyptic
discourse that posits a moment of self-present truth. It is not possible to
simply oppose or concur with Kant's attack on the mystagogues:

> Truth itself is the end, the destination, and that truth unveils itself as
> the advent of the end. Truth is the end and the instance of the last
> judgement. The structure of truth here would be apocalyptic. And
> that is why there would not be any truth of the apocalypse that is not
> the truth of truth. (OAT, 24)

The apocalyptic tone is predicated on a notion of destination to which
Derrida is opposed. In Derrida's two-handed reading, he sides *with* Kant

against the mystagogues and *against* Kant's policing of the limits of acceptable philosophical discourse which must follow.

Derrida's analysis of apocalyptic thinking echoes with allusions to John's Apocalypse for one key reason. Derrida discerns a division and multiplication of senders and addressees, similar to that which he describes in *Limited Inc*, that undermines the metaphysical notion of destination and is so important to apocalyptic thinking:

> One does not know (for it is no longer of the order of knowing) to whom the apocalyptic dispatch returns; it leaps from one place of emission to the other (and a place is always determined *starting from* the presumed emission); it goes from one destination, one name, and one tone to the other; it always refers to the name and to the tone of the other that is there but as having been there and before yet coming, no longer being or not yet there in the present of the *récit*. (OAT, 27)

This scene is the 'structure of every scene of writing in general ... in other words of the text or of the mark in general: *that is, of the divisible dispatch for which there is no self-presentation nor assured destination*' (OAT, 27–8). Derrida's opposition to this notion of eschatological presence is conveyed by his allusion to the messianic 'Come' from John's Apocalypse, which later becomes an important motif in his thinking of the *arrivant* and the New International in *Specters of Marx*. Here, however, Derrida describes how:

> 'Come' does not address itself to an identity determinable in advance. It is a drift underivable from the identity of a determination. 'Come' is *only* derivable, absolutely derivable, but only from the other, from nothing that may be an origin or a verifiable, decidable, presentable, appropriable identity, from nothing not already derivable and arrivable without *rive* [bank, shore]. (OAT, 34–5)

The 'Come' signals an 'apocalypse without apocalypse, an apocalypse without vision, without truth, without revelation, *dispatches* ... addresses without message and without destination, without sender or decidable addressee, without last judgement, without any other eschatology than the tone of the "Come," its very difference, an apocalypse beyond good and evil' (OAT, 35). It is this very sense of suspension that Habermas resists in Derrida's work; this notion is the source of his accusation of mysticism.

In conclusion it is possible to interpret Derrida's complex and multi-layered essay as a challenge to those readers who have systematically misinterpreted deconstruction's reinscription of the protocols of western rationality. Whereas Habermas's reading approaches Derrida as an irrational, neoconservative or mystical postmodernist, Derrida adopts a more complex stance. The result is a familiar double gesture that was also evident at the end of 'The Principle of Reason', where Derrida was concerned with reflecting on the foundations of rational thought rather than abandoning them.

This chapter has shown how Derridean deconstruction was damaged by its proximity to postmodern irrationalism and the idea that 1968 led to a withdrawal from an activist politics. In rejecting these arguments it is evident that Derrida was engaged in rethinking existing models of political analysis and transformation in a way that does not simply renounce these traditions, but attempts to re-examine their legacy in the light of changed conditions. This argument will be fleshed out in Chapter 6, which considers *Specters of Marx* and Derrida's thinking of inheritance. Before that, however, it is necessary to examine how the implications of Habermas's reading of deconstruction led to the interpretive violence and confusion of the de Man affair.

5
The Politics of the Proper Name: Nietzsche, Derrida and de Man Disfigured

The year 1987 saw a renewed interest in the politics of deconstruction. The discovery of a number of book and music reviews written by the young Paul de Man between 1939 and 1943 for *Jeudi: Hebdomadaire du Cercle 'Le Libre-Examen'*, *Les Cahiers du Libre Examen, Bibliographie Dechenne*, the Belgian newspaper *Le Soir* and the Flemish newspaper *Het Vlaamsche Land* prompted newspaper reports of deconstruction's culpability with antisemitism and the politics of the far right. The discovery of the articles by a young Belgian researcher, Ortwin de Graef, led to a violent and acrimonious debate that instantly became a major media event far beyond academia. De Man's silence about his wartime articles was seen to confirm the conclusions that were being drawn from the literary translation of Derrida's work.

These revelations were followed in quick succession by similar allegations about Heidegger, prompted in this instance by Victor Farias's book, *Heidegger et le Nazisme*. Heidegger's similar postwar silence about his membership of the Nazi Party between 1932 and 1945 could not be withdrawn from an analysis of his philosophy. Heidegger's understanding of *destruktion* was often identified as the most significant influence on the development of deconstruction, and Derrida was therefore seen as the main advocate of a strategy that risked continuing the potentially dreadful political implications of Heideggerian philosophy. While for Derrida and other leading French philosophers, Farias's book presented no new facts, it prompted a wide-ranging debate about Heidegger's alleged fascism in the Anglo-American academy.

Five years later in 1992, another controversy linked Derrida with the legacy of Heidegger's wartime politics. An interview given by Derrida entitled, 'Heidegger, the Philosophers' Hell', published for the first time in 1987 in the French journal, *Le Nouvel Observateur*, led to renewed allegations about deconstruction's Heideggerian influence. Richard Wolin undertook to translate the interview so that he could include it in a book he was editing about Heidegger entitled, *The Heidegger Controversy: a Critical Reader*, published by Columbia University Press in 1991. When Derrida discovered a copy of the interview in 1992 he was shocked by the poor academic standards of Wolin's English translation and subsequently protested to Columbia until it was withdrawn from further editions. Aided by Thomas Sheehan, Richard Wolin and Derrida exchanged letters in the *New York Review of Books* about the cause of Derrida's apparent censorship of the interview. While Wolin and Sheehan interpreted Derrida's reaction as one that demonstrated he had something to hide, Derrida insisted that the interview had already appeared in a number of other publications, and the idea of a cover-up was clearly untenable. Derrida's motivation sprang from the fact that Wolin's translation was too poor to merit publication.

These events were finally encapsulated by the attempt to veto the award of an honorary degree to Derrida by Cambridge University in 1992. Resistance to the vulgar conception of deconstruction by members of the Cambridge faculty led to a vote to confirm the award for the first time in thirty years. The publication of a letter in the London *Times* by an international group of philosophers attempted to influence the faculty's decision and to encourage the rejection of the award. After much discussion the faculty finally voted to accept the proposal and award Derrida the degree.

Added to the de Man affair and the Heidegger affair, the so-called Derrida affairs offer more evidence of the confusion that accompanied the cross-cultural translation of Derrida's thought. All four episodes provide a fascinating insight into the remarkable resonance of deconstruction and show how the political implications of Derrida's work suffered as a consequence of its proximity to de Man's and Heidegger's wartime involvement, some forty years earlier.

In order to develop some of the main themes of Chapter 2 this chapter will focus on Derrida's direct response to the allegations surrounding Paul de Man rather than Heidegger. What follows is divided into three sections. The first part considers Derrida's discussion of the Nazi appropriation of Nietzsche entitled, 'Otobiographies: the Teaching of Nietzsche and the Politics of the Proper Name'. This essay is an important intertext of Derrida's subsequent discussion of the fate that beset de Man's intellectual legacy. Parts 2 and 3 turn to Derrida's essays on de Man's wartime journalism, first in 'Like the Sound of the Sea Deep within a Shell: Paul de Man's War' (1988) and finally in 'Biodegradables: Seven

Diary Fragments' (1989). Derrida's involvement with the legacy of de Man prompted him to reiterate that deconstruction is an ethical injunction that mounts a sustained attack on the aesthetic ideology that underpins nationalism and xenophobia. While two of de Man's articles in particular led Derrida to condemn his antisemitism, he identified how de Man's postwar academic work is profoundly engaged in deconstructing rather than confirming the philosophical infrastructure of aesthetic ideology.

The final part of this chapter examines Derrida's discussion of the discourse of European exemplarity in *The Other Heading* (1992). Derrida's deconstruction of the logic of exemplarity and his understanding of identity based on respect for the alterity of the other – ethico-political themes that have been evident since his earliest texts – is precisely what Heidegger and the young de Man sacrificed when they identified National Socialism with the spiritual mission of European renewal. The aim is to show how Derrida's conception of a self-differentiating European identity in *The Other Heading* underpins his notion of a 'democracy to come' in *Specters of Marx*.

Translating Nietzsche

In 'Otobiographies', Derrida's reading of Nietzsche voices some of the important themes that have dogged the reception of his own proper name. The central themes of Derrida's reading of the autobiographical text, *Ecce Homo*, and *On the Future of Our Educational Institutions* are the responsibilities of interpretation, the limits of authorial intentionality and the politics of (mis)interpretation. In relation to these concerns, Derrida argues that Nietzsche's status is exemplary in that he 'was alone in treating both philosophy and life, the science and the philosophy of life with his name and in his name' (EO, 6). Although it could be argued that all literary authors run the risk that Derrida identifies, Nietzsche's special significance derives from the corruption of his signature by Nazi propagandists – the 'poisoned milk' of National Socialism which has been mixed up with his names and signatures (EO, 7). By implication Derrida's essay is also an intertext of his later readings of de Man, and a commentary on the reception of his own proper name.

Nietzsche's association with Nazism leads Derrida to ask how the German philosopher's books could have sustained such a range of misreadings? In reply Derrida does not doubt that Nietzsche has been misinterpreted; however, he does point out that the legacy of Nietzsche's works – and particularly his description of a *Führer*, a leader who should restore German students' obedience in *On the Future of Our Educational Institutions* – should not be allowed to 'resonate all by itself in its Hitlerian consonance, with the echo it received from the Nazi orchestration of the Nietzschean reference, as if the word had no other possible context' (EO, 28). Given Nietzsche's prophetic warning in *Ecce Homo* that his books would be 'born posthumously', Derrida asks: Should the author or the reader be held responsible for the future interpretations of his work? Derrida speculates that it is no accident that Nietzsche's books run the risk of their Nazi inheritance. They possess a certain quality, which enables other readers to exploit the same language, the same words and the same utterances for different purposes. But it is also true that Nietzsche understood that once his books left him his responsibility ceased. Derrida invokes the name of Nietzsche, then, to represent the risk that accompanies the relation between an author's name and the meanings that his books inherit during their movement beyond his control.

These tensions are dramatized by the title of the text – *The Ear of the Other* – from which the essay on Nietzsche is taken. As the title implies Derrida requests that his readers listen to his discourse on autobiography with another ear. Derrida first addresses this theme in 'Tympan', which prefaces *Margins of Philosophy*. The tympanum, a thin and transparent partition, which is stretched obliquely between the auditory canal and the middle ear, alludes to the borderline or *dynamis* that separates the work from the author. Derrida's use of the tympanum restates his idea that meaning is always mediated, always the product of an interpretative experience. By using one of his most persistent themes in a different context, Derrida writes that the precision of hearing, which here alludes to the notion of the self-presence of speech, is in 'direct proportion to the obliqueness of the tympanum' (MP, xix). The tympanum obliterates the division of the proper entailed by the auditory proximity of Being in speech. Derrida's point as always is to undermine any conception of self-present meaning or teleology. Derrida shows how writing makes, unmakes and disseminates the presence of meaning. This notion can be explained if we turn to Derrida's reference to the words, 'I have forgotten my umbrella', which were found enclosed in quotation marks among Nietzsche's unpublished manuscripts, in *Spurs: Nietzsche's Styles*.

Derrida's discussion of this phrase confirms one of the main theses of *Limited Inc*, namely, that there is 'no infallible way of knowing ... *for sure* what Nietzsche wanted to say or do when he noted these words, nor even that he actually *wanted* anything' (SN, 123). It is possible to see that the phrase may be 'detached as it is, not only from the milieu that produced it, but also from any intention or meaning on Nietzsche's part' (SN, 125). In other words, 'The meaning and the signature that appropriates it remain in principle inaccessible' (SN, 125). This understanding of the meaning of the fragment 'withdraw[s] it from any assured horizon of a hermeneutic question' (SN, 127). The phrase has no centre of meaning: 'Because it is structurally liberated from any living meaning, it is always possible that it means nothing at all or that it has no decidable meaning. There is no end to its parodying play with meaning, grafted here and there, beyond any contextual body or finite code' (SN, 133).

Next, Derrida extends the meaning he gleans from the fragment and applies it to Nietzsche's corpus as a whole: 'If Nietzsche had indeed meant to say something, might it not be just that limit to the will to mean, which, much as a necessarily differential will to power, is forever divided; folded and manifolded' (SN, 133). For Derrida, the idea that the 'totality of Nietzsche's text ... might well be of the type "I have forgotten my umbrella" cannot be denied' (SN, 133). Derrida summarizes his strategy of reading in 'Choreographies', suggesting that it is concerned with resisting the temptation to settle on one position or meaning, or to accept only one truth.

Now, if we return to 'Otobiographies' we will see that Derrida's strategy is not simply a one-sided attempt to undermine the historicity and specificity of a text. Derrida similarly argues that Nietzsche's books are not to be understood to be simple *presentations* of identity or self-present meaning: 'Nietzsche advances behind a plurality of masks or names, like any mask and even any theory of the simulacrum can propose and produce themselves only by returning a constant yield of protection, a surplus value in which one may still recognise the ruse of life' (EO, 7). Derrida seems willing to play with the dissimulation of the proper name of Nietzsche and the protection this affords to the author. But this is not a strategy of evasion. Derrida *does* acknowledge what cannot be absolved. The point of his reading is to highlight the problem of advancing a simple or uncomplicated interpretation. The existence of an aporetic logic in Nietzsche's texts underpins Derrida's insistence that reading is a political act. It is particularly evident in relation to Nietzsche that, 'The reader provides the signature of the text, and only the name inherits, not the author', as he explains further:

The important thing about the ear's difference ... is that the signature becomes effective ... performed and performing – not at the moment it apparently takes place, but only later, when ears will have managed to receive the message. (EO, 50)

Responsibility lies *between* reader and text. The process, however, cannot be predetermined:

> In some ways the signature will take place on the addressee's side, that is, on the side of him or her whose ear will be keen enough to hear my name, for example, or to understand my signature, that with which I sign ... Nietzsche's signature does not take place when he writes. He says clearly that it will take place posthumously ... when the other comes to sign with him, to join with him in alliance and, in order to do so, to hear and to understand him. To hear him one must have a keen ear. (EO, 35)

Nietzsche's signature, then, embodies the familiar double gesture that calls for, yet resists, translation – a double-bind that we have also seen in operation in 'Des Tours de Babel'. Texts do not therefore faithfully transport the author's intended meaning to the reader. The meaning of a text is transformed via translation, through the ear of the other, the signatory of the text. Derrida returns to this metaphorical cluster of ear and waves during the scandal that surrounded the discovery of de Man's wartime articles. The point of my analysis of Derrida's reading of Nietzsche shall now become apparent as we turn to consider the inheritance or 'posthumous' existence of de Man's signature during the late 1980s.

Paul de Man disfigured

Chapter 2 set out Norris's (1988) and Johnson's (1987) persuasive accounts of the political implications of de Man's early academic work. While both writers display a certain amount of unease with the reviews and articles that de Man wrote between 1939 and 1943, they are united in their view that the texts are profoundly at odds with his early to middle period academic essays and especially with his later deconstructive phase. Johnson, for example, claims that, 'Whatever Paul de Man is doing in these early essays, it is certainly not deconstruction. Indeed, deconstruction is precisely the dismantling of these notions of evolutionary continuity, totalization, organicism, and "proper" traditions' (Johnson, 1987, xvi). In 'Like the Sound of the Sea Deep within a Shell', Derrida also adopts this line, and quotes approvingly from Culler's measured and persuasive response to de Man's articles, entitled, ' "Paul de Man's War" and the Aesthetic Ideology' (1989). Culler argues that de Man's critique of poetry's totalizing drive is traceable to his earlier and later writings. This is especially evident in de Man's discussion of Heidegger and the way his close reading works to undermine the naive belief that poetry can achieve the reconciliation of contradictions. Furthermore, Norris (1988) argues that de Man's lack of nostalgia for Heideggerian presence, evident in his essays on 'Wordsworth and Hölderlin', and his reply to Derrida's reading of Rousseau, are testimony to his resistance to organic ideology. The main target of the de Man affair is in fact *deconstruction* or, to be more accurate, a crude but widespread misrepresentation of both Derrida's and the later de Man's understanding of the word.

In what follows my argument is based on four key assumptions:

1. In the hands of de Man and Derrida, deconstruction is a critique of aesthetic ideology and all forms of totalizing thought. It is unquestionably anti-totalitarian and has always been concerned with the analysis of the conditions of totalitarianism. Derrida profoundly rejects all views to the contrary in no uncertain terms:

   purification, purge, totalization, reappropriation, homogenization, rapid objectification, good conscience, stereotyping and nonreading, *immediate* politicization or depoliticization ... *immediate* historicization or dehistoricization ... immediate ideologizing moralization ... This is what must be deconstructed ... (LSS, 646)

2. Critics conflated early and late de Man in order to signal the end of deconstruction, which they misguidedly misread as a nihilistic challenge to the values of western philosophical and literary traditions. By 'dangerously simplifying' de Man's articles, critics claimed that his association with deconstruction was a form of 'self-exoneration'; de Man is sympathetic to deconstruction, they argued, because it retreats from historical fact and problematizes all forms of understanding. In fact, a 'deconstructive understanding of history', Derrida writes:

   consists rather (this is its very style) in transforming things by exhibiting writings, genres, textual strata ... that have been repulsed, repressed, devalorized, minoritized, delegitimated, occulted by hegemonic canons ... From this point of view, deconstructive interpretation and writing would come along, without any soteriological mission, to 'save,' in some sense, lost heritages. (B, 821)

The de Man case offers certain critics an exemplary occasion for attacking what they take to be deconstruction, a word which is variously described in their discourse as a 'threat' or 'public enemy' (B, 825). The debate was therefore more concerned with the 'prestige of deconstruction' (B, 826), than the careful pursuit of justice vis-à-vis de Man.

3. It is possible to interpret de Man's apparent pro-Nazi sympathies as effects of Henrik de Man's political biography, as it is to see his rejection of political idealism as a product of his uncle's shattered utopianism. Though this assumption may be open to the charge of biographical reductionism, both Norris and Derrida establish a powerful case for its inclusion within the debate.

4. While Derrida adopts a logic of 'recurrent alternation', as evidenced by his frequent use of the 'on the one hand' and 'on the other hand', he clearly expresses distaste at reading de Man's articles. The *'massive, immediate, and dominant* effect of all of these texts', Derrida writes, 'is that of a *relatively* coherent ideological ensemble which, *most often and in a preponderant fashion,* conforms to official rhetoric, that of the occupation forces' (B, 822). The logic of 'recurrent alternation' that Derrida identifies is the 'equivocal structure of all the politico-philosophical discourses at play' (LSS, 601) in the de Man affair and, by implication, in language itself.

Let us look at Derrida's response to de Man in more detail. The title of Derrida's first essay – 'Like the Sound of the Sea Deep within a Shell: Paul de Man's War' – derives from one of de Man's own articles, first published in *Le Soir* in 1941. With striking irony, de Man saw little future for the articles and opinions to which he, then aged twenty-one years old, penned for the Belgium newspaper. Referring to Montherlant's *Solstice de juin* in one of his review articles, de Man compares the mood of indifference that greets him when he opens wartime newspapers and journals with the 'sound of the sea' that one hears in a seashell held close to the ear (LSS, 591). Evidently, the young de Man could not have been more wrong. Far from generating a mood of indifference, as he seemed to foresee, the newspaper reports of the discovery of his wartime articles were frequently harsh and quick to reach violent conclusions.

In the face of the ignorance and sensationalism evident in many of the journalistic commentaries on the events, Derrida counters with a patient and careful response based on extended research into de Man's activities. Derrida's discussion begins with extracts from an editorial published by de Man in the journal, *Les Cahiers du Libre Examen*, founded in 1937, where he had served first as a member of the editorial committee and then later as director. Derrida quotes two passages from the editorial in order to demonstrate the emergence of an aporetic logic, a logic which at once both reassures Derrida of de Man's pro-democratic sympathies *and* unsettles them.

In the first passage from February 1940, de Man refers to the 'commonplace' assumption that the decadent values of western civilization are 'crumbling' throughout Europe. Protecting these values is no longer a merely theoretical pursuit; it has become a necessity requiring appropriate tactics and strategy (LSS, 601). Derrida tries to establish a context for these remarks by referring to what he takes to be the pro-democratic sympathies of *Cahiers* in early 1940. Referring to another editorial dated April 1937, Derrida outlines that *Cahiers* had always presented itself as 'democratic' and 'antifascist'. In the above passage, Derrida argues that de Man takes 'sides *against* Germany and *for* democracy, for "the victory of the democracies" in a war defined as a "struggle ... against barbarity" ' (LSS, 600–1). While these references reassure Derrida about de Man's democratic sympathies, therefore immediately unsettling the accusations that simply identify his complicity with Nazism, Derrida also detected the source of such allegations in de Man's reference to western decadence. The existence of such an emphasis, Derrida argues, can occasionally lead to the restoration of totalitarianism. Nevertheless, Derrida's emphasis on the word *commonplace* complicates any simplified reading. This is strikingly evident in the passage from the *Cahiers* editorial, which describes the notion of the liberation of the individual as one that defines western ethical principles. If western nations differentiate themselves from other civilizations, it is precisely as a consequence of this concept that lies near the heart of all western thought (LSS, 602). For Derrida, this passage complicates the meaning of the word *commonplace* still further, thus confirming that the underlying strategy of the editorial is deeply ironic. By emphasizing the themes of democracy, the freedom of the individual and the notion that western civilization should be prevented from sliding into decadence, Derrida argues that the 'author of this editorial ... has no taste for simplification or received ideas, for commonplaces and easy consensus' (LSS, 602).

The mood of the second passage from the *Cahiers* editorial is similarly aporetic in character, Derrida argues. While resisting what de Man identifies as the urge to 'dangerously simplify' the editorial's position on the current conflict, he contends that it can be described as the west's 'struggle' against barbarity. Looking forward to the ultimate victory of the western democracies in this struggle, de Man argues that its success hinges on its ability to re-establish a European society that once again places the values that it 'cherishes' at its centre (LSS, 603). This passage sees de Man complicating any simple reading. The effect produced is paradoxical and ultimately aporetic.

Having established the existence of the logic of recurrent alternation that prevents de Man from simplifying his relation to National Socialism, Derrida turns to a number of other articles that were published several months after the *Cahiers* editorial. The theme of European unity cuts across all of de Man's articles. Following the invasion of France and Belgium de Man is preoccupied with how unity is to be determined after the victory of Germany. In other words, the unity of Europe can only be secured by a strong Germany, as it, unlike France, lies at the heart of the continent. De Man describes the emergence of German power and the realignment of European states as a revolution for which he sees a theoretical role for himself. Acting more as what Derrida describes as a 'chronicler-commentator' de Man argues that the fundamental question of European unity can only be approached from a '*quasi-theoretical* angle' (LSS, 610).

In order to continue his reading of de Man's aporetic logic, Derrida turns to his review article on Montherlant's *Le Solstice de juir*, published in November 1941. Derrida returns to the passage that includes the title of his essay in order to note the irony of de Man's attack on Montherlant's engagement with current affairs. While Montherlant predicts complete oblivion for the newspapers and journals that concern themselves with current affairs, de Man also applies this judgement to Montherlant's own reflections. Derrida reads de Man's criticism of Montherlant as well as other social commentators such as Chardonne and Brasillach as a deliberate step back from Nazi ideologues. While de Man insists on the 'riches of German culture' and on the fundamental role it ought to play in the destiny of Europe, Derrida argues that de Man's relationship with the priority accorded to Germany in the renaissance of Europe is double-edged and at least 'very debatable' (LSS, 613). As such, to Derrida's knowledge, de Man 'at no point ... name[s] Nazism, a fortiori in order to praise it' (LSS, 613). 'In all the texts I have been able to read', Derrida comments, 'and about which the least one can say is that they were turned in the direction of politics and current affairs, the word "Nazi," "Nazi party" appears only once or twice ... and then it does so in a neutral or informative mode' (LSS, 613).

Derrida's main point here relates to de Man's apparent defence of the moral and political implications of a writer's work. This is strikingly apparent in the case of Gide. De Man's defence of Gide from a purely literary perspective – which therefore eschews his low political credibility in occupied Belgium – is for Derrida a remarkable gesture. In fact Derrida interprets de Man's views as a precursor of Jean Paulhan's similar postwar rejection of the political trial of writers who were known to have collaborated. So, Derrida detects in de Man's work a resistance to simple forms of collaboration.

In the second main section Derrida turns to de Man's understanding of nationalism, and finds great evidence of his respect for German nationalism. This theme is particularly evident in de Man's article, 'Art as the Mirror of the Essence of Nations', where he argues that European states can only eradicate conflict and develop if they are led by a state that is conscious of its 'national grandeur' (LSS, 613). Nevertheless, it is evident that de Man supports the belief in the autonomous identity of Belgium, France and Germany. So while Derrida identifies de Man's understanding of the role of German culture in the formation of the new Europe, he is also aware of the attempt to preserve national identities. This is particularly evident in de Man's understanding of the role of France in 'Le Problème français: *Dieu est-il français*, de F. Sieburg', where he writes that the impetus for maintaining the grandeur of the European ideal is closely connected to the renewal of the 'French spirit' (LSS, 620). And this is particularly true also of de Man's attachment – as a Flemish writer – to Flemish culture in 'Le Destin de la Flandre', where he is concerned with resisting the blurring of national identities and preserving the 'profound originality' of Flemish culture (LSS, 620–1).

Derrida identifies a general law that underpins the functioning of de Man's articles. De Man's allegiance to Nazism, National Socialism and antisemitism is far from straight forward. In fact, the disjunctions and cautionary undertones of de Man's text resist any simple form of allegiance. For Derrida, de Man's articles are underpinned by a rhythm that disturbs univocity. The logic of recurrent alternation shows that 'de Man's discourse is constantly split, disjointed, engaged in incessant conflicts' such that 'all the propositions carry within themselves a counterproposition' (LSS, 607). The notion of recurrent alternation reiterates Derrida's understanding of the *double-bind*.

In the final section of Derrida's analysis he turns to consider the operation of this logic in the articles that have attracted the charge of antisemitism. Of all of the articles published by de Man between 1939 and 1943, there are two passages which have attracted most critical comment. In 'Like the Sound of the Sea Deep within a Shell', Derrida discusses the significance of the passage from 'Jews in Present-day

Literature' that I referred to in Chapter 2. Derrida's first reaction to this passage recognizes all the traits of 'an antisemitism that would have come close to urging exclusions, even the most sinister deportations' (LSS, 621). This passage precisely describes a mood of xenophobia and Derrida does not try to avoid its ramifications. In addition, de Man continues, Jewish writers have rightly remained as members of the second tier, having failed to exert any significant influence on literary history to date (LSS, 622–3). Faced with this passage Derrida does not exonerate de Man, as we will see some readers have alleged. On the contrary, he is clearly shocked 'in the face of the *unpardonable* violence of these sentences' (LSS, 623). Derrida responds, however, with the logic of the double-bind, which resists reducing de Man (or any author for that matter) to one text alone. Readers must be courageous enough, Derrida argues, to be just to these texts even in the face of 'their *dominant* effect' which unquestionably takes them in the 'direction of the worst' (LSS, 623).

Detecting a certain undercurrent of ironic detachment or mockery, Derrida interprets de Man's whole article as an indictment or 'uncompromising critique of "vulgar antisemitism" ' (LSS, 624) therefore taking on what Derrida identified in his *Cahiers* editorial as an opposition to the commonplace. De Man's condemnation of 'vulgar antisemitism' leaves the door open to two interpretations. On the one hand, 'To condemn vulgar antisemitism may leave one to understand that there is a distinguished antisemitism in whose name the vulgar variety is put down' (LSS, 624). On the other hand, 'to condemn "vulgar antisemitism," *especially if one makes no mention of the other kind*, is to condemn antisemitism itself *inasmuch as* it is vulgar, always and essentially vulgar' (LSS, 625). While de Man provides no further evidence of either of these interpretations, Derrida reads such an absence as the mark of de Man's ambiguity. For Derrida, the articles should be regarded as a condemnation of vulgar antisemitism in literature or in history. Derrida imagines that de Man's purpose was to treat Judaism from a literary point of view, in the context of a page in the newspaper that was devoted to other perspectives on this subject. In fact Derrida interprets de Man's relationship with the other articles that frame his text – especially the one next to it on Freud – as 'nonconformist' and as an example of the logic of the double-edge that I have previously identified. So Derrida is content to situate de Man's views in the context of a literary thesis rather than in relation to the wider themes of antisemitism. The main focus recontextualizes de Man's understanding of vulgar antisemitism and this is further underpinned, in Derrida's eyes, by an ironic use of the word vulgar – that he detects in his other article,

'Propos sur la vulgarité artistique' [Remarks on artistic vulgarity], and in the work of Henrik de Man – 'always in a fashion that cuts both ways' (LSS, 626).

In the four paragraphs of de Man's article that follow, which Derrida identifies as the centre of the article, not the 'slightest allusion to Jews or to antisemitism' can be found (LSS, 627). Rather they set out de Man's idea that the history of art and literature is uncontaminated by sociopolitical history. De Man reserves the word vulgar for those types of ideological criticism that seek to merge literature with sociopolitical and sociohistorical determinations. Derrida points out in fact that while today they would be regarded as an example of formalism, at that time they represented an 'anticonformist attack' (LSS, 628) on popular opinion. The main body of de Man's article evidences no connection with antisemitism, neither in relation to art in general nor to its specific literary examples. In fact de Man's anticonformism is particularly evident, Derrida continues, in his literary examples which include Gide, Hemingway, Lawrence and Kafka. For Derrida, then, de Man's nonconformism 'resinscribes all of these "accursed ones" in the then protective legitimacy of the cannon and in the great literary family' (LSS, 628). De Man's nonconformism in this section of the article – that is, his opposition to vulgar antisemitism and to antisemitism in general – is primarily concerned with his literary thesis. This posits that contemporary literature cannot be viewed as an 'isolated phenomenon' that was largely the product of the 'mentality of the 20s'; such a view would in fact be 'absurd' (LSS, 629). The implication is that de Man delimits the extent of Jewish influence on contemporary literature rather than engages in unacceptable and careless antisemitism.

This theme is continued, albeit in a rather limited fashion, in what Derrida refers to as the final and most disastrous paragraph of the entire article. Here de Man seemingly states his admiration for the qualities that he identifies with the 'Jewish spirit'. De Man's unwillingness to negate this thesis at least maintains the possibility that this is indeed what he meant to convey. De Man describes the Jews in stereotypical terms, noting their 'cerebralness' and their ability to absorb doctrines while preserving a 'certain coldness'; such qualities are precisely apposite for the 'lucid style' of analysis required of the novel (LSS, 622, 630). In the absence of words to the contrary, Derrida argues that these lines emphasize de Man's *positive* view of certain stereotypical Jewish traits:

> One can hardly believe one's eyes: would this mean that what he [de Man] prefers in the novel, 'the work of lucid analysis,' and in theory,

a 'certain coldness' of intelligence, correspond precisely to the qualities of the 'Jewish spirit'? And that the 'precious qualities' of the latter are indispensable to literature and theory? (LSS, 630)

In response to his own question, Derrida implies that this is indeed one possible interpretation. Placing the above quotation in the context of the final paragraph, Derrida acknowledges the re-emergence of de Man's reference to the Jewish problem that provides most cause for concern. Derrida remarks that these lines from de Man are the only ones that express such sentiments. In all of the articles that have come to light, Derrida writes, he has 'found no remark analogous or identical to this one' (LSS, 631). Still adopting a questioning attitude, Derrida argues that in order to understand these sentiments they have to be patiently recontextualized rather than hastily and crudely interpreted. Derrida ends his reading by opening up the future of the debate. It *will* be necessary to come to terms with the significance of de Man's seemingly contradictory attitudes in these articles; it *will* be necessary to understand de Man's praise for the Dreyfusard Charles Péguy; and it *will* be necessary to understand his reference to 'a Jewish colony isolated from Europe' in the context of similar notions about solving the Jewish problem. Noting that this article was published on 4 March 1941, Derrida ends his reading with the acknowledgement that de Man stopped contributing articles to *Le Soir* at the end of 1942, at the same time as Henrik de Man left Belgium and gave up 'all public responsibility' (LSS, 632).

In the final section of his essay, Derrida turns to the attack on deconstruction that lies behind the accusations levelled at de Man. The subtitle of the essay, 'Paul de Man's War', refers not only to the events of 1939–43 but also to the aggressive debate in the American academy. Though de Man is dead, Derrida argues that readers still have responsibilities and concerns toward him. Hence it is necessary when evaluating these articles to resist the simplistic idea that Paul de Man's views, political or otherwise, can be transparently skimmed off from the surface of his books without considering the ethico-political consequences: 'Our actions with regard to what remains to us of de Man will also have the value of an example, whether we like it or not' (LSS, 650–1). Derrida's wide-ranging responses to de Man's articles, based on his careful, patient and even-handed approach, underlines above all that there can be *'no question of dissimulating them or of participating in any kind of camouflage operation'* (LSS, 635). Derrida's initial response seeks to remain sensitive to the contradictory lessons of the exchanges, which have so far determined the debate, and to alert critics to the difficulty of deciphering meaning in a monological fashion. It is simply not feasible to conclude a reading that must remain open and as differentiated as possible. In contradistinction to many of de Man's severest readers, Derrida attempts to preserve a certain openness with regard to the discussion – a stance that recognizes the continuing relevance of fresh evidence. Derrida's response to Paul de Man *cannot* be described as a simple form of defence or condemnation, as other contributors to the debate would have wished.

In 1989 *Critical Inquiry* published six responses to Derrida's essay on the discovery of de Man's wartime writings and the reaction they caused in the American academy. I will briefly examine some of the main arguments in the light of my commentary on 'Like the Sound of the Sea Deep within a Shell', before moving onto consider Derrida's more general meditation on the interpretative afterlife of publications in 'Biodegradables'.

Of the six articles, five clearly opposed Derrida's reading of de Man, describing it in terms of an apologia for the Yale critic's obvious antisemitic and fascist sympathies. Only Jonathan Culler's essay, ' "Paul de Man's War" and the Aesthetic Ideology', supports the drift of Derrida's reading. Nevertheless, it is worth recognizing the salient points of the essays written by Apostolidès, Brenkman and Law, Holdheim, Perloff, and Wiener, all of which can be broadly grouped together, before considering Culler in more detail.

It must be said at the outset that de Man's antisemitic comments in 'Jews in Contemporary Literature', which Derrida to his credit singles out for special attention, irrefutably links the young de Man with a sympathetic attitude towards Nazi ideology. These commentators are mistaken, however, if they believe that Derrida is trying to condone or excuse de Man. Their other arguments are enmeshed in a web of resistances and contradictions, which, at the very least, confirm that de Man was, as Norris argues, 'not wholly given over at any one time to the purposes of cultural propaganda' (Norris, 1988, 189).

Nevertheless, in 'Resetting the Agenda' John and Jules Brenkman and David Law dispute all of Derrida's main arguments. They challenge the idea that there is an absolute break that 'separates the later from the earlier de Man' (Brenkman, Brenkman and Law, 1989, 804); and that de Man's texts are deliberately written in an ironic mode, so that while he appears to be 'firmly committed to fascist ideology' he also 'regularly distanced himself from that ideology and even undermined its meanings' (1989, 804). The latter point is also made by Peloff, who takes issue with Derrida's insistence on the logic of recurrent alternation. For Perloff, Derrida's emphasis on the idea that de Man terminated his work for *Le Soir* at the end of 1942 and that his discourse is deliberately double edged cannot be sustained. According to Perloff censorship by the Nazis was not imposed on literary as opposed to political columns until at least August 1942. There was no need for de Man to adopt a logic of recurrent alternation as Derrida argues. This view is also advanced by Holdheim, who interprets this logic more as a sign of 'ad hoc reservations or inconsistencies, such as one would expect from a somewhat immature and occasionally (indeed) ambivalent author, writing in huge generalities under the pressure of imminent deadlines. They certainly do not add up to a basic polar opposition of any kind' (Holdheim, 1989, 787).

While I have argued that Derrida's arguments are persuasive, if only because those of de Man's critics show signs of haste and lack of rigour, it is difficult to decide if they are entirely accurate. The same applies to Holdheim's rejection of Derrida's argument that de Man mounts an anticonformist attack on existing Nazi ideology and Wiener's rejection of Derrida's notion that de Man critiques 'vulgar antisemitism' and, by implication, all forms of antisemitism (Wiener, 1989, 802). Derrida's reading of de Man offers sufficient *resistance* to the monadic reading of his opponents to merit a more thorough examination of all of the texts that impinge on the case. At the very least, Derrida introduces a measure of reasonable doubt vis-à-vis the accusations of those critics who condemn de Man outright. As Culler persuasively identifies, Derrida's argument is that 'whatever de Man's intentions, he is unable to control the resonances of the articles he publishe[d]' between 1940 and 1943 (Culler, 1989, 778). His texts generate enough evidence to condemn him – as the five respondents show – but they also provoke Derrida's patient and careful teasing out of resistances to monadic readings of this kind. Derrida's emphasis on de Man's relative immaturity is also a point which should not readily be dismissed; de Man wrote articles for *Le Soir* when he was between twenty and twenty-two years of age. What is really at issue here is the resonance of deconstruction; here at least it *is* possible to determine the accuracy of the arguments advanced.

It is in relation to the meaning of deconstruction that it is possible to give unequivocal support to Derrida's argument. Near the centre of the debate stands an interpretation of deconstruction that is wholly unsupportable. Around this issue, a number of points converge: deconstruction is described as ahistorical. Apostolidès, for example, argues that 'It is difficult to excuse ... [de Man's] clear affiliation with the anti-Semitic collaborators who took over *Le Soir* at this point' (Apostolidès, 1989, 766), and directly relates this point to deconstruction's profound antipathy to history: 'What is indeed striking in deconstruction is that it escapes confrontation with historical development ... [and] that this method rarely confronts historicity' (1989, 766). As has already been established in my reading of Habermas (1987), deconstruction is profoundly historical, and there are no grounds for levelling accusations of this type. Similar responses apply to the idea that deconstruction rejects historical context, withdraws from political analysis, or undermines the grounds of rationality to absolutely no effect.

Culler's article, ' "Paul de Man's War" and the Aesthetic Ideology', merits longer consideration as it returns to my argument about de Man's politics in Chapter 2. Culler refers to the antisemitic elements in the articles mentioned by Derrida as an 'aberration' (Culler, 1989, 780). 'The other articles', he writes:

> for *Le Soir*, though written in a context that would have encouraged any anti-Semitism, bear no traces of such views, although they do repeatedly speak of national traditions, national characters, national habits of mind. (1989, 780)

But it is de Man's wartime writings, Culler argues, that 'give a new dimension to much of de Man's work in America, helping one to understand more plainly what is implied by his critique of the aesthetic ideology' (1989, 780). To support this view, Culler quotes from Alice Yaeger Kaplan's study of fascism and her understanding of the fascist conception of the state. Kaplan argues that fascism articulated a poetic language of self-presence that sought to reduce the distance between the people and the state, and challenged the modern experience of alienation and fragmentation. Culler interprets the political context which Kaplan establishes as adding a 'new dimension to de Man's attempt – from the early critiques of Heidegger to his late critiques of phenomenality – to undo totalizing metaphors, myths of immediacy, organic unity, and presence, and to combat their fascinations' (1989, 781). In these late essays, de Man finds in 'Kant's work on the aesthetic a critique of the ideology of the aesthetic developed, for instance, by Schiller and applied, or misapplied, both in humanistic conceptions of aesthetic education and in fascist conceptions of politics as an aesthetic project' (1989, 781). Whereas aesthetic objects classically establish a union between traditional antinomies such as language and thing, subject and object, de Man conceived of literature's reliance on figurative language as a way of demystifying such unities:

> Literature ... offer[s] evidence of the autonomous potential of language, of the uncontrollable figural basis of forms, which cannot therefore serve as the basis of reliable cognition, or, as de Man

argues ... allegorically expose the violence that lies hidden behind the aesthetic and makes aesthetic education possible. (1989, 782)

This is where the importance of de Man's wartime writings is most powerfully felt:

> The fact that de Man's wartime juvenilia had themselves on occasion exhibited an inclination to idealize the emergence of the German nation in aesthetic terms gives special pertinence to his demonstration that the most insightful literary and philosophical texts of the tradition expose the unwarranted violence required to fuse form and idea, cognition and performance. (1989, 783)

De Man's use of deconstruction, as Derrida argues at the end of 'Like the Sound of the Sea', provides further evidence of his commitment to deconstruct oppositions that, in the name of unity, purity and hierarchy, attempt to eliminate difference. So rather than see de Man's apparent silence on his wartime writings as a strategy of evasion, it is necessary to understand that his later essays are attempts to come to terms with the dangerous political potential of an aesthetic ideology that conjoined language, culture and national destiny.

The remains of the proper name

In Derrida's second response to the debate about de Man's articles, 'Biodegradables', he considers the way future readers are likely to represent the events by turning to embrace a number of questions about inheritance, translation and the nature of a literary or philosophical archive. Derrida had already approached this theme in 'Like the Sound of the Sea Deep within a Shell', through his reference to Montherlant's description of the biodegradability of wartime newspaper reports. In 'Biodegradables' Derrida takes up this latter theme by speculating upon the fate of a young librarian or researcher who is handed the task of summarizing the events of the de Man affair at some point in the future. Contemplating such a task, Derrida is not merely concerned with reiterating what he stated in 'Paul de Man's War', but also, and more importantly, with describing similarities between the 'figure of the biodegradable' and the interpretative 'afterlife' of publications. 'Preliminary question', Derrida writes near the beginning:

> Can one say, figuratively, that a 'publication' is biodegradable and distinguish here the degrees of degradation, the rhythms, the laws, the

aleatory factors, the detours and the disguises, the transmutations, the cycles of recycling? Can one transpose onto 'culture' the vocabulary of 'natural waste treatment' – recycling, ecosystems, and so on – along the whole legislative apparatus that regulates the 'environment' in our societies? (B, 813–14)

The biodegradable is of course not a natural thing, in fact, as Derrida points out, the word is used to describe 'an artificial product, most often an industrial product, whenever it lets itself be decomposed by micro-organisms' (B, 813). It is not a thing – something which remains present to itself and unchanging through time – on the contrary, it is an 'essentially decomposable thing, destined to pass away, to lose its identity as a thing and to become again a non-thing' (B, 813). Derrida answers his initial question in the affirmative and sets about relating the figure of biodegradability to a number of the principal themes of his previous work, particularly the notion of the double-bind and its implications for the legacy of a proper name. The contaminated 'pluri-etymology' (B, 815) of the word, biodegradable, itself 'a modern and unstable graft of Greek and Latin', exemplifies Derrida's concerns with the relationship between the proper name and the problem of translation:

> this parasitic nonbelonging and this character of artificial synthesis that render the word less biodegradable than some other word; because it does not belong to the organic compost of a single natural language, this strange thing may be seen to float on the surface of culture like the wastes whose survival rivals that of the masterpieces of our culture and the monuments that we promise to eternity. (B, 815)

Applied to the domain of cultural production, Derrida outlines the double-bind of the biodegradable. *On the one hand*, a biodegradable text would be 'assimilated ... by a culture that it nourishes, enriches, irrigates, even fecundates but on the condition that it lose its identity, its figure, or its singular signature, its proper name' (B, 824). *On the other hand*, the biodegradable poses the question of *resistance* to assimilation: 'Is it not the case that, as "nonbiodegradable," the singularity of a work resists, does not let itself be assimilated, but stays on the surface and survives like an indestructible artefact' (B, 824). This double-bind effectively restates the problematic of translation and the proper name function which Derrida first outlined in 'Living On: Border Lines' and then subsequently in 'Des Tours de Babel'. There is a requirement to understand the untranslatability or unreadability of publications; the proper name function lies beyond the text and beyond the corruption of translation as a process of transformation. There is also a duty to translate and to read a text; the proper name offers itself to be read, therefore risking its own inevitable reduction and corruption. Derrida attempts, then, to use this understanding of the double movement of the figure of the biodegradable, of resistance *and* assimilation, as a way of explaining the interpretive afterlife of published works. 'What is it in a "great" work', Derrida asks:

> let's say of Plato, Shakespeare, Hugo, Mallarmé, James, Joyce, Kafka, Heidegger, Benjamin, Blanchot, Celan, that resists erosion? What is it that, far from being exhausted in amnesia, increases its reserve to the very extent to which one draws from it, as if expenditure augmented the capital? This very thing, this singular event that, enriching the meaning and accumulating memory, is nevertheless not to be reduced to a totality or that always exceeds interpretation. (B, 845)

The great works have been able to survive successive waves of interpretation because they have been able to resist decades, or even centuries, of interpretation, in the case of Shakespeare. The proper name like the text, or the fragment from the historical archive, loses its singularity but:

> must also resist it, contest it, question and criticize it enough (dare I say deconstruct it?) and thus it must not be assimilable ([bio]degradable, if you like). Or at least, it must be assimilated as inassimilable, kept in reserve, unforgettable because irreceivable, capable of inducing meaning without being exhausted by meaning, incomprehensibly elliptical, secret. (B, 845)

Derrida's analysis of the biodegradable allows him to discuss the complex singularity of an intellectual legacy. In the context of the debate about de Man's wartime articles, it allows Derrida to adopt a historical timescale that is sorely missing from the hurried responses of the other main contributors.

Derrida's response to the allegations that surrounded de Man in 'Like the Sound of the Sea Deep within a Shell' and 'Biodegradables' reiterates his insistence that deconstruction is a critique of aesthetic ideology. Both of Derrida's responses are admirable in that they attempt to condemn those passages that require condemnation while also keeping open the possibility of an incalculable future for the debate about de Man.

The articles written by de Man that are marked by antisemitic sentiments are different in kind to the rigorous scholarly essays he produced during his later academic career. One can have understood little about deconstruction – either in terms of the form it takes in Derrida or in the postwar work of de Man – if one fails to see it as a powerful and interminable critique of the misguided philosophy that led to German National Socialism.

By way of a conclusion to this chapter I intend to examine Michael B. Naas's essay on Derrida's critique of the political example – an idea that emerges from his discussion of the future of European identity in *The Other Heading*. Derrida's concern with the simultaneous singularity and commonalty of European identity and his thinking of democracy will serve as a preface to the discussion of the promise of democracy and the New International in the next chapter. In the context of this chapter, however, *The Other Heading* restates Derrida's detailed rejection of the universality of European culture, a discourse which as he shows has been powerfully in evidence in a number of European thinkers, from Hegel, Husserl and Valéry, to Heidegger and the young de Man. This theme was evident in Derrida's reading of de Man's 'L'Exposition "Histoire d'Allemagne" au Cinquantenaire' published in *Le Soir* in 1942, in which he focused on the *exemplary* place of German culture. In *The Other Heading* Derrida reiterates the connection between deconstruction and the attempt to remain faithful to the ideal of enlightenment rationality. He establishes that the ethical relation that underpins deconstruction's notion of identity is profoundly incompatible with de Man's comments on European, and specifically German, exemplarity.

The Other Heading

Published in 1992, *The Other Heading* consists of two articles, 'The Other Heading: Memories, Responses, and Responsibilities', and an interview, 'Call it a Day for Democracy', and marks Derrida's response to the debate about European integration. Derrida situates this debate in its historical context, relating it to the tremor that is shaking Central and Eastern Europe in the aftermath of the events of 1989. These events are grouped 'under the very problematic names *perestroika, democratization, reunification*' (OH, 19), as well as the consolidation of the market economy and political and economic liberalisms. Derrida's main target is the discourse of European universalism that continues to permeate contemporary discussions of Europe, whether in the form of official documents from the French government or Francis Fukuyama's end-of-history thesis.

As an example of this discourse, Derrida quotes from the then President of France, François Mitterrand, who declared that the debate about the future of Europe showed that, historically and geographically, it is returning home. Derrida also quotes from an official document from France's State Secretary on International Cultural Relations about the centrality of France to the development of the European Community, especially to its concept of solidarity. In both instances Derrida singles out the idea that France should play an avant-garde role in promoting European self-consciousness and integration. This exemplary logic makes France a safe-guard of European culture and the European spirit. The logic of these passages is indicative of a discourse that has a rich resonance in western philosophy:

> I note only that from Hegel to Valéry, from Husserl to Heidegger, in spite of all the differences that distinguish these great examples from each other ... this *traditional* discourse is *already* a discourse of the *modern* world ... This old discourse about Europe, a discourse at once exemplary and exemplarist, is already a *traditional discourse of modernity.* (OH, 27–8)

As Derrida's quotation from Mitterrand indicated, this '*traditional discourse of modernity*' is alive and well in modern Europe. In order to develop further historical parallels, Derrida focuses in particular on the existence of this theme in the work of Paul Valéry.

Valéry was not only a European intellectual but a Mediterranean spirit who made the characteristics of the Mediterranean basin into an exemplary form for a future European identity. As Naas argues, Valéry attempts to 'articulate a logic whereby the example or exemplar would become a universal heading for all the nations or peoples of the world' (OH, xxvi). Derrida deliberately uses the word heading in his title to allude to Plato's *Republic* where a political state is identified as a ship. This allusion also animates Valéry's idea that Europe determines the universal heading of mankind. In 'The European', for example, Valéry advances European culture as a universal culture. Out of all of the achievements of mankind, Valéry contends, the most significant have been the work of European civilization and the spirit of European man in particular. In another of Valéry's essays from *History and Politics* the same trend is evident. Here, however, he is more specific in that he identifies the exemplary place of French thinkers as 'men of universality'.

Derrida's point is to contrast the singularity of two historical contexts. Valéry's essays on European exemplarity are therefore compared with the French government's documents, and more generally with the mood of contemporary Europe on the verge of realignment. Derrida describes an 'imminence whose repetition we seem to be living, but whose irreducible singularity we should now, in an even more imperative way, recover from against the backdrop of analogy and resemblance' (OH, 61). For Valéry – as for the young de Man – the end of 1939 seemed to mark a 'tremor that was not only going to reduce to rubble ... what was called Europe. It was also going to destroy Europe in the name of an idea of Europe, of a young Europe that attempted to assure its hegemony' (OH, 62). While what followed was the victory of the western democracies, the victory over Nazism installed another conception of Europe which in turn was based on a 'succession of exclusions, annexations ... exterminations' and the 'quasi-naturalization of borders' (OH, 62). With the destruction of the Berlin Wall and the democratic revolutions in Eastern Europe, there is the 'same feeling of imminence, of hope and of danger, of anxiety before the possibility of other wars with unknown forms, the return to old forms of religious fanaticism, nationalism, or racism' (OH, 63). The post-1989 order was beset by the 'greatest uncertainty concerning the borders of Europe itself', especially its 'geographico-political' and spiritual borders (OH, 63).

Naas argues that *The Other Heading* 'raise[s] the question of politics from within a coherent and consistent critique of the logic of the example' (OH, xv), describing a constant coupling of politics and the example in Derrida's work that is evident in 'his persistent questioning of the relationship between nationalism and philosophical nationality, between national and supranational identity and the logic of identity itself' (OH, xviii). Rather than being simply one example among others, the discourse of European exemplarity is linked with Derrida's early resistance to western metaphysics and ethnocentrism in *Of Grammatology*. While Naas's thesis should be familiar by now, he quotes Derrida's understanding of the tension between universality and singularity from the 'Exergue' to *Of Grammatology*. Writing about the exemplary status that he attributes to his reading of Rousseau, Derrida indicates that: 'This is the moment, as it were, of the example, although strictly speaking, that notion is not acceptable within my argument' (OG, lxxxix). Derrida's recurrent reference to the tension between singularity and generality is directly concerned with responding to the west's 'political thinking of spirit and capital [that] has always depended upon or entailed a mere mentioning and mere use of examples' (OH, xxiii).

The point of Derrida's comparison between Valéry and contemporary Europe is to consider the question of European identity. How will it be possible to preserve the singularity of European nations *and* negotiate the consequences of the much-vaunted idea of European integration? The notion of identity that emerges in response to these questions reiterates Derrida's understanding of the repetition of sameness and the interruption of alterity: '*what is proper to a culture*', Derrida writes, '*is to not be identical to itself*' (OH, 9). Hence Derrida describes the 'proper name effect' in terms of the law of differance:

> there is no self-relation, no relation to oneself, no identification with oneself, without a culture, but a culture of oneself *as* a culture *of* the other, a culture of the double genitive and of the *difference to oneself.* (OH, 10)

Derrida contrasts his notion of identity as 'difference-to-oneself' with the Heideggerian idea that difference is '*gathered*' (OH, 11). According to Derrida the problematic that faces contemporary Europe is this: ' "How can a European cultural identity" respond, and in a responsible way – responsible for itself, for the other, and before the other – to the double question of *le capital*, of capital, and of *la capitale*, of the capital?' (OH, 16). The purpose behind Derrida's word play in this passage is to indicate the possibility of a different (or 'other') heading for Europe: 'there is another heading, the heading being not only ours but the other, not only that which we identify, calculate, and decide upon, but the *heading of the other*, before which we must respond, and which we must *remember, of which* we must *remind ourselves*' (OH, 15). Unlike Valéry, Derrida is concerned with maintaining an excess or outside in the face of this totalizing concept of European universality. This excess relates to the possibility of a completely other future: 'to the to-come [*à-venir*] of the *event*, to that which *comes* [*vient*], which comes perhaps and perhaps comes from a completely other shore' (OH, 69).

In order to achieve a different direction, Derrida reiterates the familiar logic of the *double-bind* – of repetition and alterity – confirming Beardsworth's emphasis on the contradictory logic of the aporia. 'I will ... venture to say', Derrida writes, 'that ethics, politics, and responsibility, *if there are any*, will only ever have begun with the experience and experiment of the aporia' (OH, 41). The future 'should be anticipated *as* the unforeseeable, the *unanticipatable*, the non-masterable, non-identifiable, in short, as that of which one does not yet have a memory' (OH, 18). In contrast, Derrida insists that those whose task it is to form the direction of the new Europe should be 'suspicious of *both* repetitive memory *and* the completely other of the absolutely new; of *both* anamnestic capitalization *and* the amnesic exposure to what would no longer be identifiable at all' (OH, 19). Derrida's task is to advance an idea of European intellectuals as the:

> guardians of an idea of Europe, of a difference of Europe, *but* of a Europe that consists precisely in not closing itself off in its own identity and in advancing itself in an exemplary way toward what it is not, toward the other heading or the heading of the other ... (OH, 29)

This double injunction is predicated on the aporia of time and the call toward the other that Derrida believes is taking place now.

Faced with these two imperatives, Derrida is concerned with outlining a notion of responsibility, which attempts to '*invent* gestures, discourses, politico-institutional practices that inscribe the alliance of these two imperatives, of these two promises or contracts: the capital and the acapital, the other of the capital' (OH, 44). Derrida outlines the need for a 'strategy that tries to organize cultural identity around a capital that is all the more powerful for being mobile, that is, European in a hyper- or supra-national sense' (OH, 47). He imagines a self-differentiating European identity that is national *and* supra-national, in which citizens are 'more national for being European ... [and] all the more European for being trans-European and international' (OH, 48).

Derrida's response reiterates the need for a vigilant attitude in the face of the best intentioned of European projects that are founded on democracy and tolerance, wherever they occur, whether in newspapers, magazines, or the space of the university. Derrida is intent on disrupting the apparent transparency and naturalness of the cultural discourse of European integration. While he invokes the logic of the example in Valéry and Husserl, he is also concerned with displacing that logic by identifying the singularity of the context that frames their work.

Having addressed the theme of a European capital city – *la capital* – Derrida turns to the need for a new thinking of *le capital*, to the question of what links capital to the theme of European identity. In a speculative vein, Derrida argues that the new European identity that he imagines should 'invent another way of reading and analyzing *Capital*, both Marx's book and capital in general' (OH, 54). Derrida's return to Marx is based on a resistance to the totalitarian dogmatism or Marxist intimidation and the counter-dogmatism that attempts to ban the use of the word capital. In passages of this kind it is possible to see the intellectual framework of *Specters of Marx* taking shape, especially in Derrida's attempt to respond in a responsible way to the 'neo-capitalist exploitation of the breakdown of an anti-capitalist dogmatism' (OH, 57).

In the closing sections of *The Other Heading*, Derrida clarifies the ethico-political imperatives behind his attempt to discern *another* heading for Europe's notion of identity. Bearing in mind Derrida's critique of exemplarity, each of the examples that he advances – whether it relates to his notion of democracy or duty – simultaneously disrupts its exemplary status. Derrida identifies a notion of *duty* and *responsibility* that 'recall[s] what has been promised under the name Europe, to re-identify Europe' (OH, 76). This concept of *duty* means opening Europe 'onto that which is not, never was, and never will be Europe' (OH, 77) and 'welcoming foreigners in order not only to integrate them but to recognize and accept their alterity' (OH, 77). Hence duty is linked to the respect for 'differences, idioms, minorities, singularities' (OH, 78), and also at the same time, for 'the universality of formal law, the desire for translation, agreement and univocity, the law of the majority, opposition to racism, nationalism, and xenophobia' (OH, 78). *Duty* is linked to the recurrent need for critical or deconstructive thinking. This indebtedness to a notion of deconstruction as a form of interminable critique is especially evident in the case of Marxism. 'The *same duty*', Derrida writes:

> dictates *criticizing* ... a totalitarian dogmatism that, under the pretense of putting an end to capital, destroyed democracy and the European heritage. But it also dictates criticizing a religion of capital that institutes its dogmatism under new guises ... (OH, 77)

This double critique is conjoined to a particular understanding of democracy and international law that depends on an incalculable future:

> The *same duty* dictates assuming the European, and *uniquely* European, heritage of an idea of democracy ... something that remains to be thought and *to come* [*à venir*]: not something that is certain to happen tomorrow, not the democracy (national or international, state or trans-state) of the *future*, but a democracy that must have the structure of a promise – *and thus of a memory of that which carries the future, the to-come, here and now.* (OH, 78)

In 'Call It a Day for Democracy' the double imperative of deconstruction is linked to the 'responsibility to think through the axioms or foundations of democracy ... [and to] analyze unrelentingly its historical determinations'

(OH, 95). This 'double contradictory imperative' means that Derrida 'remain[s] faithful to the ideal of the Enlightenment, the *Aufklärung*, the *Illuminismo*, while yet acknowledging its limits, in order to work on the Enlightenment of this time' (OH, 79). Derrida reiterates the conclusion of 'The Principle of Reason' and 'Of an Apocalyptic Tone Recently Adopted in Philosophy' in that he is concerned with 'tolerating and respecting all that is not placed under the authority of reason' (OH, 78). This double duty both attempts to 'think reason and the history of reason' while also at the same time thinking what 'necessarily exceed[s] its order, without becoming, simply because of this, irrational, and much less irrationalist' (OH, 79).

Derrida's discussion of the discourse of European exemplarity indicates how deconstruction intervenes to disrupt the functioning of an exclusionary logic. The ethics of the *other* heading is precisely what the young de Man forgot when he argued that western civilization, its history and continued existence, relies on the 'people who are its center' (LSS, 609). Nevertheless, in his postwar work de Man's deconstruction of aesthetic ideology *is* based on such an understanding. While de Man could have provided more direct evidence of his intellectual opposition to totalitarian forms of thought, the reaction to the discovery of his articles indicates the immense personal risk that he would have faced had he done so. While this does not exonerate de Man – as Derrida has argued, it is neither a case of simply exonerating nor simply condemning de Man – it does perhaps grant us an insight into the personal motives that lay behind his complex appropriation of deconstructive thinking. In Derrida's hands, deconstruction has always been advanced as a critique of totalizing forms of thought. Further evidence of this emerges in Derrida's long-awaited engagement with the inheritance of Marx in *Specters of Marx*.

6
Maintaining the Presence of Marx: Marxism and Deconstruction

In reply to Houdebine's and Scarpetta's careful questioning in *Positions* Derrida argued that his encounter with Marx and the 'theoretical elaboration' (POS, 62) constantly required of him remained 'still to come' and could not 'be immediately given' (POS, 63). In order to understand Derrida's attitude to Marxism, his response must be set in the context of a broader political realignment that took place among postwar intellectuals on the French left. In the decades that followed May 1968 French intellectuals from Lyotard to Debray rejected the main theoretical supports of Marxism. In 1976 the French Communist Party conformed to the trend by renouncing its belief in the dictatorship of the proletariat and committed itself to the democratic road to socialism. The rise of the 'New Philosophers' in the late 1970s and the infamous 'silence of the intellectuals' in 1981 added to the demise of the revolutionary left in the French academy.

While Derrida's engagement with these developments was not immediately apparent in his work, his sympathetic yet critical attitude to the Marxist tradition was. As leading intellectuals renounced their belief in revolutionary transformation, the Leninist conception of the working class and the Sartrean ideal of the engaged intellectual, Derrida publicly expressed his sympathy with Marxism in a paper presented at the Cerisy colloquium on 'The Ends of Man' in 1980. Derrida spoke clearly about the significance of his 'tormented silence' on Marx, maintaining once more, as Nancy Fraser argues, that 'he had deliberately not produced a discourse against revolution or Marxism in order to avoid contributing to the "anti-Marxist concert" of the *circa* 1968 period' (Fraser, 1984, 133). Derrida said that he 'did not and *does* not want to weaken "what Marxism and the proletariat can constitute as a force in France" ' and that he had adopted a 'complex', 'encumbered' strategy which staked out a series of 'virtual differences or divergences' from the Marxist 'revolutionary project' (1984, 133). His apparent silence, Derrida stressed, was not to be understood as a neutral response to Marxism, but rather as a 'perceptible political gesture' (1984, 134).

The publication of Alan Bass's English translation of *Positions* in 1981 added fresh momentum to the reception of Derrida's work. Critical readers such as Eagleton and Said, however, were not slow to describe Derrida's response to his Marxist interlocutors as evasive or to invent a range of political implications for deconstruction that in time would be shown to be sharply at odds with Derrida's resistance to the Haby Reform, his essays on apartheid and nuclear weapons, and his thinking of the principle of reason, law and justice. Such readers promptly dismissed deconstruction as the latest form of 'textual idealism', as a 'liberalism without a subject' or as an example of 'postmodern irrationalism' (Eagleton, 1981, 138). While those on the left derided deconstruction's neoconservative politics, those on the right attacked it as a product of the late 1960s, focusing on its relentlessly negative implications for institutions of higher education and canonical texts. In both cases they failed to contextualize Derrida's resistance to the metaphysical aspects of Marxism vis-à-vis its decline among a generation of French intellectuals, and their rejection of its models of social and political analysis and transformation.

With the publication of *Specters of Marx* in 1994 Derrida presented his clearest understanding of deconstruction's implications for Marxism. The title fastens onto the first noun of the *Communist Manifesto* – 'A *specter* is haunting Europe' – in order to reinvoke the revolutionary inheritance of Marx at a time when 'so many raised voices ... are attempting to conjure [it] away' (SM, 96). Echoing Michael Ryan's (1982) sympathetic discussion of deconstruction as a type of open or critical Marxism, Derrida outlines how Marx called for the transformation of his own theses. The development of his own thinking, Derrida explains, owes a *debt* to a 'certain *spirit* of Marx' which means that 'deconstruction would have been impossible and unthinkable in a pre-Marxist space' (SM, 92). 'Deconstruction', Derrida writes, 'has never had any sense or interest, in my view at least, except as a radicalization, which is to say also *in the tradition* of a certain Marxism ...' (SM, 92). The disappearance of the 'dogma machine' and the Marxist ideological apparatuses provides Derrida with an opportunity to reassess the Marxist inheritance. Describing the need to read and reread Marx as a responsibility for contemporary scholars, Derrida strikingly underlines the point that there will be no future 'without Marx, without the memory and the inheritance of Marx' (SM, 13). Arguing in opposition to Francis Fukuyama's 'end of history' thesis that Marx's texts 'live on' and continue to engage the responsible reader in critical exegesis, Derrida reiterates the requirement to deal justly with an intellectual inheritance. This process of reading justly is dependent on the injunction to choose by filtering, sifting and critizing the corpus of works:

> 'One must' means *one must* filter, sift, criticize, one must sort out several different possibles that inhabit the same injunction. And inhabit it in a contradictory fashion around a secret. If the readability of a legacy were given, natural, transparent, univocal, if it did not call for and at the same time defy interpretation, we would never have anything to inherit from it ... (SM, 16)

Reiterating one of the main questions of 'Biodegradables' Derrida asks: How is it possible to do *justice* to an inheritance? Though it is possible to see the seeds of Derrida's response to this question in his discussion of de Man in 'Like the Sound of the Sea Deep within a Shell', here the question of justice is related to the differential logic of spectrality. While Derrida's complex reading of *The German Ideology* identifies Marx's attempt to exorcize the logic of spectrality, Derrida shows how his thinking is at the same time intimately associated with it. Derrida is able to reject Marx's notion of the end of the political, a notion that depends on the end of conflict after the final victory of communism, and to outline a conception of the political that is based on spectrality. The logic of hauntology or spectrality allows Derrida to play on the similar sounding French word *ontologie* rather like he did with *difference* and *differance*, and to remain faithful to a *certain* spirit of Marx whose untimely spectres can always return to haunt the metaphysical conception of time or politics. Spectrality echoes with allusions to Derrida's discussion of the discourse of European exemplarity in *The Other Heading* and is the basis of the link he establishes between European identity and the 'promise of democracy'.

Having already traced a number of aspects of the debate about Marxism and deconstruction in the previous chapters, this section will focus in particular on Derrida's Levinisian understanding of the law and justice in 'Before the Law' (1992) and 'Force of Law: the "Mystical Foundation of Authority" ' (1992). This understanding will be shown to provide the key to comprehending Derrida's connection between the 'aporia of time' and a 'democracy to come' in *Specters of Marx*.

Spectrality

Spectrality is one of the main organizing principles of Derrida's notion of inheritance and indebtedness in *Specters of Marx* (Kamuf,

2005; Wolfreys, 2004). At the literal level of the text, spectrality emerges from Derrida's renarration of the murder of Hamlet's father. By overlaying his text with Shakespeare's *Hamlet* Derrida dramatizes the haunting of Fukuyama's eschatological discourse by the spectre of Marx. Derrida compares Fukuyama's notion of a post-Cold War Europe that has banished Marxism to the rotten state that prevailed after the death of Hamlet's father. Consequently, the reappearance of the ghost of Hamlet's father on the battlements of Elsinore Castle is likened to the haunting of Europe by Marx's ghost.

On another level, Derrida identifies himself with Hamlet's cry, 'The time is out of joint. O cursèd spite,/That ever I was born to set it right!' (SM, 20–1). Hamlet curses his destiny, Derrida argues, as fate leads him to inherit a situation that he must put in order. Similarly, Derrida implies that deconstructionists are best placed to deal with the spirit of the Marxist inheritance. In the apparent absence of political conflict that has settled after the death of Hamlet's father or, by analogy, in contemporary Europe after the fall of the Berlin Wall, Derrida's intervention emphasizes that it is necessary to deal with the Marxist inheritance now – the ghost of a certain spirit of Marxism – when so many raised voices are denying the very possibility of a new politics, least of all a revolutionary one. While Derrida self-reflexively identifies with Hamlet by voicing the accusations of procrastination and paralysis that have frequently been aimed at his own response to Marx, he also compares himself to Horatio, who is confronted with the ghost of Hamlet's father. Derrida quotes Marcellus's plea: 'Thou art a Scholler; speake to *it* Horatio ... Question it' (SM, 175). Moreover, Derrida speculates that what he calls the 'scholar of the future' or 'intellectual of tomorrow' (SM, 176) should be defined by his ability to speak with spectres, or 'to give them back speech' and thereby to challenge the metaphysical distinction between the real and the unreal effectively.

In relation to Marx's texts the theme of spectrality is more complex. Derrida identifies that Marx both recognizes the existence of spectrality and attempts to exorcize it, therefore falling back upon a 'pre-deconstructive' ontology of presence:

> On the one hand, Marx insists on respecting the originality and the proper efficacity, the autonomization and automatization of ideality as finite-infinite processes of difference ... But, on the other hand ... Marx continues to want to ground his critique or his exorcism of the spectral simulacrum in an ontology. It is a – critical, but pre-deconstructive – ontology of presence as actual reality and as objectivity. (SM, 170)

By the title, 'Specters of Marx', Derrida writes that he 'will name from now on certain figures whose coming Marx will have been the first to apprehend, sometimes to describe. Those that herald the best and whose event he will have greeted, those that arise from or threaten the worst, whose testimony he will have rejected' (SM, 98–9). From the first noun of the *Manifesto* – 'A specter is haunting Europe' – Marx conjures up the 'terror that this specter inspires in all the powers of old Europe' (SM, 99). Haunting is also associated in Derrida's mind with that of hunting or a 'holy hunt' which is taking place against the threat of communism. Multiplying his allusions to his theme of the '*non-contemporaneity with itself of the living present*' (SM, xix) – which I previously identified as originary repetition or the aporia of time – Derrida finds a parallel between Pope John Paul II's post-communist belief in the founding of a Christian Europe and the Holy Alliance that confronted communism in 1848 – a complex configuration of metaphors and allusions that derives from Fukuyama's *The End of History and the Last Man*.

Fukuyama and the end of history

Published in 1992 Fukuyama's text epitomized the mood of euphoria that followed the fall of the Berlin Wall in 1989 and the idea that western liberal capitalism had won a historic victory over the spectre of communism. The emergence of post-Marxism was a recurrent theme of the early 1990s, and this mood was expressed by further democratic elections in China, and encapsulated by George Bush's optimistic phrase 'the New World Order', following the emergence of *perestroika* and *glasnost* in the former Soviet Union. The much-heralded disintegration of the Soviet Union, Fukuyama argued, led to the triumph of liberal democracy and market capitalism and the emergence of a post-historical period that was free of ideological conflict.

To confirm Derrida's point about the spectre of the Holy Alliance of 1848, he identifies how Fukuyama's discourse is underpinned by a Hegelian-Kojevian Christian logic of presence and incarnation – an apocalyptic and eschatological tone that Derrida has consistently criticized. Derrida identifies the '*neo-evangelistic*' (SM, 59) language of the 'new gospel' (SM, 56), the 'good news' (SM, 57) and the 'Promised Land' (SM, 58) that structures Fukuyama's discourse on the geopolitical victory of economic liberalism, rejecting the idea that the universalization of western liberal democracy has been achieved.

Far from having produced a smooth transition to pluralist democracy, the collapse of Soviet Communism led to a resurgence of nationalist, ethnic and religious conflicts in Eastern Europe, particularly in the former Yugoslavia. Neither in the USA nor in the member states of the European Union, Derrida argues, has this perfect state of liberal democracy been realized, or even come close to realization. In contradistinction to Fukuyama, Derrida shows the real state of post-communist Europe. 'Under the heading of international or civil-international war', Derrida asks:

> is it still necessary to point out the economic wars, national wars, wars among minorities, the unleashing of racisms and xenophobias, ethnic conflicts, conflicts of culture and religion that are tearing apart so-called democratic Europe and the world today? (SM, 80)

The affirmative response to this question comes in Chapter 3, 'Wears and Tears (Tableu of an Ageless World)', where Derrida outlines a detailed response to Fukuyama's euphoric praise for the state of western liberal democracy. In fact liberal democracy of the parliamentary form has never been so marginalized in the world. The emergence of 'techno-tele-media apparatuses' and the new discourses of information and communication have amplified the undermining of parliamentary democracy. Television has magnified the role of professional politicians, while at the same time taking away from them their former power and status in the public sphere and making them into mere marionettes engaged in soundbite politics or a rhetoric adequate for politics by television. This risks making politicians no more than TV actors who willingly forsake unpopular principles for an effective media performance. Alluding to the Painter from *Timon of Athens* Derrida replaces Fukuyama's idealistic vision with a black picture of the world. Accompanying this, Derrida outlines his own vision of the ten plagues of the so-called new world order, focusing progressively on unemployment, homelessness, the economic war among countries of the European Community, the worst ramifications of the free market for the environment and employment conditions, foreign debts in Third World countries, the global arms trade, the dissemination of nuclear weapons, inter-ethnic wars, the mafia and drug cartels, and the present crisis in international law. Combining all of these elements, Derrida passionately declares that such a glib understanding of social and political events must never be allowed to efface the reality:

> For it must be cried out, at a time when some have the audacity to neo-evangelize in the name of the ideal of a liberal democracy that

has finally realized itself as the ideal of human history: never have violence, inequality, exclusion, famine, and thus economic oppression affected as many human beings in the history of the earth and of humanity. Instead of singing the advent of the ideal of liberal democracy and of the capitalist market in the euphoria of the end of history, instead of celebrating the 'end of ideologies' and the end of the great emancipatory discourses, let us never neglect this obvious macroscopic fact, made up of innumerable singular sites of suffering: no degree of progress allows one to ignore that never before, in absolute figures, never have so many men, women, and children been subjugated, starved, or exterminated on the earth. (SM, 85)

Given Derrida's powerful challenge to the 'new world order', he turns next to the unique status claimed by Fukuyama's eschatological themes. There is in fact nothing new in Fukuyama's thesis; it merely reiterates the 'end of history' thesis that was prominent at the end of the 1950s. This apocalyptic tone derived from an increasing awareness of the atrocities of the Stalinist period. By recalling these events, Derrida locates Fukuyama's ahistorical thesis within historical time, subjecting it to deferral and disjunction and cleverly turning Fukuyama's apocalyptic accusation back upon his own text. Fukuyama's 'youthful enthusiasm' about the victory of liberal democracy is not the first occasion on which such a thesis has been proclaimed with such vigour. What is being proposed here by Derrida is the idea that we have not reached the end of history so much as the end of a certain concept of history. The promise of 'some historicity as future-to-come' is what he calls 'the messianic without messianism' (SM, 73). Deconstruction, Derrida spells out in perhaps his clearest terms, 'consisted from the outset in putting into question the onto-theo- but also archeo-teleological concept of history – in Hegel, Marx, or even in the epochal thinking of Heidegger' (SM, 74). This process of questioning did not derive from the attempt to oppose or end history; rather it signalled how onto-theo-archeo-teleology 'neutralizes' or 'cancels' an effective theory of history. In its place Derrida's deconstructed notion of history relies on 'an affirmative thinking of the messianic and emancipatory promise' (SM, 74), which by challenging the onto-theological and teleo-eschatological opens history to the incalculable.

Fukuyama's ideal good news, then, is 'inadequate to any empiricity' (SM, 64). But Derrida's rejection of Fukuyama's Hegelian neo-evangelism is also based on a complex allusion to Marx. Derrida purposively alludes to Marx's similar denunciation of Max Stirner's Hegelian rhetoric in *The German Ideology*. Marx's work, Derrida comments, is also distinguished by the 'frequentation of specters' (SM, 101). Derrida's use of the word spectre, unlike Marx, who thereby announces and calls for the presence of communism, describes 'the persistence of a present past, the return of the dead which the worldwide work of mourning cannot get rid of' (SM, 101). Unlike Derrida, then, Marx's understanding of the spectre was supposed to correspond to the end of the political, that is to say, the spectre of communism would be the 'motor of the revolution, the transformation, the appropriation then finally the destruction of the State' (SM, 102). Marx advances the spectre of communism as a threat to Europe that will manifest itself in the realization of the party above all.

Derrida, in contrast, rejects both Marx's teleology and the continued relevance of the party for modern politics. Derrida is principally interested in Marx's struggle with the logic of spectrality, a logic which he is at once aware of and at the same time attempts to conjure away. To pursue this analysis, Derrida examines Marx's famous passage from *The Eighteenth Brumaire of Louis Bonaparte* about revolutionary inheritance in order to make his point about the residual metaphysical elements in his work. Marx indicates that revolutionary periods borrow from the spirits of the past in what Derrida identifies as a regeneration of the past and of the spirit of the past. Thinking in particular of the French Revolution of 1789, Marx describes how bourgeois society was accomplished with the aid of Roman costumes, symbolism and language. Historical anachrony is necessary for such a process to take place. No time, Derrida writes, is 'contemporary with itself, neither the time of the Revolution, which finally never takes place in the present, nor the times that follow or follow from it' (SM, 111). Bourgeois society 'can *present itself* only through the Roman haunting, in the anachrony of antique costume and phrases' (SM, 111). Though Marx recognizes this anachrony, he is concerned with breaking with this notion of inheritance altogether. In the social revolution of the nineteenth century, the time will still be out of joint, there will still be the anachrony that Marx identifies; however, it will be identifiable precisely because it no longer tries to imitate the past.

Spectrality amounts to a thinking through of the ontology of totalitarianism. This allows Derrida to foreground the double refusal inherent in the logic of spectrality both within Marxist thought, which, as Derrida movingly registers, has been responsible for some of the worst atrocities of the twentieth century, and against Marxism, in the thought of Fukuyama's end of history thesis.

Another associated aspect of Derrida's reading of Marx's and Stirner's attempt to conjure away the logic of spectrality relates to the origin of exchange-value and use-value. Marx's analysis of commodities attempts to show how their mystical character owes little or nothing to use-value. Marx's example is a simple wooden table. For Marx, use-value has nothing mysterious about it: he believes that it is possible to speak of it in simple and even pure terms. However, when the table becomes a commodity, it assumes a quite different form:

> the ordinary, sensuous thing is transfigured, it becomes someone, it assumes a figure. This woody and headstrong denseness is metamorphosed into a supernatural thing ... The ghostly schema now appears indispensable. (SM, 150)

As Derrida further observes, 'commodities transform human producers into ghosts' (SM, 156). Marx transgresses the borders between use-value and exchange-value: it is not a case of negating use-value, Derrida argues, 'But of doubting its strict purity' (SM, 160). Furthermore, and this is the main conclusion of Derrida's reading, the concept of use-value was always already, in advance, haunted by its other, 'namely, what will be born from the wooden head of the table, the commodity-form, and its ghost dance' (SM, 160). As Marx actually realizes, 'the first use-value is an exchange-value' (SM, 161).

Derrida's point here is to identify Marx's ironic dismissal of Stirner's similar allusions to the logic of spectrality. Marx, then, 'reproduce[s] the literal language of Stirner, which he himself cited in *The German Ideology* and turned back, in some way, against its author' (SM, 159). Marx surely wants to see the back of the logic of spectrality in the commodity form, and he believes that with the passing of the bourgeois economy it will disappear, taking commodity fetishism and religion with it.

Derrida's understanding of spectrality, in contrast, which draws upon the allusion he makes throughout to the act of parricide and vengeance in *Hamlet*, returns us to his thinking of the originary violence of the law and the institution. In *Hamlet* vengeance is the origin of law. In opposition to this notion Derrida describes a Levinisian understanding of justice in *Specters of Marx* that is based on the:

> singularity of an-economic ex-position to others. 'The relation to others – that is to say, justice,' writes Lévinas. Whether he knows it or not, Hamlet is speaking in the space opened up by this question ... the coming of the event, the excessive or exceeded relation to the other – when he declares 'The time is out of joint.' (SM, 23)

Derrida's notion of inheritance is similarly underpinned by his conception of justice. The very possibility of deconstruction is related to a concept of justice that answers to the call of the absolute singularity of the other, rather than to a Heideggerian understanding of presence that is based on 'sameness' or 'gathering'. Importantly, Derrida expands on his understanding of justice in 'Before the Law' and 'Force of Law: the "Mystical Foundation of Authority" '.

'Before the Law'

The notion of the aporia can be viewed as the organizing principle of Derrida's work, especially when one turns to consider the political implications of deconstruction. The meaning of aporia is close to Derrida's understanding of originary repetition – and it refers to the condition of judgement rather than its suspension. Let me reiterate Beardsworth's important connection between aporia and law once again as it is a key theme of *Specters of Marx*:

> Derrida's philosophy only makes sense politically in terms of the relation 'between' aporia and decision and neither in terms of a unilateral philosophy of decision: in other words, aporia is the very locus in which the political force of deconstruction is to be found. (Beardsworth, 1996, xiv)

Similarly, the aporia is profoundly related to Derrida's deconstruction of the metaphysical conception of time. The significance Derrida attributes to the aporia is to be found in his ' "temporal" deconstruction of the logics which inform traditional determinations of politics and the political' (1996, xiv). Both of these aspects underpin Derrida's understanding of spectrality and the promise of democracy in *Specters of Marx*. As a prelude to my discussion of this key aspect of the text it is necessary to examine 'Before the Law' in greater detail.

'Before the Law' discusses Kafka's short story of the same name which describes a man's attempt to acquire access to the law – though he does not specify what kind of law, whether, for example, it is moral, judicial, political, or natural. In the opening paragraph, Kafka sets the scene, describing how the law is guarded by a doorkeeper who will not let a countryman enter at this time. While admission may be possible, it is not possible at the moment. The countryman believes that the law should be accessible at all times and to everyone, but the doorkeeper – who is one of many others, each of whom is more powerful and potentially terrifying than the last – will not let him enter. The doorkeeper does not say no to his request; but makes it known that his request shall be deferred. The man stays outside the door for many years and though he frequently talks to the doorkeeper he remains indifferent to his pleas for admittance. After many years, as the countryman approaches death, he is led to question the doorkeeper for the final time, asking why he is the only one who has ever asked for admittance to the gate? The doorkeeper finally asserts that the door was in fact only made for him, and closes it in his face.

The main conflict that Derrida examines here is that between the law of singularity and the general or universal essence of the law. For the law to be general 'the law must be without history, genesis, or any possible derivation. That would be *the law of the law*. Pure morality has no history' (BL, 191). The law 'yields by withholding itself, without imparting its provenance and its site' (BL, 192). The law is transcendent.

Through his deconstruction of idealism Derrida is concerned, as Beardsworth writes, with the attempt to 're-relate the law to history' and at the same time to 'exempt the law from any history' (Beardsworth, 1996, 28). This double-bind is a familiar Derridean move vis-à-vis western metaphysics and its dual role – which makes the law of law exterior to history/determination and nothing but the differance of history/ determination – is evident in Derrida's detour through Freud's discussion of the history of law and the origin of morality in *Totem and Taboo*.

In *Totem and Taboo* Freud attempts to account for the origin of morality and the law by focusing on the existence of taboos in primitive cultures. Derrida is concerned in particular with the passage in which Freud describes the emergence of morality in terms of the murder of a father by his sons. The parricide springs from their simultaneous love and hate of their father's superior position, and especially in response to the obstacle that he presented to their desire for power and sexual fulfilment. Freud describes how, rather than feel empowered by their actions, the sons felt a mixture of remorse and guilt that ultimately led to repression. Freud places the sons' knowledge of guilt after the act of parricide. While Freud continues to believe that the story marks the real origin of morality, Derrida argues that the story 'inaugurates nothing since repentance and morality had to be possible *before* the crime' (BL, 198). The story is spun from fiction and does not mark the origin of the moral law:

> It resembles a fiction, a myth, or a fable, and its relation is so structured that all questions as to Freud's intentions are at once inevitable and pointless ... The structure of this event is such that one is compelled neither to believe nor disbelieve it. Like the

question of belief, that of the reality of its historical referent is, if not annulled, at least irremediably fissured. Demanding and denying the story, this quasi-event bears the mark of fictive narrativity (fiction *of* narration as well as fiction as narration: fictive narration as the simulacrum of narration and not only as the narration of an imaginary history). (BL, 199)

Derrida's point is that the origin of fiction is the origin of law. It is at this stage that it is possible to reconnect with Beardsworth's argument again:

> The aporia of law emerges from the impossibility of finding, or inventing the origin of law. The origin of law is an 'impossible' invention, and the condition of all inventions of law. (Beardsworth, 1996, 31)

The meaning of the aporia stems from its relationship to Derrida's notion of temporality. Derrida's interest in Kafka's short story relates to his concern with the theme of time vis-à-vis the origin of law. Permission for the man of the country to come before the law is not refused – it is 'delayed, adjourned, deferred' (BL, 202). The doorkeeper does not say no but defers the entry of the man indefinitely. It is not a prohibition as much as an example of differance. For our purposes it is an example of the 'non-derivability of the law' and of the 'aporia of law' (Beardsworth, 1996, 34). As Derrida argues:

> It is prohibition: this does not mean that it prohibits, but that it is itself prohibited, a prohibited place. It forbids itself and contradicts itself by placing the man in its own contradiction: one cannot reach the law, and in order to have a *rapport* of respect with it, *one must not* have a rapport with the law, *one must interrupt the relation*. One must *enter into relation* only with the law's representatives, its examples, its guardians. (BL, 203–4)

The disjunction of time is further enhanced because of the father's increased significance after his death. 'Furthermore, if the dead father is more alive when dead,' Beardsworth argues, 'the murder of the father is not only an act performed in vain, but the aporia of law which emerges out of the inability to give a genealogy of the son's affect of remorse constitutes at the same time an aporia of time and of place' (Beardsworth, 1996, 34). Against the ahistorical reading of the law which Derrida encounters, his reading of Kafka argues that, in order to account for the origin of law, one must locate it in time and space. The origin, however, is always already differance. As a subject of the law the man of the country is before the law; however, as the story reveals, because he cannot enter the law he is also outside it. The law is differance because the subject of the law can never determine its essence. He can never say, 'There it is' (BL, 205). As a subject before the law, the judgement is 'always in preparation and always being deferred' (BL, 206). The law 'neither arrives nor lets anyone arrive' (BL, 211). The subject is before the law and at the same time subject to the law's non-identity with itself – its differance.

Derrida's special concern with literature also emerges at this point. Literature's significance resides in its ability not to efface the knowledge of the aporia of law. Instead of ignoring the temporality of the law, literary writing re-marks the law. To quote once again the above passage from Derrida: 'Demanding and denying the story, this quasi-event bears the mark of fictive narrativity (fiction *of* narration as well as fiction as narration: fictive narration as the simulacrum of narration and not only as the narration of an imaginary history)' (BL, 199). The aporia or double-bind of the law is neither a pure event nor pure fiction; it is the middle way between the two. Literature is in a privileged position to account for the fictive narrativity of all myths of origin because its understanding of writing is always determined as the excess or remainder of any horizon or origin. As Beardsworth writes, the 'aporia of law is nothing else than the aporetic relation between aporia, judgement and failure' (Beardsworth, 1996, 37). 'Declarations of Independence' also reiterates that Derrida is concerned with re-marking the violence of the metaphysical origin that is determined by disavowing time or effacing differance. Derrida's reading of 'Before the Law' shows, through the man of the country's inability to gain access to the law, the suspension of the law but importantly not the suspension of judgement. The possibility of the law (as we know from our understanding of Derrida's logic of contamination) is also its impossibility. There is therefore a direct connection with Derrida's critique of horizonal or messianic forms of thought. It is this understanding of the aporia of law which Beardsworth relates to Derrida's notion of the 'promise of democracy'. Before reconnecting with this theme in *Specters of Marx*, it is worth pursuing this theme a little further in Derrida's other prominent discussion of the law in 'Force of Law: the "Mystical Foundation of Authority" '.

'Force of Law: the "Mystical Foundation of Authority" '

In 'Force of Law' Derrida insists that deconstruction shakes the normative criteria that makes it possible to distinguish between law (*droit*) and justice. In a familiar gesture, Derrida identifies how the German word *Gewalt*, which appears in *Zur Kritik der Gewalt*, the text by Benjamin that he discusses, normally signifies violence, but can also mean legitimate power. Having established this moment of undecidability, Derrida returns to one of the main questions of 'Declarations of Independence': How is it possible to distinguish between the force of law and the originary violence that must have established its authority? The founding or inauguration of law is based on a performative and therefore interpretive violence which cannot be said to be either just nor unjust. This origin cannot appeal to any exterior moment beyond itself to guarantee or on the contrary invalidate it. Derrida demonstrates that he is concerned with the violence that has been established around the founding act of the law. By implication every institution of law is always already a non-natural instituting of law.

There can be no justice that is separate from force as Derrida's approving allusions to Pascal's *Pensées* indicate. Pascal's use of Montaigne's phrase, *fondement mystique de l'authorité* – the mystical foundation of authority – is the source of Derrida's title. From Montaigne, Pascal is led toward a critique of the authority of law based on a divine mandate. Justice is shown to be the product of custom. By tracing it to its source, its mystical character is revealed; its legitimacy is annihilated. Derrida's interest in the Pascalian critique provides the impetus for a critical philosophy and furthermore for a critique of juridical ideology that seeks to examine the superstructures of law and the socioeconomic forces that underpin them. This critique is pursued via the mystical limit at the origin of the originary violence of the law. In a crucial passage, Derrida relates the nonfoundation of law – the idea that the law is a violence without a ground – to the possibility of deconstruction. Continuing to distinguish between law and justice, Derrida argues that deconstruction relies on an undeconstructible concept of justice. To explain this experience of justice, Derrida returns to the notion of the aporia. There is no justice, Derrida argues, without the experience of the aporia. It is this experience that makes justice possible. Whereas law, in contrast, is the element of calculation, justice is the incalculable. The moment of the aporia thus occurs when one understands that the moment of the decision, between what is just and unjust, is never determined by any rule. This means that justice is always tied to the problem of language. Derrida is concerned with how it is possible to reconcile the act of justice that must always concern singularity – individuals in a unique situation – with the general rule of justice. Three aporias arise as a result of Derrida's attempt to be just to the singularity of the other, while also recognizing the existence of restrictions imposed by pre-existing normative criteria. First, the singularity of the other can only be maintained if the law is subject to reinvention or fresh judgement. As each case is different, each requires an absolutely unique interpretation. A decision can only be a just one if it both adheres to the law and reinvents it in each case.

The second aporia relates to the function of undecidability. This reinvention or 'other-ing' of law, insofar as it is incalculable, exemplifies what Derrida calls the 'ordeal of the undecidable'. This process is not, as is frequently assumed, tantamount to the endless deferral of meaning. On the contrary, the experience of the undecidable, like that of the aporia, is the prerequisite of responsibility, judgement and justice. Without this passage by way of the undecidable a decision might be legal, but it would not be just. The experience of the undecidable, like that of differance, has a *ghostliness* that deconstructs from within any certitude of presence, or of the absolute justice of any decision. The figure of the ghost looks forward to *Specters of Marx*, where, as we have seen, its purpose is to describe the tension between differance and a pre-deconstructive ontology in Marx's work. Whereas in *Specters of Marx* it indicates, as Critchley suggests, both the possibility and impossibility of any conceptual order, here its appearance signifies that the law is both possible and impossible, violent and non-violent. At this point Derrida returns to the main theme of his discussion of Kafka in 'Before the Law'. Deconstruction operates on the basis of an infinite idea of justice. These ideas clearly converge in Levinas's understanding of ethics, as Derrida acknowledges, in which justice is a function of the dissymmetry that structures the relation with others.

The third aporia concerns Derrida's resistance to a messianic promise that is evident, for example, in Judaism, Christianity, Islam and Marxism. Derrida of course refuses all such messianisms as he would all forms of teleology or eschatology. In place of messianism Derrida places his understanding of a 'to-come' (*à venir*) which he carefully distinguishes from the future that can always reproduce the present. Justice exceeds calculation, rules and programs; it cannot be anticipated. Drawing on Levinas's ethical thinking Derrida describes it as the 'experience of absolute alterity' which as such is unpresentable. However, this does not mean that such thinking should function as an alibi for hindering an engagement with political or institutional matters. And this is precisely Derrida's concern in *Specters of Marx*, where this understanding of justice underpins a configuration of themes, principally the relation between non-horizonal thinking and the 'promise of democracy'.

Derrida's critique of the ontology of totalitarianism is based on the rejection of an account of justice that would seek to restrict responsibility to the living present. Spectrality is directly related to justice as differance. In the more overtly political context of Derrida's discussion of Marx, the question again arises whether the differential understanding of justice is tantamount to the endless deferral of action or judgement. For Beardsworth, as we have already seen, the aporia does not suspend judgement; rather it shows itself as the condition of judgement in such a way that does not retreat from ethical decision making. In an interview with Beardsworth that was published prior to *Specters of Marx* entitled, 'The Deconstruction of Actuality', Derrida attempts to clarify the affirmative understanding of the aporia of the law. 'The theme of différance', he argues:

> is often accused of encouraging procrastination, neutralization, and resignation, and therefore of evading the needs of the present, especially ethical and political ones. But I have never seen any conflict between différance and the pressing urgency of present need. (DOA, 31)

On the contrary, Derrida rejects the negative association of difference as deferral, arguing instead that he has always focused on the regenerative aspects of the term:

> Différance points to a relationship (a 'ferance') – a relation to what is other, to what differs in the sense of alterity, to the singularity of the other – but 'at the same time' it also relates to what is to come, to that which will occur in ways which are inappropriable, unforeseen, and therefore urgent, beyond anticipation: to precipitation in fact. The thought of différance is also, therefore, a thought of pressing need, of something which, because it is different, I can neither avoid nor appropriate. (DOA, 31)

Derrida is concerned with the need to think of justice as an obligation, pledge, promise, engagement or injunction: 'There would be no différance without urgency, emergency, immediate, precipitation, on the ineluctable, the unforeseen arrival of the other, to the other to whom reference and deference are made' (DOA, 32). The injunction of Marx is here related to the injunction of justice – the absolute singularity of a justice without presence which gives us an insight into Derrida's understanding of the word maintaining (*maintenant*) with which the text opens. The word is a neologism which incorporates the idea of maintaining and sustaining – thus 'Maintaining now the specters of Marx' (SM, 3) – with a form of presence which is irreducible to absolute presence. This idea precisely reiterates the logic of Derrida's figure of differance or, in the context of the translation of Marx, the figure of iterability. In challenging Fukuyama's quasi-religious language of the end, Derrida's reading of Marx crucially depends upon this complex connection between justice as an irreducible respect for the radical alterity of the other and the translation of differance or the trace as *maintenant*. Derrida argues that this understanding of justice is inherent in the text of Marx – it is he writes in fact, 'an *ineffaceable* mark' (SM, 28) that neither can nor should be ignored by those engaged with Marx's legacy.

This reading of 'Before the Law' fastens on to Derrida's belief in the singularity of the law and Freud's discussion of vengeance as the origin of the law. The later essay, 'Force of Law', extends Derrida's thinking of the relationship between deconstruction and justice, especially in relation to the idea of an 'undeconstructible' notion of justice. These themes presuppose a grasp of Derrida's debt to Levinas's thinking of the ethical relation.

The promise of democracy

Derrida's resistance to horizonal forms of thinking is evident in his incorporation of the notion of differance into his idea of a democracy which is not yet present – of a 'democracy to come'. This notion of democracy is heavily indebted to Levinas's conception of the ethical relation and his thinking of community. It is here that we can establish a link between Derrida's understanding of justice and democracy. Levinas discusses his ethical notion of community in 'The Other and Others' in *Totality and Infinity* and at much greater length in *Otherwise than Being*.

For Levinas, the ethical relation, the relation between an ego and an Other, is an encounter based on justice and always takes place in public. In other words, it is irreducibly political. This political dimension is evident in Levinas's understanding of *le tiers*, the third party, which enables him to pass beyond the I–thou relation. Through the face-to-face encounter, the interruption of the Saying in the Said and the notion of *le tiers*, Levinas is able to describe his idea of a community as a double structure. This is especially true of his notion of human fraternity which possesses a double aspect. On the one hand, this relates to 'individualities' whose singularity refers only to itself. On the other hand, this notion relies on the asymmetry or non-coincidence of the Same and the Other. The double structure, as Critchley argues, attests to the fact that the community is a 'commonality among equals which is at the same time based on the inegalitarian moment of the ethical relation' (Critchley, 1992, 227).

Critchley picks up this thread again in his reading of *Otherwise than Being*. The notion of *le tiers*, Levinas writes, inaugurates a moment of conflict or contradiction in the Saying; prior to this moment, its movement was in only one direction. The subsequent two-directional traffic defines the moment of justice, described in terms of a 'an order of co-presence' as before a court. Individuals are given the authority to call others to account for their actions.

One of the main questions confronting Levinas's understanding of ethics is: 'How is the Saying, my exposure to the Other, to be Said, or given a philosophical exposition that does not utterly betray this Saying?' (Critchley, 1992, 7). Levinas's answer to this question relies on a conception of the trace, in which the Said is able to maintain a trace of the Saying within itself. A just community would be based on the constitutive existence of dissension and conflict. The trace of the Saying in the Said disrupts all immanent or totalitarian forms of political organization; this is what Levinas identifies as the double structure. All forms of injustice or racism emerge when the organization of a polity fails to recognize the transcendence of the Other and 'forgets that the State, with its institutions, is informed by the proximity of my relation to the Other' (Critchley, 1992, 233). Importantly, Levinas relates this understanding to the purpose of philosophical questioning itself. Philosophy is the name given by Levinas to the relation between ethics and politics – between the Other and the search for justice and control. The final commitment to the wisdom of love, rather than to the more traditional notion of the love of wisdom, reinforces Levinas's respect for the Saying. As Critchley writes, 'Love is therefore ethical Saying, whereas philosophy is that language of the Said and justice that is called on to serve love' (Critchley, 1992, 235). This notion of philosophy restates Levinas's idea of the double structure of the community. On the one hand, Levinas argues, philosophy is compelled to serve justice in a double gesture in which differance is 'thematized' and the thematized is subject to differance. On the other hand, philosophy must criticize the laws of being. Philosophy is both the Saying and the Said. Its commitment to justice, however, means that it will always be called to interrogate the '*polis* in the name of what it excludes or marginalizes, the pre-rational one-for-the-other of ethics' (Critchley, 1992, 235).

Derrida's first mention of justice in the 'Exordium' in *Specters of Marx* develops this understanding of the ethical relation in terms of a configuration of related themes: spectrality, the *arrivant* and the 'promise of democracy'. In each case the target is horizonal thinking or absolute self-presence. The concept of justice with which he is concerned seems in fact impossible or unthinkable without a realization of the responsibility to the 'ghosts of those who are not yet born or who are already dead' (SM, xix). This restatement of the logic of spectrality extends the notion of responsibility to a political context: the conversation with ghosts – whether they be the victims of capitalist, colonial or totalitarian conflicts – takes place 'in the name of justice' (SM, xix). It is this conception of justice that re-opens politics as contestation in the face of Fukuyama's end of history thesis. Derrida's conception of justice is the 'undeconstructible condition of any deconstruction', but it is also a 'condition that is itself in deconstruction' (SM, 28).

In *Politics of Friendship* Derrida clarifies this understanding of spectrality still further in relation to a futural notion of friendship. Derrida relates his open-ended notion of democracy – 'democracy ... never exists, it is never present, it remains the theme of a non-presentable concept' (POF, 306) – to a reconsideration of the Graeco-Roman model of friendship, showing how this model is indebted to finite or metaphysical thinking that attempts to 'place friendship above the law and politics' (POF, 278). In place of this logic, Derrida outlines the need for a new model of friendship which is based on Levinas's notion of a 'non-reappropriable alterity' (POF, 288). Derrida situates his rethinking of friendship and humanitarianism in relation to the main concerns of *Specters of Marx*: international law, nationalism, the return of the religious, and ethnocentrism. A reconsideration of these areas, Derrida writes, 'cannot be done without a systematic, and *deconstructive*, coming to terms with the tradition of which we are speaking here' (POF, 273); these areas all rely on a conception of the virtue of fraternity.

Derrida's discussion of friendship fastens onto the phrase, 'O my friends, there is no friend', frequently attributed to Aristotle, but echoing with philosophical allusions to Cicero, Montaigne, Kant and Nietzsche. In their work, Derrida discerns a link between their discussion of friendship and 'all laws and all logics of universalization, to ethics and to law or right, to the values of equality and equity, to all the political models of the *res publica* ... and especially in regard to democracy' (POF, 3). The temporal disjunction or *contretemps* that Derrida identifies either side of the comma in this phrase – therefore reiterating his concern with the opposition between universality and singularity that I highlighted in 'Before the Law' – enables him to reinvoke the theme of spectrality and a future to come. Derrida's closing line – 'O my democratic friends' (POF, 306) – renarrates Aristotle's mourned lament as a critique of Fukuyama's horizonal thinking: O my democratic friends, there is no democratic friend. Derrida turns the feeling of lament into anticipation and an injunction: as yet there is no truly democratic friend! As he says: 'May we have it one day!' (POF, 284).

In the final chapter, 'For the First Time in the History of Humanity', Derrida elaborates on *'the great philosophical and canonical discourse on friendship'*, a theme which 'explicitly tie[s] the friend-brother to virtue and justice, to moral reason and political reason' (POF, 277). The Graeco-Roman or metaphysical model of friendship that Derrida identifies is founded on a familiar logic of exclusion: in this instance, it has been able to 'exclude the feminine or heterosexuality, friendship between women ... [and] friendship between men and women' (POF, 277). The history of friendship reiterates two of Derrida's main deconstructive themes: the deconstruction of the history of concepts and the question of logocentrism and phallogocentrism. Derrida's analysis of this model is aimed at a form of politics that could be founded on a notion of friendship 'which exceeds the measure of man, without becoming a theologem' (POF, 294). Whereas the Graeco-Roman model is 'homological, immanentist, finitist' (POF, 290), Derrida stresses the need for an infinite, dissymeterical and heterological notion of friendship. Nietzsche's discussion of the spectral effect of 'the friend to come, the *arrivant* who comes from afar, the one who must be loved in remoteness and from afar' (POF, 288) is crucial in this context. Belonging neither to the past nor the present, the effect reinforces Derrida's notion of the 'absolute singularity of the other' (POF, 276) or 'nonreappropriable alterity' that is 'resistant to the very generality of the law' (POF, 277). Nietzsche outlines a notion of spectral friendship based on justice that echoes Derrida's own discussion of de Man in 'Biodegradables' and *Specters of Marx*. This concept of friendship urges the arrival, not of the 'past friend, but [of] the friend to come ... what is coming is still spectral, and it must be loved as such' (POF, 288). In his discussion of friendship, then, Derrida is able to place his injunction from *Specters of Marx* – 'It is necessary to speak of the ghost' (SM, xix) – in relation to his continuing deconstruction of the metaphysical oppositions that lie at the heart of western political thought.

Returning to *Specters of Marx*, it is possible to see Levinas's thinking of community as the basis of Derrida's notion of the democracy to come: 'The space of the *polis* is not an enclosed or immanent structure, but rather a multiplication of spaces, a structure of repeated interruptions, in which the social totality is breached by the force of ethical transcendence'

(Critchley, 1992, 238). This kind of ahorizonal thinking – effectively Derrida's ever-present concern with the limit of metaphysical closure – is clearly in evidence in his rejection of Fukuyama. In contradistinction to Fukuyama, then, Derrida posits a process of democratization that is without an end or final realization. Beardsworth's thinking of the aporia of law and the aporia of time is particularly indebted to Derrida's understanding of the promise of democracy in *Specters of Marx*. The following passage from Derrida's text reworks all of Beardsworth's main themes:

> The democratic promise, like that of the communist promise, will always keep within it, and it must do so, this absolutely undetermined messianic hope at its heart, this eschatological relation to the to-come of an event *and* of a singularity, of an alterity that cannot be anticipated. Awaiting without horizon of the wait, awaiting what one does not expect yet or any longer, hospitality without reserve, welcoming salutation accorded in advance to the absolute surprise of the *arrivant* ... and this is the very place of spectrality. (SM, 65)

This fascinating passage successfully conveys the idea that the democracy to come will never present itself in the form of full presence. As such it registers Derrida's requirement to respect the singularity and infinite alterity of the other and to relate the open possibility of the other to a form of political organization. The messianic is also related to Derrida's thinking of decision: 'This messianic hesitation does not paralyze any decision, any affirmation, any responsibility. On the contrary, it grants them their elementary condition. It is their very experience' (SM, 169). The experience of the messianic without messianism is similarly connected to the condition of justice which we have already examined.

In *Specters of Marx* Derrida's notion of the *arrivant* reiterates his deconstruction of messianism – as distinct from the messianic – or horizonal form of thinking. What Derrida describes as 'undeconstructible justice' is related to the 'coming of the other, the absolute and unpredictable singularity of the *arrivant as justice*' (SM, 28). The messianic 'designate[s] a structure of experience rather than a religion ... where no figure of the *arrivant*, even as he or she is heralded, should be pre-determined, pre-figured, or even pre-named' (SM, 168). Consequently, Derrida is able to contemplate his commitment to the promise that is not based on an 'Abrahamic messianism' (SM, 167). These ideas are strongly in evidence in Derrida's attempt to envisage a new form of political organization – what he calls the 'New International'.

The New International

By far the most important element in Derrida's discussion of the ten plagues of the modern world is international law. Derrida signals the crisis of international law by attacking the emergence and global significance of the super-state. For Derrida, the new powers of the super-state must be curtailed by a universal understanding of human rights. Faced with this requirement Derrida argues that the Marxist spirit can still inspire an effective political engagement, especially in the face of the increasing power of the nation state and the evident concentration of juridical, financial and techno-scientific capital. The New International is his attempt to reappraise international law in the light of these crimes.

The New International is described as 'a link of affinity, suffering, and hope, a still discreet, almost secret link, as it was around 1848, but more and more visible' (SM, 85). The enigmatic tone signalled by the end of the last sentence is continued by Derrida's description of the New International as 'without status, without title, and without name, barely public even if it is not clandestine, without contract, "out of joint," without coordination, without party, without country, without national community ... without co-citizenship, without common belonging to a class' (SM, 85). The New International clearly rejects the new world order and the idea that Derrida is squarely opposed to enlightenment rationality as it calls for 'an alliance without institution' (SM, 85) that is inspired by the Marxist spirit.

As Derrida explains, this fidelity to the inheritance of a certain Marxist spirit of the Marxist inheritance remains a task and a duty for the following two reasons. First, this adherence remains an urgent one in that it is necessary to 'adjust "reality" to the "ideal" in the course of a necessarily infinite process' (SM, 86).

Secondly, remaining faithful to a certain spirit of Marx is necessary in order to call into question the ideal notion of the market, the laws of capital, the determination of human rights and liberty. His clearest commitment to the spirit of Marxism is apparent in this further passage:

> Now, if there is a spirit of Marxism which I will never be ready to renounce, it is not only the critical idea or the questioning stance ... It is even more a certain emancipatory and *messianic* affirmation, a certain experience of the promise that one can try to liberate from any dogmatics and even from any metaphysico-religious determination, from any *messianism*. (SM, 89)

The New International thus combines Derrida's thinking of justice, the promise of democracy and the spirit of Marxism. Breaking with the party form does not imply that every structure of effective political organization should be renounced.

It is here, however, that we turn to one of the most important questions of the debate about the status of Derrida's Marx. Critics who have not understood the importance of Derrida's deconstruction of western metaphysics' conception of temporality – what we have been calling 'originary repetition' (Beardsworth, 1996, 18) – ask whether it is possible to found a politics without ontology? Or, more to the point, is it possible to found a recognizably Marxist politics without ontology? Following Bennington (1994) and Beardsworth (1996) this chapter has set out reasons why it is. Derrida's thinking of the aporia of time is the condition of his notion of justice and of a democracy to come.

In contrast, Habermas (1987), McCarthy (1989), Ahmad (1994) and Soper (1995) all answer this question in the negative. Evidence for their conclusion is provided by the following passage in which Derrida states quite clearly that he 'opposed, to be sure, de facto, "Marxism" or "communism"' (the Soviet Union, the International of Communist Parties, and *everything* that resulted from them' (SM, 14). Later in the text Derrida distinguishes his understanding of the spirit of Marxist critique from all forms of Marxism that failed to resist ontology, such as is evident in dialectical or historical materialism, as well as the forms of Marxism that give rise to the party, Marxist State or workers' International. In response to these passages, Aijaz Ahmad, for example, argues that Derrida's use of the word everything is so all encompassing that he is not sure what kind of spirit or Marxist inheritance continues to haunt the post-1989 world. Derrida's emphasis on a New International that would be 'without country, without national community (International before, across, and beyond any national determination), without co-citizenship, without common belonging to a class' (SM, 85), seems to close down the possibility of prescribing any form of political resistance or organization.

Kate Soper goes further than Ahmad, arguing that in *Specters of Marx* Derrida seems to suggest that:

> [W]e must never ontologize, must remain no more than haunted by the spirit of an emancipatory politics, must never seek to incarnate it in any set of goods, institutions or strategies, since to do so – it is implied – is inevitably to betray the spirit itself. (Soper, 1995, 27)

Soper rejects the idea that it is possible to have a legitimate form of political resistance once ontology has been deconstructed in the fashion that Derrida suggests.

Though Critchley (1995) is more sympathetic to Derrida's understanding of the New International, he also recognizes that this concept is rather vague and could therefore be accused of an empty universalism. It is simply not clear, he argues, how the New International is to achieve hegemony when its apparent flexibility does not specify who is to act as an agent of change and against whom it is targeted. In this vein, he points out with some justification that Derrida's idea that 'Whether they wish it or know it or not, all men and women, all over the earth, are today to a certain extent the heirs of Marx and Marxism' (SM, 91) could equally apply to conservative or liberal thinkers such as Adam Smith and John Locke; Derrida's notion of inheritance lacks specificity. Though Derrida is concerned in passages of this kind with breaking down the boundaries between left and right, it is difficult to imagine American Republicans or British Conservatives subscribing to the idea that they are heirs of Marx. For Soper and Ahmad, Derrida's attempt to preserve the spirit of Marx risks turning it into an apologia that effectively refutes every aspect of the Marxist inheritance in order to maintain some semblance of contemporary relevance.

Such an argument, however, ignores Derrida's own awareness of precisely this criticism. Derrida indicates that in *Specters of Marx* he is concerned with the future identity of Marxism. His whole text, he writes, could be described as an attempt to determine the form of a Marxist utterance. There is enough evidence in *Specters of Marx* not to doubt Derrida's sincerity about his attempt to 'avoid the neutralizing anesthesia of a new theoreticism, and to prevent a philosophico-philological return to Marx from prevailing' (SM, 32).

Here, however, two paths present themselves. By collapsing the existing boundaries of political thought, Derrida is either dismissed as an irresponsible anarchist – this is the reading of Habermas (1987) and McCarthy (1989) – or it is understood that Derrida is concerned with the attempt to reinvent the political (Bennington, 1994; Critchley, 1995; Beardsworth, 1996). The latter position depends on the link I have established between Derrida's thinking of time and the promise of democracy. Beardsworth makes the point precisely once again thereby refuting Ahmad and Soper and aligning Derrida more appropriately with a democratic tradition of Marxism:

> When Derrida places his thinking under the term 'democracy', it is not with regard to a specific political regime, although it is not

opposed to it either. It is with regard to an absolute future that informs all political organizations, but which is heard most, despite their legal form, within democratic organizations of power. This absolute future is the promise that the 'we' of the community (family, nation, world, even, as Derrida says … humanity) – qua the 'we's' radical lack of identity – will have returned from the beginning to haunt any determination of the community. (Beardsworth, 1996, 146)

This chapter has argued that Derrida's thinking of justice and the 'promise of democracy' emerge from his deconstruction of the metaphysical notion of time. The idea of a 'democracy to come' marks Derrida's commitment to a form of political organization that is based on originary repetition. McCarthy and Habermas, who refuse this reading of deconstruction, do so as I argued at the outset, because they continue to rely on a metaphysical understanding of the political that effectively 'close[s] down the space opened by original thinking' (Critchley, 1992, 189).

Afterword: Legacy

In his readings of Benjamin, de Man, Kant, Nietzsche and Marx, to name but five prominent examples from the preceding chapters, we have seen that Derrida has been engaged with the question of an intellectual legacy and inheritance. With the notion of *spectrality* Derrida gathers these themes together to perhaps greatest effect. His thoughts in the related areas of the proper name, the signature, mourning, inheritance and spectrality are all the more significant when they are used, as suggested here, to consider the reception of Derrida's own work, especially that of the word deconstruction and all that it has been heir to over the last four decades.

As readers of Derrida we occupy very much the same ground as he identified with regard to Paul de Man. In Derrida's own words: Paul de Man *'himself, he is dead*, and yet, through the specters of memory and of the text, he lives *among us* and, as one says in French, *il nous regarde* – he looks at us, but also he is our concern, we have concerns regarding him more than ever without his being here' (LSS, 593). This also applies to us – to me, you – as readers and translators of Derrida, now, and in the future to come. Readers of Derrida are urged, as Peggy Kamuf identifies in her commentary on *Specters of Marx*, to reject the traditional scholar's fear of phantoms and ghosts, and to embrace Derrida's injunction to 'redefine altogether the role of scholars' (Kamuf, 2005, 239). The 'intellectual of tomorrow' is called to 'speak of, to, and with ghosts' thus defining the 'scholar's sense of justice' (2005, 239). The reading of Derrida's reception that has been undertaken here underlines the relationship between reading, response and responsibility. By understanding this relationship it is possible to concur with Julian Wolfreys's recent study and to resist premature reports that there 'is no longer any need to work with any patience with Derrida other than, yet again, in some pedagogical, propaedeutic manner, where whatever goes by the names *difference, supplement, deconstruction, writing, text,* and so on, are all subsumed within, subordinated to a form of technical competence and calculation' (Wolfreys, 2004, 11). Derrida's work – as well as the reception of his own work – continually reiterates that reading is concerned with a responsibility to remain vigilant in the face of institutionalization, ontologization and the interpretive violence that they entail.

The figure of the 'biodegradable' plays a similarly important role in clarifying the interpretive afterlife of deconstruction itself. *On the one hand,* a biodegradable text is assimilated and enriched by a culture 'but on the condition that it lose its identity, its figure, or its singular signature, its proper name' (B, 824). *On the other hand,* the biodegradable poses the question of *resistance* to assimilation: 'Is it not the case that, as "nonbiodegradable," the singularity of a work resists, does not let itself be assimilated, but stays on the surface and survives like an indestructible artefact' (B, 824). There is, then, a requirement to understand the untranslatability of publications; the proper name function lies beyond the text and beyond the corruption of translation as a process of transformation. At the same time, there is also a duty to translate and to read a text; the proper name offers itself to be read, therefore risking its own inevitable reduction and corruption. The great works of literature and philosophy have been able to survive successive waves of interpretation due to this process. Can we not also now add the name Jacques Derrida to this list of great authors? Only time – decades of interpretive time perhaps – will tell.

Derrida's readings of Nietzsche in particular were also concerned with the responsibilities toward an intellectual inheritance. Responsibility here lies *between* reader and text as Derrida makes clear:

> In some ways the signature will take place on the addressee's side, that is, on the side of him or her whose ear will be keen enough to hear my name, for example, or to understand my signature, that with which I sign ... Nietzsche's signature does not take place when he writes. He says clearly that it will take place posthumously. (EO, 35)

Reader and author sign together in an alliance of mutual responsibility that does not permit the reader to impose just any interpretation. Translation for sure is a political process. Deconstruction challenges the idea that translation entails the transport of pure signifieds between source and target texts, replacing translation with a notion of *regulated transformation* that does not disregard context or responsibility.

By tracing the translation and transformation of deconstruction the previous chapters have identified how the debate about the politics of deconstruction has been determined by the word's inscription in 'conflictual and differentiated contexts' (LINC, 141) – in American literary criticism (Chapter 2), in relation to pedagogical institutions (Chapter 3), postmodernism (Chapter 4), the de Man affair (Chapter 5) and Marxism (Chapter 6). In each case, deconstruction attacks both the political left and the political right: it is neither conservative nor revolutionary; it is not determinable within the codes of such oppositions.

In order to come to terms with the political implications of Derrida's thought it has been necessary to understand metaphysics' disavowal of time – a notion that lies at the very heart of Derrida's conception of iterability as was evident in 'Signature, Event, Context'. Derrida's thinking of time underpins his conception of justice, his understanding of the Marxist inheritance, his commitment to the principle of reason, the New International, and a 'democracy to come'. When Derrida aligns his thinking with democracy, it is not with regard to a particular political regime, as is the case with Fukuyama. Derrida aligns deconstruction with the notion of a 'future-to-come' that determines the horizon of *all* political organizations. Deconstruction challenges *all* forms of political authenticity.

Two questions were posted in the Introduction to which we can now return: Why has deconstruction been identified with a modern form of immorality or of irresponsibility? And how has deconstruction been associated with numerous political strategies, from anarchism to left-reformism, from totalitarianism to fascism? The answers to both of these questions are determined by the narrative of Derrida's reception that has been outlined.

Derridean deconstruction emerged as a challenge to structuralism, phenomenology and Marxism in the French academy at the end of the 1950s. During the late 1960s deconstruction became a prominent literary methodology at a time when a successor to the New Criticism was being sought. A selective reading of Derrida's early work and personal political involvement overemphasized his understanding of the dissemination of meaning transforming it into *mis en abyme*, freeplay and a thorough-going epistemological relativism that viewed language as an autonomous and self-referential system. From here it was a relatively short step to associate deconstruction's particular brand of textual iconoclasm with immorality, amorality and irresponsibility.

Having established this misunderstanding of Derrida's metaphysical critique, we have also seen the growing demands and pressure for deconstruction to become ethically and politically responsible. Habermas's reading of postmodernism's attack on enlightenment rationality advanced Derridean deconstruction as a continuation and intensification of the later Heidegger's mystical philosophy, therefore crudely raising the spectre of fascism and political evasion. Nevertheless, it proved to be influential. Derrida represented a new generation of French philosophers whose dangerous influence coincided with the emergence of neo-conservatism. Again deconstruction suffered by association with a particularly prominent reading of postmodern irrationalism and its apparent withdrawal from political activism.

Prior to Ryan's *Marxism and Deconstruction* (1982) Marxist critics largely followed this trend, and deconstruction was wrongly represented as an ambivalent strategy: a combination of anarchism, left-reformism, nihilism and textual idealism. This stance, again taking its lead largely from Habermas, underestimated deconstruction's usefulness as a political strategy for feminist theorists and activists – as my reading of Johnson (1987) and Elam (1994) argued – as well as for post-colonialists, Afro-Americanists and gays and lesbians. This reading profoundly overlooked Derrida's work with GREPH and the International College of Philosophy, and the essays that have been discussed here: 'The Principle of Reason: the University in the Eyes of Its Pupils', 'Of an Apocalyptic Tone Recently Adopted in Philosophy', 'Languages and Institutions of Philosophy', 'Declarations of Independence', 'Sendoffs' and 'Mochlos, or The Conflict of the Faculties'. The selective reading of deconstruction by the first wave of literary critics added to Habermas's influential understanding of postmodernism, and marginalized the politico-institutional context of Derrida's early thought.

The de Man affair represented the high point of the profound and violent implications of this misreading of deconstruction. Derrida's careful and rigorous intervention, however, argued that it was possible to establish a clear connection between de Man's deconstructive critique of aesthetic ideology in his middle and later period essays and his own anti-systematizing and anti-totalizing notion of deconstruction. By foregrounding this connection Derrida was able to resist the reinvention of deconstruction as an irrational and apolitical postmodern strategy. In the wake of the de Man affair, Derrida set about clarifying the ethico-political aspects of deconstruction still further in 'Like the Sound of the Sea Deep within a Shell: Paul de Man's War', 'Biodegradables', *The Other Heading*, 'Force of Law: the "Mystical Foundation of Authority" ', 'Before the Law', *Specters of Marx* and *Politics of Friendship*. Based on a reading of these important works deconstruction is more appropriately described as a form of anti-totalitarian critique that is heavily indebted to a Levinisian conception of ethics and a rethinking of the post-Kantian tradition of enlightenment rationality. Deconstruction, as Eagleton recognized, is an attempt to 'dismantle the logic by which a particular system of thought, and behind that a whole system of strategies and social institutions, maintains its force' (Eagleton, 1983, 148). This reading is substantiated in particular by 'The Principle of Reason', 'Declarations of Independence' and Derrida's notion of a 'democracy to come' in *Specters of Marx*.

It is entirely against the grain of Derrida's thinking to attempt to calculate in advance the future reception of Derrida or of this extraordinary word *deconstruction*. For sure, it will continue to give rise to many 'posthumous' lives as Nietzsche remarked in a different context. Nevertheless, Derrida's ability to transcend the reductive and profoundly misleading accusations levelled at his work during the de Man affair is evidenced by deconstruction's new-found prominence in Departments of Law, Architecture and Theology. In 'Force of Law' Derrida explained in fact that deconstruction has no *natural* relationship with philosophy and especially not with Literary Studies, where it has often been thought to belong (FL, 8). It is here that a future study of the reception of deconstructive questioning could continue to examine what Derrida identified in 'Letter to a Japanese Friend' as deconstruction's 'very different connotations, inflections, and emotional or affective values' (LJF, 1).

Bibliography

Abrams, M. H. (1989). *Doing Things with Texts: Essays in Criticism and Critical Theory* (New York: Norton).

Ahmad, Aijaz (1992). *In Theory: Nations, Languages, Literatures* (London: Verso).

—— (1994). 'Reconciling Derrida: "Specters of Marx" and Deconstructive Politics.' *New Left Review* 208, 87–106.

Althizer, T., Myers, M., Rascke, C., Scharelmann, R., Taylor, M., and Wimquist, C., eds (1982). *Deconstruction and Theology* (New York: Continuum).

Apostolides, Jean-Marie (1989). 'On Paul de Man's War.' *Critical Inquiry* 15:4, 765–6.

Bannet, Eve Tavor (1989). *Structuralism and the Logic of Dissent: Barthes, Derrida, Foucault, Lacan* (Urbana and Chicago: University of Illinois Press).

—— (1992). *Postcultural Theory: Critical Theory after the Marxist Paradigm* (London: Macmillan).

Bassnet, Susan, and Lefevere, Andre, eds (1990). *Translation, History and Culture* (London and New York: Pinter Publishers).

Baudelaire, Charles (1976). *Oeuvres complètes* (Paris: Pléiade).

Beardsworth, Richard (1996). *Derrida and the Political* (London and New York: Routledge).

Benedikt, Michael (1991). *Deconstructing the Kimbell: an Essay on Meaning and Architecture* (New York: Sites Books).

Benjamin, Andrew (1989). *Translation and the Nature of Words: a New Theory of Words* (London and New York: Routledge).

Benjamin, Walter (1970). 'The Task of the Translator: an Introduction to the Translation of Baudelaire's Tableaux Parisiens.' *Illuminations*, trans. Harry Zohn (London: Jonathan Cape).

Bennington, Geoffrey (1988). 'Deconstruction and the Philosophers (The Very Idea).' *Oxford Literary Review* 10, 73–130.

—— (1994). *Legislations: the Politics of Deconstruction* (London: Verso).

—— and Derrida, Jacques (1993). *Jacques Derrida*, trans. Geoffrey Bennington (Chicago: Chicago University Press).

Berman, Art (1988). *From the New Criticism to Deconstruction: the Reception of Structuralism and Post-Structuralism* (Urbana and Chicago: University of Illinois Press).

Bernasconi, Robert, and Critchley, Simon, eds (1991). *Re-Reading Levinas* (Bloomington: Indiana University Press).

Boyne, Roy (1990). *Foucault and Derrida: the Other Side of Reason* (London: Unwin Hyman).

Brenkman, John, Brenkman, Jules, and Law, David (1989). 'Resetting the Agenda.' *Critical Inquiry* 15:4, 804–11.

Brunette, Peter, and Wills, David, eds (1989). *Screen/Play: Derrida and Film Theory* (Princeton, New Jersey: Princeton University Press).

Callinicos, Alex (1989). *Against Postmodernism: a Marxist Critique* (London: Polity Press).

Callinicos, Alex (1990). 'Reactionary Postmodernism?' *Postmodernism and Society*, eds Roy Boyne and Ali Rattansi (London: Macmillan), 97–118.
—— (1995). 'Messianic Ruminations: Derrida, Stirner and Marx.' *Radical Philosophy* 77, 37–41.
Champagne, Roland B. (1995). *Jacques Derrida* (New York and Oxford: Macmillan).
Chow, Rey (1993). 'Ethics after Idealism.' *Diacritics* 23:1, 3–22.
Clark, Timothy (1992). *Derrida, Heidegger, Blanchot: Sources of Derrida's Notion and Practice of Literature* (Cambridge: Cambridge University Press).
Cornell, Drucilla (1992). *The Philosophy of the Limit* (London: Macmillan).
Cornell, Drucilla, Rosenfield, Michael, and Carlson, David Gray, eds (1992). *Deconstruction and the Possibility of Justice* (London and New York: Routledge).
Critchley, Simon (1992). *The Ethics of Deconstruction: Derrida and Levinas* (London: Blackwell).
—— (1995). 'On Derrida's *Specters of Marx.*' *Philosophy and Social Criticism* 21:3, 1–30.
Culler, Jonathan (1980). *On Deconstruction* (London: Routledge & Kegan Paul).
—— (1989). ' "Paul de Man's War" and the Aesthetic Ideology.' *Critical Inquiry* 15:4, 777–83.
de Man, Paul (1979). *Allegories of Reading: Figural Language in Rousseau, Nietzsche, Rilke, and Proust* (New Haven and London: Yale University Press).
—— (1983). 'The Temptation of Permanence', trans. Dan Latimer. *Southern Humanities Review* 17, 209–21.
—— (1984). *The Rhetoric of Romanticism* (New York: Columbia University Press).
—— (1986). *The Resistance to Theory* (Minneapolis: University of Minnesota Press).
—— (1988a). *Blindness and Insight* (Minneapolis: University of Minnesota Press).
—— (1988b). *Wartime Journalism, 1939–1943*, eds Werner Hamacher, Neil Hertz and Thomas Keenan (Lincoln and London: University of Nebraska Press).
Eagleton, Terry (1981). *Walter Benjamin or Towards a Revolutionary Criticism* (London: Verso).
—— (1983). *Literary Theory* (Oxford: Blackwell).
—— (1984). *The Function of Criticism: from 'The Spectator' to Post-Structuralism* (London: Verso).
—— (1986). *Against the Grain: Essays 1975–1985* (London: Verso).
—— (1995). 'Marxism without Marxism.' *Radical Philosophy* 73, 35–7.
Elam, Diane (1994). *Feminism and Deconstruction: Ms. en Abyme* (London and New York: Routledge).
Farias, Victor (1989). *Heidegger and Nazism* (Philadelphia: Temple University Press).
Fawkner, H. W. (1990). *Deconstructing Macbeth, the Hyperontological View* (London: Associated University Presses).
Fraser, Nancy (1984). 'The French Derrideans: Politicising Deconstruction or Deconstructing Politics.' *New German Critique* 33, 127–54.
—— (1995). 'From Redistribution to Recognition? Dilemmas of Justice in a Post-Socialist Age.' *New Left Review* 212, 68–93.
Freud, Sigmund (1913). 'Totem and Taboo.' *The Standard Edition of the Complete Psychological Works of Freud*, Vol. 13, ed. James Strachey (London: Hogarth Press), 1–161.
Fukuyama, Francis (1992). *The End of History and the Last Man* (London: Hamish Hamilton).

Gasché, Rodolphe (1979). 'Deconstruction as Criticism.' *Glyph* 6, 177–216.

—— (1986). *The Tain of the Mirror: Derrida and the Philosophy of Reflection* (Chicago: University of Chicago Press).

—— (1995). *Inventions of Difference: On Jacques Derrida* (London: Harvard University Press).

Gilligan, Carol (1982). *In a Different Voice: Psychological Theory and Women's Development* (London: Harvard University Press).

Godzich, Wlad, and Waters, Lindsay, eds (1989). *Reading de Man Reading* (Minneapolis: University of Minneapolis Press).

Gouldner, Alvin (1979). *The Future of Intellectuals and the Rise of the New Class* (New York: Seabury Press).

Grosz, Elizabeth (1995). 'Ontology and Equivocation: Derrida's Politics of Sexual Difference.' *Diacritics* 25:2, 115–24.

Habermas, Jürgen (1987). *The Philosophical Discourse of Modernity: Twelve Lectures* (Cambridge: Polity Press).

—— (1989). 'Work and Weltanschaung: the Heidegger Controversy from a German Perspective.' *Critical Inquiry* 15:4, 431–56.

—— (1996). 'Modernity – an Unfinished Project.' *Habermas and the Unfinished Project of Modernity*, eds, Maurizio Passerin d'Entrèves and Seyla Benhabib (Cambridge: Polity Press), 38–55.

Hartman, Geoffrey, ed. (1979). *Deconstruction and Criticism* (New York: Seabury Press).

Harvey, Irene E. (1986). *Derrida and the Economy of Différance* (Bloomington and London: Indiana University Press).

Heller, Agnes, and Fehér, Ferenc (1988). *The Postmodern Political Condition* (Oxford: Basil Blackwell).

Helmling, Steven (1994). 'Historicizing Derrida.' *Postmodern Culture* 4.3: 34 pars Online. 10 August 2005. Available: http://muse.jhu.edu/journals/ postmodern_culture/toc/pmc4.3.html

Holdheim, Wolfgang W. (1989). 'Jacques Derrida's Apologia'. *Critical Inquiry* 15:4, 784–96.

Holub, Robert (1985). 'Counter-Epistemology and Marxist Deconstruction.' *Southern Review* 18, 206–14.

—— (1992). *Crossing Borders: Reception Theory, Poststructuralism, Deconstruction* (Madison, Wisconsin: University of Wisconsin Press).

Irzik, Sibel (1990). *Deconstruction and the Politics of Criticism* (New York: Garland).

Johnson, Barbara (1980). *The Critical Difference: Essays in the Contemporary Rhetoric of Reading* (Baltimore: Johns Hopkins University Press).

—— (1987). *A World of Difference* (Baltimore: The Johns Hopkins University Press).

—— (1995). *The Wake of Deconstruction* (Baltimore: The Johns Hopkins University Press).

Judt, Tony (1986). *Marxism and the French Left: Studies in Labour and Politics in France, 1830–1981* (Oxford: Clarendon Press).

—— (1992). *Past Imperfect: French Intellectuals, 1944–56* (Berkeley, Los Angeles: University of California Press).

Kafka, Franz (1978). 'Before the Law.' *Wedding Preparations in the Country and Other Stories*, trans. Willa and Edwina Muir (Harmondsworth: Penguin).

Kamuf, Peggy (2005). *Book of Addresses* (Stanford: Stanford University Press).

Kamuf, Peggy, ed. (1991). *A Derrida Reader: Between the Blinds* (New York: Columbia University Press).

Kant, Immanuel (1979). *The Conflict of the Faculties*, trans. Mary J. Gregor (Lincoln and London: University of Nebraska Press).

Kaplan, Alice Yaeger (1986). *Reproductions of Banality: Fascism, Literature, and French Intellectual Life* (Minneapolis: University of Minneapolis Press).

Kearney, Richard (1984). *Dialogues with Contemporary Continental Thinkers* (Manchester: Manchester University Press).

Khilnani, Sunil (1993). *Arguing Revolution: the Intellectual Left in Postwar France* (New Haven: Yale University Press).

Lacoue-Labarthe, Phillippe (1989). 'Neither an Accident nor a Mistake.' *Critical Inquiry* 15:4, 481–4.

—— (1990). *Heidegger, Art, and Politics*, trans. Chris Turner (Oxford: Blackwell).

Lacoue-Labarthe, Phillippe, and Nancy, Jean-Luc, eds (1981). *Les fins l'homme: à partir du Travail Jacques Derrida* (Paris: Galilée).

Lacoue-Labarthe, Phillippe, Nancy, Jean-Luc, Balibar, E., Lyotard, J. F., and Ferry, L. (1981b). *Rejouer le politique* (Paris: Galilée).

Lacoue-Labarthe, Phillippe, Nancy, Jean-Luc, and Sparks, Simon (eds) (1983). *Retreating the Political* (New York and London: Routledge).

Lehman, David (1992). *Signs of the Times: the Rise and Fall of Paul de Man* (New York: Poseidon).

Lehmann, Jennifer M. (1993). *Deconstructing Durkheim, a Post-Structuralist Critique* (London: Routledge).

Leitch, Vincent B. (1980). 'The Lateral Dance: the Deconstructive Criticism of J. Hillis Miller.' *Critical Inquiry* 6:4, 593–607.

—— (1983). *Deconstructive Criticism: an Advanced Reader* (New York: Columbia University Press).

—— (1992). *Cultural Criticism, Literary Theory, Poststructuralism* (New York: Columbia University Press).

Lentricchia, Frank (1980). *After the New Criticism* (London: Athlone Press).

Levinas, Emmanuel (1969). *Totality and Infinity*, trans. A. Lingis (Pittsburgh: Duquesne University Press).

—— (1981). *Otherwise than Being or beyond Essence* (The Hague: Martinus Nijhoff).

—— (1989). 'As if Consenting to Horror.' *Critical Inquiry* 15:4, 485–8.

Llewelyn, John (1986). *Derrida on the Threshold of Sense* (Basingstoke: Macmillan, now Palgrave Macmillan).

Lloyd, Fran (1993). *Deconstructing Madonna* (London: Batsford).

Lorrain, Jorge (1994). 'The Postmodern Critique of Ideology.' *The Sociological Review* 42:2, 289–314.

McCarthy, Thomas (1989). 'The Politics of the Ineffable: Derrida's Deconstructionism.' *The Philosophical Forum* 21:1–2, 146–68.

—— (1993). 'Deconstruction and Reconstruction in Contemporary Critical Theory.' *The Canadian Journal of Philosophy*, Supplementary Volume 19, 263–4.

Macksey, Richard, and Donato, Eugenio, eds (1972). *The Structuralist Controversy: the Languages of Criticism and the Sciences of Man* (Baltimore: The Johns Hopkins University Press).

McClintock, Anne, and Nixon, Rob (1986). 'No Names Apart: the Separation of Word and History in Derrida's "Le Dernier Mot du Racisme".' *Critical Inquiry* 13:1, 140–54.

MacRobbie, Angela (1994). *Postmodernism and Popular Culture* (London and New York: Routledge).

Mouffe, Chantal (1993). *The Return of the Political* (London: Verso).
—— (1995). 'Politics, Democratic Action, and Solidarity'. *Inquiry* 38:1–2, 99–108.
Mulhall, Stephen (1995). 'Critic and Messiah: Derrida's Inheritance from Marx.' *The Times Literary Supplement* 23 June, 12.
Nietzsche, Friedrich (2004). *On the Future of Our Educational Institutions*, Eng. trans. Michael W. Genke (South Bend, Indiana: St. Augustine's Press). Norris, Christopher (1981). *Deconstruction: Theory and Practice* (London: Methuen).
—— (1984). 'On Marxist Deconstructors: Problems and Prospects.' *Southern Review* 17, 203–11.
—— (1985). *The Contest of the Faculties* (London: Methuen).
—— (1987). *Derrida* (London: Fontana).
—— (1988). *Paul de Man: Deconstruction and the Critique of Aesthetic Ideology* (London: Routledge).
—— (1989). *Deconstruction and the Interests of Theory* (London: University of Oklahoma Press).
—— (1992a). *Uncritical Theory: Postmodernism, Intellectuals and the Gulf War* (London: Lawrence and Wishart).
—— (1992b). 'Deconstruction, Postmodernism and Philosophy: Habermas on Derrida.' *Derrida: a Critical Reader*, ed. David Wood (Oxford: Blackwell), 165–92.
—— (1992c). *Deconstruction: Theory and Practice*, 2nd edn (London: Methuen).
—— (1993a). *The Truth about Postmodernism* (London: Basil Blackwell).
—— (1993b). 'Lost in the Funhouse: Baudrillard and the Politics of Postmodernism.' *Postmodernism and Society*, eds Roy Boyne and Ali Rattansi (London: Macmillan), 119–53.
—— (1993c). 'Old Themes for New Times: Postmodernism, Theory and Cultural Politics.' *Principled Positions: Postmodernism and the Rediscovery of Value*, ed. Judith Squires (London: Lawrence and Wishart), 151–88.
—— (1996). 'Deconstruction, Postmodernism and Philosophy: Habermas on Derrida.' *Habermas and the Unfinished Project of Modernity*, eds Maurizio Passerin d'Entrèves and Seyla Benhabib (Cambridge: Polity Press), 97–123.
Papadakis, Andreas C., ed. (1988). *Deconstruction in Architecture* (London: Architectural Design; New York: St. Martin's Press).
Parker, John, and Shotter, John (1990). *Deconstructing Social Psychology* (London: Routledge).
Pascal, Blaise (1962). *Pensées* (Paris: Editions du Seuil).
Perloff, Majorie (1989). 'Response to Jacques Derrida.' *Critical Inquiry* 15:4, 767–76.
Proust, Marcel (2004). *Swann's Way* (London: Penguin Books).
Ramprogus, Vince (1995). *The Deconstruction of Nursing* (Aldershot: Avebury).
Rapaport, Herman (1989). *Heidegger and Derrida: Reflections on Time and Language* (Lincoln and London: University of Nebraska Press).
—— (1995). 'Deconstruction's Other: Trinh T. Minh-Ha and Jacques Derrida.' *Diacritics* 25:2, 98–113.
Readings, Bill (1989). 'The Deconstruction of Politics.' *Reading de Man Reading*, eds Lindsay Walters and Wlad Godzich (Minneapolis: University of Minnesota Press), 223–43.
—— (1995). 'Dwelling in the Ruins.' *Oxford Literary Review* 17:1–2, 15–28.
Readings, Bill, and Schaber, B., eds (1993). *Postmodernism across the Ages: Essays for a Postmodernity That Wasn't Born Yesterday* (New York: Syracuse University Press).

Rée, Jonathan (1993). 'Hell's Angels: Derrida and the Heidegger Controversy.' *Radical Philosophy* 64, 61.

Rose, Gillian (1984). *Dialectic of Nihilism: Post-Structuralism and Law* (Oxford: Basil Blackwell).

Rose, Margaret A. (1991). *The Postmodern and the Post-Industrial: a Critical Analysis* (Cambridge: Cambridge University Press).

Ross, Andrew, ed. (1988). *Universal Abandon? The Politics of Postmodernism* (Edinburgh: Edinburgh University Press).

Royle, Nicholas (1995). *After Derrida* (Manchester: Manchester University Press).

—— (1997). 'Phantom Review.' *Textual Practice* 16:2, 386–98.

—— (2003). *Jacques Derrida* (London and New York: Routledge).

Royle, Nicholas, ed. (1992). *Afterwords* (Tampere: Outside Books).

Ryan, Michael (1980). 'Self-Evidence.' *Diacritics* 10:2, 2–16.

—— (1982). *Marxism and Deconstruction: a Critical Articulation* (Baltimore and London: Johns Hopkins University Press).

Said, Edward W. (1978). *Orientalism* (London: Routledge & Kegan Paul).

—— (1984). *The World, the Text, and the Critic* (Cambridge, Mass.: Harvard University Press).

—— (1994). *Representations of the Intellectual: the 1993 Reith Lectures* (London: Vintage).

Salusinszky, Imre (1987). *Criticism in Society* (London and New York: Methuen).

Satzewich, Vic, ed. (1992). *Deconstructing a Nation: Immigration, Multiculturalism and Racism in '90s Canada* (Halifax, Nova Scotia: Fernwood).

Schulte, Raines, and Biguenet, John, eds (1992). *Theories of Translation: an Anthology of Essays from Dryden to Derrida* (Chicago and London: University of Chicago Press).

Searle, John R. (1977). 'Reiterating the Differences: a Reply to Derrida.' *Glyph* 1, 198–208.

—— (1983). 'The World Turned Upside Down.' *The New York Review of Books* 27 October, 74–9.

Shapiro, Michael J. (1992). *Reading the Postmodern Polity: Political Theory as Textual Practice* (Minneapolis and Oxford: University of Minnesota Press).

Shelley, Percy B. (1981). *The Complete Poems* (Boston: Houghton Mifflin).

Silverman, Hugh J. (1989). *Derrida and Deconstruction* (New York and London: Routledge).

Silverman, Maxim (1992). *Deconstructing a Nation: Immigration, Racism and Citizenship in Modern France* (London: Routledge).

Simons, Jon (1995). *Foucault and the Political* (London and New York: Routledge).

Smart, Barry (1992). *Modern Conditions: Postmodern Controversies* (London: Routledge).

—— (1993). *Postmodernity* (London and New York: Routledge).

Soper, Kate (1995). 'The Limits of Hauntology.' *Radical Philosophy* 77, 26–31.

Spivak, Gayatri C. (1980). 'Revolutions That as Yet Have No Model.' *Diacritics* 10:4, 29–49.

—— (1987). 'Subaltern Studies: Deconstructing Historiography.' *In Other Worlds: Essays in Cultural Politics* (New York: Methuen), 197–221.

—— (1990). *The Post-Colonial Critic: Interviews, Strategies, Dialogues* (New York and London: Routledge).

—— (1995). 'Ghostwriting.' *Diacritics* 25:2, 65–84.

Squires, Judith, ed. (1993). *Principled Positions: Postmodernism and the Rediscovery of Value* (London: Lawrence and Wishart).

Thwaites, Tony (1995a). 'Between Games: Literary and Cultural Studies, and the Logics of Disagreement.' *Southern Review* 28:1, 10–19.

—— (1995b). 'Facing Pages: On Response, a Response to Steven Helmling'. *Postmodern Culture* 6.1: 35 pars. Online. 10 August 2005. Available: http://muse.jhu.edu/journals/postmodern_culture/toc/pmc6.1.html

Ulmer, Gregory L. (1985). *Applied Grammatology: Post(e)-Pedagogy from Jacques Derrida to Joseph Beuys* (Baltimore and London: Johns Hopkins University Press).

Valéry, Paul (1962). *History and Politics*, trans. Denise Folliot and Jackson Mathews (New York: Bollingen).

Warren, Rosanna, ed. (1989). *The Art of Translation: Voices from the Field* (Boston: Northeastern University Press).

Weber, Samuel (1981). 'After Eight: Remarking Glyph.' *Glyph* 8, 232–8.

—— (1984). 'The Debts of Deconstruction and Other, Related Assumptions.' *Taking Chances: Derrida, Psychoanalysis and Literature*, eds Joseph H. Smith and William Kerrigan (Baltimore and London: Johns Hopkins University Press), 37–41.

—— (1987). *Institution and Interpretation* (Minneapolis and London: University of Minnesota Press).

Wiener, Jon (1988). 'Deconstructing de Man.' *The Nation* 9 January, 2.

—— (1989). 'The Responsibilities of Friendship: Jacques Derrida on Paul de Man's Collaboration.' *Critical Inquiry* 15:4, 797–803.

Wolfreys, Julian (2004). *Occasional Deconstructions* (Albany: State University of New York Press).

Wolin, Richard (1992). *The Terms of Cultural Critique: the Frankfurt School, Existentialism, Poststructuralism* (New York: Columbia University Press).

Wolin, Richard, ed. (1993). *The Heidegger Controversy: a Critical Reader* (Cambridge, Massachusetts, and London: The MIT Press).

Wood, David (1991). 'Opening Time.' *Radical Philosophy* 58, 36.

Wood, David, ed. (1992). *Derrida: a Critical Reader* (Oxford: Basil Blackwell).

Wood, David, and Bernasconi, Robert, eds (1988). *Derrida and Différance* (Evanston, Illinois: Northwestern University Press).

Wordsworth, William (1960). *The Prelude*, ed. Ernest de Selincourt (Oxford: Clarendon Press).

Yeats, W. B. (1983). *The Collected Poems* (London: Macmillan).

Young, Robert (1990). *White Mythologies: Writing History and the West* (London and New York: Routledge).

Young, Robert, ed. (1981). *Untying the Text: a Post-structuralist Reader* (London: Routledge & Kegan Paul).

Zelechow, Bernard (1983). 'The Myth of Translatability: Translation as Interpretation.' *Translating Religious Texts: Translation, Transgression and Interpretation*, ed. David Jasper (London: Macmillan).

Index of Works
by Jacques Derrida

Index of Proper Names and Key Words